Communications in Computer and Information Science   2244

AF166332

Rationale

The CCIS series is devoted to the publication of proceedings of computer science conferences. Its aim is to efficiently disseminate original research results in informatics in printed and electronic form. While the focus is on publication of peer-reviewed full papers presenting mature work, inclusion of reviewed short papers reporting on work in progress is welcome, too. Besides globally relevant meetings with internationally representative program committees guaranteeing a strict peer-reviewing and paper selection process, conferences run by societies or of high regional or national relevance are also considered for publication.

Topics

The topical scope of CCIS spans the entire spectrum of informatics ranging from foundational topics in the theory of computing to information and communications science and technology and a broad variety of interdisciplinary application fields.

Information for Volume Editors and Authors

Publication in CCIS is free of charge. No royalties are paid, however, we offer registered conference participants temporary free access to the online version of the conference proceedings on SpringerLink (http://link.springer.com) by means of an http referrer from the conference website and/or a number of complimentary printed copies, as specified in the official acceptance email of the event.

CCIS proceedings can be published in time for distribution at conferences or as post-proceedings, and delivered in the form of printed books and/or electronically as USBs and/or e-content licenses for accessing proceedings at SpringerLink. Furthermore, CCIS proceedings are included in the CCIS electronic book series hosted in the SpringerLink digital library at http://link.springer.com/bookseries/7899. Conferences publishing in CCIS are allowed to use Online Conference Service (OCS) for managing the whole proceedings lifecycle (from submission and reviewing to preparing for publication) free of charge.

Publication process

The language of publication is exclusively English. Authors publishing in CCIS have to sign the Springer CCIS copyright transfer form, however, they are free to use their material published in CCIS for substantially changed, more elaborate subsequent publications elsewhere. For the preparation of the camera-ready papers/files, authors have to strictly adhere to the Springer CCIS Authors' Instructions and are strongly encouraged to use the CCIS LaTeX style files or templates.

Abstracting/Indexing

CCIS is abstracted/indexed in DBLP, Google Scholar, EI-Compendex, Mathematical Reviews, SCImago and Scopus. CCIS volumes are also submitted for the inclusion in ISI Proceedings.

How to start

To start the evaluation of your proposal for inclusion in the CCIS series, please send an e-mail to ccis@springer.com.

Wenying Feng · Nick Rahimi ·
Venkatasivakumar Margapuri
Editors

Software and Data Engineering

33rd International Conference, SEDE 2024
San Diego, CA, USA, October 21–22, 2024
Proceedings

 Springer

Editors
Wenying Feng
Trent University Durham GTA
Oshawa, ON, Canada

Nick Rahimi
University of Southern Mississippi
Hattiesburg, MS, USA

Venkatasivakumar Margapuri
Villanova University
Villanova, PA, USA

ISSN 1865-0929   ISSN 1865-0937 (electronic)
Communications in Computer and Information Science
ISBN 978-3-031-75200-1   ISBN 978-3-031-75201-8 (eBook)
https://doi.org/10.1007/978-3-031-75201-8

This Springer imprint is published by the registered company Springer Nature Switzerland AG
The registered company address is: Gewerbestrasse 11, 6330 Cham, Switzerland

If disposing of this product, please recycle the paper.

Preface

We are pleased to present the proceedings of the 33rd SEDE Conference: Software and Data Engineering (SEDE 2024), held on October 21–22, 2024, at the Hilton San Diego Airport/Harbor Island in San Diego, California, USA. SEDE 2024 was proudly organized as part of the conference series of the International Society for Computers and Their Applications (ISCA), a not-for-profit organization dedicated to promoting the advancement of science and engineering in the area of computers and their applications.

This conference, one of the most established in the field, brought together researchers and professionals from the domains of Software Engineering and Data Engineering to share and discuss high-quality research results and outcomes. SEDE 2024 aimed to facilitate cross-fertilization of ideas in Software and Data Engineering, with a particular focus on research integrating both domains.

The conference featured a rigorous peer-review process, with each paper reviewed by at least two experts in the field. This single-blind review process ensured the selection of high-quality papers that reflect the current state and future directions of software and data engineering.

We received 25 submissions covering a wide range of topics within software and data engineering. After careful evaluation, the Program Committee selected the presented in these proceedings, representing cutting-edge research and innovative ideas in the field.

The conference program included presentations of accepted papers, keynote speeches by distinguished researchers, and engaging panel discussions. A highlight of the event was the presentation of the Best Paper Award during the conference banquet, recognizing outstanding contributions to the field.

We would like to express our gratitude to all the authors who submitted their work to SEDE 2024, the Program Committee members and additional reviewers for their thorough and timely reviews, and all the attendees for their active participation. Special thanks go to Springer Nature for publishing these proceedings.

We hope that these proceedings will serve as a valuable resource for researchers and practitioners in the fields of software and data engineering, fostering further advancements and collaborations in these crucial areas of computer science. Furthermore, we encourage readers to explore the extended versions of these papers in the ISCA journal, furthering the impact of this research.

October 2024

Wenying Feng
Nick Rahimi
Venkatasivakumar Margapuri

Organization

General Chair

Wenying Feng   Trent University Durham GTA, Canada

Program Chairs

Nick Rahimi   University of Southern Mississippi, USA
Venkatasivakumar Margapuri   Villanova University, USA

Program Committee

Somenath Chakraborty   West Virginia University Institute of Technology,
                                       USA
Wei Dai   Purdue University Northwest, USA
Takaaki Goto   Toyo University, Japan
Karan Gupta   SunPower Corporation, USA
Xiaolan Huang   Southern Illinois University, USA
Swathi Kaluvakuri   Southern Illinois University, USA
Mirsalar Kamari   University of Southern Mississippi, USA
Koushik Maddali   Southern Illinois University, USA
Jose Martinez   University of Southern Mississippi, USA
Majid Memari   Utah Valley University, USA
Md. Saef Ullah Miah   American International University, Bangladesh
Saydul Akbar   University of Southern Mississippi, USA
Abu Jafar Md   University of Tennessee, USA
Abhay Paroha   Schlumberger, USA
Niketa Penumajji   CivicPlus, USA
Chinmay Rajguru   GKN Aerospace, USA
Robert Stewart   Kansas State University, USA
Ning Yang   Southern Illinois University, USA

Contents

Software Engineering and Data Science

Artificial Intelligence

Software Engineering and Data Science

Adversarial Attack Optimization and Evaluation for Machine Learning-Based Dark Web Traffic Analysis

Nyzaireyus Harrison, Heather Broome, Yaju Shrestha, Alexander Robles, Aayush Gautam, and Nick Rahimi[✉]

University of Southern Mississippi, Hattiesburg, MS 39402, USA
{nyzaireyus.harrison,heather.d.broome,yaju.shrestha,
alexander.robles,aayush.gautam,nick.rahimi}@usm.edu

Abstract. Machine learning (ML) is quickly becoming one of the most transformative technologies in the field of computing. Applications of ML are wide-spread and growing exponentially, revolutionizing the future of major industries such as finance, healthcare, automotives, and more. This has made it more necessary than ever to recognize the instability created by adversarial attacks—the deliberate manipulation of data to mislead ML models. This instability must be addressed through researching the effects of adversarial attacks and how they can be better recognized. Our research explored the use of adversarial attacks in dark web network traffic analysis by first improving our understanding of how adversarial attacks could be optimized. We manipulated a dataset of dark web traffic data through the analysis of confusion matrices and Euclidean distances, aiming to cause maximum confusion for each of our models. We then trained and tested each model in a variety of scenarios to further our understanding of weaknesses in both the traffic data and the machine learning techniques employed.

Keywords: Dark web · Machine learning · Adversarial attacks · Network traffic analysis

1 Introduction

In recent years, the scope of machine learning applications has grown to a remarkable scale. It is used for cybersecurity monitoring, self-driving cars, biometric authentication, and much more. The impact of these applications has created palpable excitement surrounding the field, further expediting growth. Simultaneously, there has been a growing sentiment that this momentum has inadequately assessed the risks of ML. It is necessary for research to address the weaknesses of ML models. Specifically, it is necessary to address the danger of adversarial attacks.

An adversarial attack is the deliberate manipulation of data to create misclassifications within a model. Such an attack is especially effective in cases where changes are subtle enough to bypass human analysis. A common example of this could be spray painting part of a stop sign. While a human may see this sign and recognize its intended

W. Feng et al. (Eds.): SEDE 2024, CCIS 2244, pp. 3–13, 2024.
https://doi.org/10.1007/978-3-031-75201-8_1

meaning, a self-driving car may struggle to classify the sign and pass it without stopping. While this particular problem may be counteracted by diversifying training data to include such issues, there are many cases which would be much harder to foresee, detect, and solve. This is especially troubling in cases where malicious actors have designed attacks to be indistinguishable to the human eye.

Cybersecurity is a major target of adversarial attacks, as its goals have drawn the attention of bad actors for decades. Not only is it a target, but it also often relies on datasets that are vast and impossible to be fully deciphered by a human [1]. In the case of network traffic analysis, the manipulation of TCP headers can cause misclassifications of suspicious and benign traffic. Network traffic analysis is necessary for intrusion detection, data loss prevention, and firewalls, each of which being necessary for major systems. Systems of concern include those of cybersecurity companies, healthcare providers, financial institutions, and infrastructure. Our research will specifically focus on improving network traffic analysis through the study of adversarial attacks on dark web data, though its interpretations may be widely applicable.

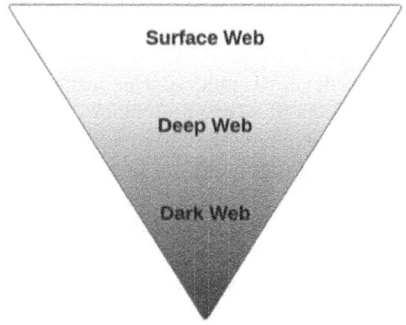

Fig. 1. Composition of the world wide web

The World Wide Web (WWW) consists of the surface web, deep web, and dark web. The deep web is the portion of the WWW that is intentionally hard to access, making up 95% of the WWW [2]. The organization and relationship of these domains are conveyed in Fig. 1. The nature of the dark web, on the other hand, makes its size immeasurable. Law enforcement and cybersecurity agencies have become heavily involved in analyzing traffic across the dark web, as it has become a hub for malicious activity. The entirety of the deep web consists of web pages and IP addresses that are not indexed within search engines, while the dark web builds upon this anonymity by also requiring encryption software for access. The anonymous and decentralized hosting of servers can make content removal largely impossible, and the concerns created by such features make researching the dark web necessary. Understanding how malicious users may use adversarial attacks to evade detection is critical for cybersecurity as a whole.

The anonymity provided by the dark web, combined with the difficulty of its accessibility, creates a hotspot of criminal activity [3]. Common crimes being facilitated by the dark web include:

- Arms, drug, and human trafficking
- Markets for stolen personal data
- Distribution of malware and ransomware
- Terrorist communications
- Orchestrations of security attacks.

It's important to note that not all traffic on the dark web is related to illegal activities, and many legitimate users employ it to counteract concerns regarding privacy. The dark web originally provided spies and dissidents with necessary channels for communication. However, the anonymity provided by the dark web quickly made it a useful platform for hackers, criminals, and extremists to communicate, trade, and launch attacks. This has led to the monitoring of certain traffic becoming necessary.

In the scope of cybersecurity, the dark web is a major facilitator for malware. It is common for users to download something legitimate from the dark web and still be infected with malware, as content is largely unregulated. Hackers may disguise malware as being legitimate, making it difficult for users to distinguish between the two. Once downloaded and executed, such malware can take control of the user's computer, steal sensitive information, or carry out other harmful activities. This poses a major threat for individuals and corporations alike [4, 5].

Machine learning is a useful tool for automating the detection of darknet attacks. Algorithms can analyze an attack's characteristics and detect similar threats in the future. However, bad actors are aware of this and frequently respond with adversarial attacks, manipulating the appearance of their network activity to evade detection. Anti-virus applications, including those pre-installed on operating systems, commonly rely on a hybrid approach of signature-based detection and ML to detect malicious traffic. So, if bad actors use adversarial training to manipulate traffic data, these applications lose efficacy.

This study aims to comprehensively evaluate the robustness and efficacy of various machine learning (ML) classification methods in detecting dark web traffic, particularly in the presence of adversarial attacks. The research is divided into two phases:

- Phase 1: Baseline Model Performance Evaluation

In the first phase, we trained and evaluated several ML classifiers on the unaltered CICDarknet2020 dataset [6]. This dataset contains a diverse collection of network traffic data captured from across the dark web, labeled into seven distinct traffic types: Audio-Stream, Browsing, Chat, Email, Peer-to-Peer (P2P), Transfer, Video-Stream, and Voice over Internet Protocol (VoIP). After extensive experimentation, we identified the top-performing classifiers for this dataset: Decision Tree (DT) [7], Multilayer Perceptron (MLP) [8, 9], and Random Forest (RF) [9]. Our initial findings revealed that the decision tree model demonstrated superior performance compared to numerous other algorithms.

- Phase 2: Adversarial Attack Simulation and Evaluation

In the second phase, we simulated three distinct adversarial attack scenarios to assess the resilience of the selected ML models against adversarial perturbations in the data. To achieve this, we crafted an adversarially poisoned dataset by strategically modifying the class labels of the CICDarknet2020 dataset. This poisoning process aimed to maximize the confusion and misclassification rate of our chosen algorithms (DT, MLP, and RF).

The poisoning strategy involved analyzing the confusion matrices and computing the sum of statistical distances (e.g., Euclidean distances) between the feature vectors of different classes. Based on these analyses, we carefully relabeled each class in a manner that would cause the most overall confusion for the three algorithms. This process was iteratively repeated, progressively degrading the accuracy of our classifiers until their performance reached a minimal level. Consequently, we obtained two distinct datasets: the original, unaltered data and the adversarially poisoned data.

Using these datasets, we constructed three adversarial attack scenarios:

1. Scenario 1: Train on original data, test on poisoned data. This scenario simulates an attacker modifying the traffic features to evade detection by our trained models.
2. Scenario 2: Train on poisoned data, test on original data. This scenario simulates an attacker compromising our training data by tampering with the classifiers during the training phase.
3. Scenario 3: Train and test on poisoned data. This scenario presents a novel defense strategy, where both the training and testing data are assumed to be adversarially manipulated.

By meticulously optimizing these adversarial attacks and evaluating the performance of our ML models under each scenario, we have paved the way for future research aimed at recognizing and defending against even the most sophisticated adversarial threats in the context of dark web traffic analysis.

The rest of this paper is organized as follows: Section 2 provides an in-depth description of our research methods. Section 3 discusses the results of our current research and defines the next step in its progress. Section 4 concludes the paper by summarizing our key findings.

2   Training Methods

In the initial research phase, we utilized the CICDarknet2020 dataset to train and evaluate the performance of three machine learning models: Decision Tree, Random Forest, and Multilayer Perceptron. These baseline experiments served as a foundation for the subsequent phases of our research. The models exhibited the following classification accuracies on the unaltered dataset:

- Decision Tree: 92.02%
- Multilayer Perceptron: 66.86%
- Random Forest: 92.64%.

The Random Forest model achieved the highest accuracy of 92.64%, closely followed by the Decision Tree model at 92.02%. However, the Multilayer Perceptron model lagged behind with a comparatively lower accuracy of 66.86%. These results highlighted the potential strengths and weaknesses of the selected models in the context of dark web traffic classification, guiding our exploration of adversarial attack scenarios in the subsequent phases.

The Decision Tree algorithm divides data hierarchically through Boolean evaluations. As the tree branches, each new split aims to distinguish its small section of data into another split. These decisions aim to separate the dataset as much as possible with both efficiency and accuracy. Trees continue to grow as they search for the lowest entropy possible, dividing small subsets of data to further minimize impurity in leaf nodes. Entropy reduction is represented in the following equation. Additionally, the algorithm prioritizes attributes with higher information gain, contributing to the model's performance optimization.

$$\text{entropy}(P_1, P_2) = -P \times \log_2 P_1 - P_2 \times \log_2 P_2 \tag{1}$$

where P1 represents the weight of the first decision and P2 represents the weight of the second decision [7].

The Multilayer Perceptron algorithm takes a much different approach than the previously discussed algorithms. MLP forms an artificial neural network with multiple layers of nodes. As the model trains, data is passed through the network's layers and each node's weight is adjusted in small increments. This model is typically most useful for datasets exhibiting non-linear patterns. Below is a simplified representation of the algorithm:

$$y = f(z) \text{ and } z = \sum_{i=0}^{n} w_i x_i \tag{2}$$

where n represents the number of inputs, w represents the weight of the neuron, x represents the input feature, and y represents the predicted class [8].

The Random Forest algorithm uses a more complex approach than decision tree by creating multiple root nodes based on a randomly selected subset of features. Following the initialization of roots, random forest branches further out as it searches for the minimal entropy. Both decision tree and random forest are highly accurate algorithms for many datasets. For random forest, however, its inefficiency is certainly a major downside. The initialization of a random root nodes is represented below, where $\Theta_1 \ldots, \Theta_M$ represents random features and Θ resamples each tree's dataset.

$$m_n(x; \Theta_j, D_n) = \sum_{i=D_n^*} \frac{\{x_i \in A_n(x; \Theta_j, D_n)\} Y_i}{N_n(x; \Theta_j, D_n)} \tag{3}$$

where $m_n(x; \Theta_j, D_n)$ represents the approximated value of query point x, $D_n^*(\Theta_j)$ represents the randomly selected subset of each tree, $A_n(x; \Theta_j, D_n)$ contains x, and $N_n(x; \Theta_j, D_n)$ represents the total points within set $A_n(x; \Theta_j, D_n)$ [9].

Following the training of the selected models in the initial phase, we proceeded to the second phase of our research. In this phase, we leveraged the models' performance results to generate confusion matrices and compute sums of statistical distances. By analyzing the confusion matrices and calculating the Euclidean distances [10] between different classes, we strategically switched the labels of the dataset to maximize confusion for the models. The label switches were determined based on the classes that were most frequently misclassified as one another. Table 1 presents the normalized Euclidean distances between the classes.

Table 1. Euclidean distances

Class	Browsing	Chat	Email	File-transfer	P2P	Video-streaming
Audio-streaming	0.2248	0.225239	0.231601	0.228245	0.222593	0.23287
Browsing	0.2273	0.231137	0.222617	0.21348	0.233966	0.217702
Chat	0.2084	0.220522	0.205472	0.235625	0.157475	
Email	0.2356	0.22447	0.232218	0.215725		
File-transfer	0.2137	0.244379	0.215141			
P2P	0.2263	0.197132				
Video-streaming	0.2573					

Our analysis revealed that the misclassification of network traffic classes was primarily attributed to similar patterns within the packets' TCP headers, which contain essential information about the transferred packet. Based on the Euclidean distances and the observed misclassification patterns, we determined the following label switches to be the most effective in maximizing confusion:

- Browsing → P2P
- Transfer → Chat
- Audio-Streaming → Email
- Chat → Audio-Streaming.

The creation of our poisoned dataset led us into the final phase of the research, which consisted of three scenarios.

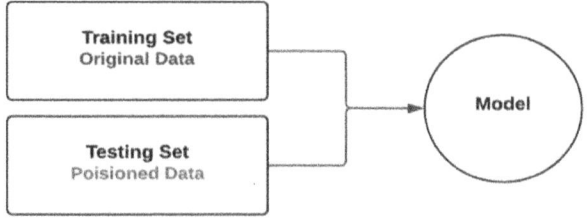

Fig. 2. Scenario 1

In the first scenario, depicted in Fig. 2, we trained each of the selected machine learning algorithms (Decision Tree, Random Forest, and Multilayer Perceptron) using the original, unaltered CICDarknet2020 dataset. However, for the testing phase, we employed the poisoned dataset, which had been strategically manipulated to maximize confusion and misclassification. This scenario represents the most common and straight-forward form of an adversarial attack, where the simulated attacker's primary objective is to evade detection by the trained models. By modifying the features of the network traffic data in the testing set, the attacker aims to exploit the models' vulnerabilities and generate incorrect predictions.

The purpose of this scenario is to evaluate the robustness and resilience of the trained models against adversarial examples that are crafted specifically to deceive them. It helps us understand how well the models can generalize to unseen, potentially malicious data points that differ from the distribution of the training data.

By assessing the performance of the models in this scenario, we can gain insights into their ability to maintain accurate classifications even when faced with adversarially manipulated data. This knowledge is crucial for developing effective defense strategies and improving the security of machine learning-based systems in the face of evolving adversarial threats.

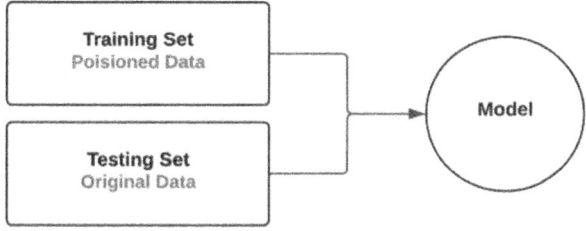

Fig. 3. Scenario 2

In scenario 2, as depicted in Fig. 3, we reversed our previous scenario, training each algorithm on the poisoned dataset and using the original dataset for testing. This scenario represents a more sophisticated and insidious form of adversarial attack, where the simulated attacker aims to manipulate the training data itself, thereby poisoning the models' learning process. By deliberately introducing misleading patterns and labels into the training set, the attacker's goal is to fundamentally corrupt the models' understanding of the data and compromise their ability to make accurate predictions. This scenario allows us to assess the resilience of the machine learning models against poisoning attacks and evaluate the extent to which they can maintain their performance when their learning process is contaminated by adversarial influence.

In the third scenario, depicted in Fig. 4, we conducted a novel experiment to assess the consistency and effectiveness of our poisoned dataset. We used the poisoned data as both the training and testing sets for the machine learning algorithms. This approach allowed us to evaluate how well the models performed when trained and tested on data that had been deliberately manipulated to introduce confusion and misclassification.

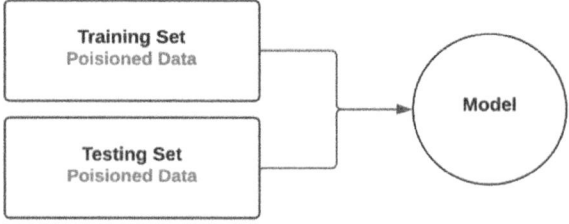

Fig. 4. Scenario 3

Interestingly, the results obtained from this scenario revealed that the models achieved accuracies very similar to those obtained when trained and tested on the original, unaltered dataset. This finding suggests that the poisoned dataset, despite being crafted to deceive the models, maintained a consistent level of performance across the different algorithms.

This scenario represents a highly complex and sophisticated adversarial attack, where the simulated attacker manages to control both the training and testing data, feeding the models poisoned information from both sources. By manipulating the entire data pipeline, the attacker aims to create a false sense of confidence in the models' performance while potentially compromising their ability to generalize to real-world scenarios.

The insights gained from this scenario provide valuable information about the efficacy and consistency of our adversarial attacks. It demonstrates that even when the models are trained and tested on manipulated data, they can still achieve comparable accuracies to those obtained on the original dataset. This finding raises important questions about the robustness and reliability of machine learning models in the face of advanced adversarial attacks that target both the training and testing phases.

Furthermore, this scenario highlights the need for developing more sophisticated techniques to detect and mitigate the effects of poisoned data in machine learning systems. It underscores the importance of implementing robust data validation, anomaly detection, and model evaluation strategies that identify and address potential inconsistencies and vulnerabilities introduced by adversarial manipulation.

3   Results and Discussion

After preparing our datasets and selecting the algorithms, we built and trained the models using a Python script. Throughout the scenarios, we observed a significant decline in accuracy, highlighting the vulnerability of machine learning to adversarial attacks.

In Scenario 1, where the models were exposed to manipulated data during the testing phase, the performance of all three algorithms deteriorated considerably. When presented with carefully mislabeled data, the models failed to serve as an effective means of network traffic detection. This emphasizes the susceptibility of machine learning-based detection systems to subtle data manipulation, raising critical concerns for cybersecurity.

Scenario 2, which exposed the models to manipulated data during the training phase, exhibited a performance reduction remarkably similar to Scenario 1. This underscores the equal importance of securing accurate training data, a process that could be easily compromised considering the prevalence of malicious actors on the dark web.

The collection of traffic data, both from the dark web and surface web, must be conducted meticulously. Thoroughness is crucial not only due to the evident consequences of a breach but also considering the inevitable rise of manipulated traffic data over time.

As the applications of machine learning continue to expand, the incentive for malicious actors to release noisy, corrupt data across their operating domain will steadily increase. The impact of such corruption on model accuracies, as demonstrated by Scenario 2, is just as detrimental as testing a high-performing model on specially disguised data. In practice, this would be of paramount concern, as the corruption of training data would degrade performance across all testing samples.

Scenario 3, which utilized manipulated data for both training and testing, achieved accuracies comparable to our initial models. The accuracies for all scenarios are presented in Table 2. Although the performance of these models is impressive, interpreting their meaning is a complex process. It is essential to consider how, if at all, these results could help us understand adversarial attacks. The performance is biased towards patterns present in the manipulated dataset. While this bias may initially seem arbitrary, it is necessary to consider its potential uses.

Table 2. All scenario accuracies

	Scenario 1 (%)	Scenario 2 (%)	Scenario 3 (%)
DTC	13.76	13.76	92.06
MLP	06.70	09.83	57.86
RFC	13.76	13.76	92.53

Similar to how a typical model may be overfit to certain patterns in a dataset, the overfitting of models that utilize manipulated data for both training and testing could potentially provide researchers with insights to aid in recognizing adversarial attacks:

- Since overfitting typically occurs with highly influential features within a model, it may accentuate patterns unique to attacked data. This could contribute to the development of more effective detection mechanisms and guide future research.
- When introduced to accurate data, a model overfit to manipulated data may exhibit anomalies and inconsistencies. Data patterns that do not cause such anomalies could potentially be repurposed as indicators of adversarial activity within detection models.
- A model overfit to manipulate data could be used to generate synthetic adversarial samples. These samples may be valuable for evaluating and improving the robustness of detection models, providing researchers with the freedom to simulate attacks of specific types and sizes.

Beyond overfitting, it may be worth considering a model created and tested exclusively with adversarial data. Such a model could be useful alone or especially when applied inversely with a conventional detection model. Rather than detecting adversarial data like a conventional model, an adversarial model could aim to detect non-adversarial data. This could be particularly useful when the primary, conventional model does not produce a confident classification for a certain instance of network activity. The adversarial trained model could help provide primary models with more confidence in classifying ambiguous data samples. However, it should be noted that the models created in Scenario 3 may not be the best fit for such an application, as it would be vital to include a variety of real-world adversarial data while continually implementing recent attack methods.

Another useful metric for evaluating the effects of these attacks is found in each model's F1 scores, as shown in Table 3.

Table 3. All scenario F1 measures

	Scenario 1 F1 score (%)	Scenario 1 F1 score (%)	Scenario 3 F1 score (%)
DTC	16.34	11.18	92.08
MLP	06.58	06.00	58.82
RFC	16.35	11.19	92.49

The models face considerable challenges in accurately classifying instances, particularly in the context of adversarial scenarios involving manipulated data. This indicates potential limitations in their robustness for detecting network traffic under adversarial conditions. The low F1 scores, especially in precision and recall, underscore the models' difficulties in minimizing false positives and capturing all relevant instances during adversarial attacks. This struggle highlights the importance of effectively generalizing the data in the presence of adversarial manipulation. Across all three scenarios, the models have low accuracy, emphasizing the need for enhanced robustness in network traffic detection to mitigate the impact of adversarial attacks.

Each scenario provides valuable insights into improving adversarial attack detection systems. In the future, our research could implement these observations to further explore their viability. However, this research specifically aims to explore a broader interpretation of adversarial attacks and their impact across general detection outcomes.

Future research could also consider the alteration of real traffic features within live network traffic and the investigation of feature dependencies to proactively anticipate counterattacks. This may be more challenging for MLP to perform, as its performance was much slower than other algorithms.

4   Conclusion

This research makes significant contributions to the field of adversarial machine learning by providing a comprehensive exploration of the vulnerabilities within machine learning models subjected to adversarial attacks. The results highlight critical concerns and opportunities for improvement in cybersecurity.

One notable insight is the surprising resilience exhibited by the models in Scenario 3, where both the training and testing data were manipulated. This finding opens new avenues for recognizing adversarial patterns and enhancing model performance. Furthermore, the research emphasizes the importance of securing both the training and testing data in machine learning-based detection systems, as demonstrated by the consistent degradation of model performance across Scenarios 1 and 2.

The findings provide a solid foundation for future research in adversarial machine learning. By shedding light on vulnerabilities and potential countermeasures, this work paves the way for the development of more resilient and adaptive models capable of withstanding evolving threats in the complex landscape of cybersecurity. The insights gained can guide researchers in designing novel architectures, training methodologies, and defense mechanisms that proactively address the challenges posed by adversarial attacks.

In conclusion, this research makes a significant contribution to the understanding and mitigation of adversarial attacks in machine learning-based cybersecurity systems. By building upon the knowledge gained from this study, the cybersecurity community can work towards creating a more secure and resilient digital ecosystem.

References

1. Rahimi, N., Maynor, J., Gupta, B.: Adversarial machine learning: difficulties in applying machine learning to existing cybersecurity systems. In: Proceedings of the 35th International Conference on Computers and Their Applications, pp. 40–47. ISCA, San Francisco, California, USA (2020)
2. Essien, E.: Relevance of the deep web to academic research. Int. J. Nat. Appl. Sci. **12**, 107–113 (2020)
3. Finklea, K.: Dark Web. Congressional Research Service, https://sgp.fas.org/crs/misc/R44101.pdf. Last accessed 22 July 2024
4. Broome, H., Shrestha, Y., Harrison, N., Rahimi, N.: SMS malware detection: a machine learning approach. In: Proceedings of the 2022 International Conference on Computational Science and Computational Intelligence, pp. 936–941. IEEE Computer Society, Las Vegas, Nevada, USA (2022)
5. Gautam, A., Rahimi, N.: Viability of machine learning in android scareware detection. In: Proceedings of the 38th International Conference on Computers and Their Applications, pp. 19–26. ISCA, Virtual (2023)
6. Lashkari, A.H., Kaur, G., Rahali, A.: DIDarknet: a contemporary approach to detect and characterize the darknet traffic using deep image learning. In: Proceedings of the 10th International Conference on Communication and Network Security, pp. 1–13. ACM, Tokyo, Japan (2020)
7. Yang, F.J.: An extended idea about decision trees. In: Proceedings of the 2019 International Conference on Computational Science and Computational Intelligence, pp. 349–354. IEEE Computer Society, Las Vegas, Nevada, USA (2019)
8. Bosque Sendra, J.: Geomatic Approaches for Modeling Land Change Scenarios (2019)
9. Biau, G., Scornet, E.: A random forest guided tour. TEST **25**(2), 197–227 (2016)
10. Penchala, S., Murad, S.A., Roy, I., Gupta, B., Rahimi, N.: Unveiling text mining potential: a comparative analysis of document classification algorithms. In: Proceedings of 39th International Confer, vol. 98, pp. 103–115 (2024)
11. Murad, S.A., Rahimi, N., Muzahid, A.J.M.: PhishGuard: machine learning-powered phishing URL detection. In: 2023 Congress in Computer Science, Computer Engineering, & Applied Computing (CSCE), pp. 2279–2284. IEEE (2023)

Enhancing Software Requirements Classification with Machine Learning and Feature Selection Techniques

Daniel Lanfear[✉], Mina Maleki, and Shadi Banitaan

Department of Electrical and Computer Engineering and Computer Science, University of Detroit Mercy, 4001 W McNichols Rd, Detroit, MI 48221, USA
{lanfeadb,malekim,banitash}@udmercy.edu

Abstract. Requirements engineers have the responsibility for classifying software requirements into functional and nonfunctional variants. As software architects need quality requirements to be known to get their job done, machine learning is employed to speed up and add consistency to the process of identifying and categorizing requirements so that effort may be spent more effectively. We experimented with the effects of different machine learning algorithms, as well as different pre-processing and feature selection techniques. It was determined that, for this application, stop words should not be removed and that performing lemmatization on words provides the most effective features for classification. Furthermore, after finalizing our choices of pre-processing techniques and algorithm to use, we proposed a modification to the Extensive Feature Selector by gathering the most distinctive words in each category and using a list of those as our main features. By using a threshold of 0.013, we obtained an F1 score of 0.787, which is an improvement on the base Enhanced Feature Selector's F1 score of 0.761 with the same number of word features.

Keywords: Machine learning · Requirements engineering · Supervised learning · Classification · Feature selection · Natural language processing

1 Introduction

The software development life cycle is made up of many steps. One of the most important steps is requirements engineering, where requirements are elicited, analyzed, processed, modeled, and validated [1, 2]. Within the task of requirement engineering, the requirements must be identified and classified so the features and the attributes of the system are clearly labeled. With this classification, stakeholders can understand the kind of system they are investing in and the development team can have guidelines to deliver a quality product [1]. The process of requirement classification can be tedious, time-consuming, and challenging to do by hand. For these reasons, automated classification is necessary.

In this application, the requirements are given as pairs of the requirement string and the class that it is associated with. Requirements can be defined as either functional or non-functional [2]. Functional requirements are defined as the features a system may

W. Feng et al. (Eds.): SEDE 2024, CCIS 2244, pp. 14–30, 2024.
https://doi.org/10.1007/978-3-031-75201-8_2

provide. The other category is non-functional requirements, which are the constraints on the behaviors the system shall have. The non-functional requirement category can be split further into sub-categories that are more specific in which respects the system should behave, such as security, performance, reliability, and others [2]. In most requirement engineering processes, functional requirements are prioritized over non-functional requirements; meanwhile, the system constraints are not specified well, if at all. This leads to either poor system design or a delay in system design until the constraints are specified [3]. One way the requirements engineers can tell if they are specifying all the proper constraints is through recognition and correct classification of the requirements.

A widely used method of automatically categorizing requirements is text classification using machine learning [4]. Text classification is a machine learning application that is used for many different purposes, from spam identification to sentiment analysis. Using natural language processing, the text data is transformed from its unstructured form into data that is understandable by a computer [5]. However, it is challenging to turn a natural language sentence into a set of features that a computer can analyze and use to make classification decisions. This is usually broken into steps, such as pre-processing, feature extraction, and classification [5]. The classification can be done as a binary classification, such as functional and non-functional requirement, or it can be done as a multiple-choice classification, such as splitting up non-functional requirements into their sub-categories [4, 6].

In this application, We aim to explore different methods of improving the ability of machine learning to distinguish between multiple classes of software requirements. We determine effective natural language processing (NLP) techniques, such as stop word removal, stemming, and lemmatization. We also review the effectiveness of a few machine learning algorithms, such as K-Nearest-Neighbors (KNN), Decision Tree (DT), Random Forest (RF), Multinomial Naive Bayes (MNB), Logistic Regression (LR), and Support Vector Machine (SVM). Our main contribution is in the feature selection space, where we propose a new way of determining discriminatory terms within the documents and compare them to other effective methods of feature selection, such as Extensive Feature Selector (EFS) [18] and Class-Index Corpus-Index (CICI) [19].

The rest of the paper is structured as follows. Section 2 conducts a review of related literature to the classification of functional and non-functional requirements. Section 3 describes the material used and the methodology followed. Section 4 discusses the results of the research. Section 5 concludes the paper and discusses future avenues for research.

2 Literature Review

Many of the studies used an open-access dataset named the PROMISE repository [7], so they can be compared rather easily. However, some authors used the data for binary classification, some attempted multi-class classification, and one used a hybrid approach.

2.1 Binary Classifiers

Plenty of work was done differentiating between functional and non-functional requirements, which led to interesting innovations. A comparison of the binary classifiers is shown in Table 1.

Of the binary classifiers, the most innovative was [8] which used a small set of linguistic dependency features to enhance the ability to generalize the models performance to other classification problems. In addition, [8] used other private requirement datasets to test their works efficacy. They used a support vector machine (SVM) classifier, which is popular in the field of text classification [4]. Reference [9] had two methods of classification, so both are listed in Table 1. For both, stop words had been removed, punctuation had been removed, and the words were lemmatized. For the first method, only word features were used with no feature selection. For the second method, the top 500 words were selected using information gain and syntax features were added. Both methods used an SVM classifier, receiving F1 scores of 0.92 and 0.87 respectively. Reference [10] used an upgraded version of the PROMISE dataset, which is the PROMISE exp dataset [11]. It adds more instances of every class and reduces the imbalance compared to the original PROMISE repository. Reference [10] did not do much pre-processing differently, but had changes in feature extraction and selection. First, instead of using the raw term frequency, they used a different formula known as term frequency-inverse document frequency. They also used Chi-Squared statistical analysis for selecting the amount of word features to use. Reference [10] got an F1 score of 0.91 using this data configuration with both the logistic regression and SVM classifiers.

2.2 Multi-class Classifiers

Less work has been done in the realm of multi-class requirement classification. It is a more difficult problem and therefore resulted in lower scores, but Logistic regression was the popular choice for this application for [10, 12]. Stop word removal as well as lemmatization continued to be popular techniques for normalizing the data. With those, as well as using TF-IDF and Chi-squared a logistic regression algorithm can obtain a 0.78 F1 Score for multi-class classification. Reference [13] tested the efficacy of these preprocessing techniques while proposing a hybrid algorithm that combines a rule-based approach with the popular k-nearest-neighbors. The authors did not use an F1 score as a metric but obtained a 0.86 accuracy score with their efforts.

3 Material and Methodology

In this research, we take many different techniques and algorithms used in NLP and experiment to determine which techniques are useful specifically for requirement classification. This is different from other forms of text classification as most requirements are single sentences and can have domain-specific nomenclature. The steps we take to classify requirements are shown in Fig. 1.

Table 1. Classifier performance comparison.

References	Classification	Dataset	Norm	Stop word removal	Word processing	Features	Feature selection	Algorithm	Results
[8]	Binary	PROMISE	X	X	None	Linguistic dependencies	Interpretable ML	SVM	F1: 0.79
[9]	Binary	PROMISE	✓	✓	Lemmatization	BoW	None	SVM	F1: 0.92
[9]	Binary	PROMISE	✓	✓	Lemmatization	BoW, syntax features	Information Gain	SVM	F1: 0.87
[10]	Binary	PROMISE exp	✓	✓	Lemmatization	TF-IDF	CHI2	LR, SVM	F1: 0.91
[10]	Multi-class	PROMISE exp	✓	✓	Lemmatization	TF-IDF	CHI2	LR	F1: 0.78
[12]	Multi-class	PROMISE	X	✓	Stemming	BoW	None	LR	F1: 0.75
[13]	Multi-class	PROMISE exp	✓	✓	Lemmatization	TF-IDf	None	Hybrid rule based KNN	ACC: 0.85

3.1 Technology Used

These experiments were done using Python, Kaggle, and multiple libraries within Python for machine learning. The Natural Language Toolkit (NLTK) [15] was used to pre-process the data. This included any modifications to the dataset itself before we extracted features from it. To extract features, run the algorithms, and evaluate the performance of the classifiers, we used the SciKit-Learn package. For data analysis and manipulation, we used the pandas package.

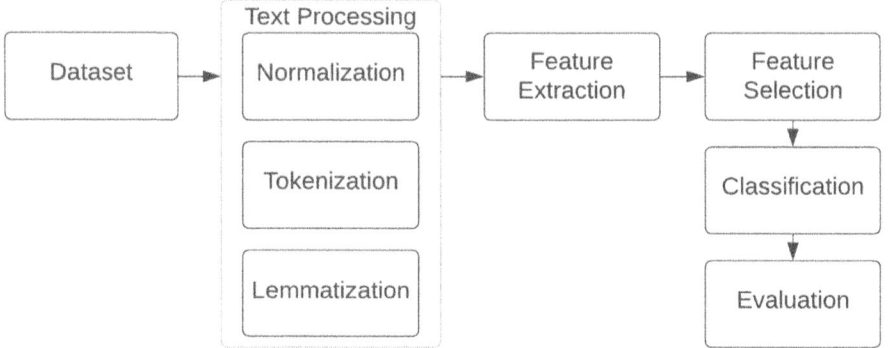

Fig. 1. The Requirement Classification framework.

3.2 Text Pre-processing

In the text pre-processing space, plenty of techniques are employed to achieve good results. These techniques range from what to include to how to represent parts of the requirement. The main outcome of the preprocessing step is to input the requirement text and produce a document that can be easily and efficiently read by a machine learning algorithm.

3.2.1 Tokenization

An important step in making a document readable by a computer is turning the requirement sentence into a list of its words.

3.2.2 Normalization

In this context, normalization is the process of lower casing, fixing spelling errors, and removing punctuation and non-alphabetic characters [13]. These processes are performed together in many text classification applications so they are labeled as one action, rather than multiple separate actions.

3.2.3 Stop Word Removal

There are plenty of terms known in natural language as stop words, which have been shown to have very little impact on classification and should be removed [15, 24]. For example: a, the, and is are all stop words and can be removed to produce a more efficient feature set. In some applications, numbers, and punctuation are removed as well, leaving just the words that do not appear in the list of stop words.

3.2.4 Stemming

Words have many different forms that come from the same base or stem. Stemming reverts a word to its base form without taking into account the part of speech the word has [16]. This may produce errors in stemming and may, for example, reduce the word 'caring' to 'car'.

3.2.5 Lemmatization

Different from stemming, lemmatization reduces a word to its lemma, which requires the word's part of speech to be understood before reduction [16, 26]. The main difference with this and stemming is that inflected words are also reduced to the same base word [27]. As an example, this would reduce the word 'caring' to 'care'.

3.3 Feature Extraction

After normalization, the following step is to extract features from the requirements. This is also known as vectorization. The most popular vectorization techniques found were Bag of Words (BoW) and Term Frequency-Inverse Document Frequency (TF- IDF).

3.3.1 Bag of Words

One of the simplest methods of feature extraction, BoW makes each distinct word in the corpus a feature with the value being the number of occurrences in each requirement. BoW is also known as term frequency, as it stores the frequency of each term in a certain requirement as its feature vector. The labeled requirement is expressed as this vector and used to train a classifier. One downside of BoW is that it gives a high weight to common words that may not be valuable [14, 23].

3.3.2 Term Frequency-Inverse Document Frequency

Term Frequency-Inverse Document Frequency [17] is more complicated as it combines two metrics. The first metric is the frequency of the word in a requirement. The second is the inverse of the document frequency of that term. This is computed by dividing the total number of requirements in the document by the total requirements with that term within the entire list of requirements. This value has logarithmic scaling done to it, then it is multiplied by the first value to extract features. The process is described well in [10] using the following equations.

$$inverse\_doc\_freq_i = \log \frac{total\_reqs}{total\_req\_with\_term\_i} \tag{1}$$

$$TFIDF\left(term_{i,j}\right) = term\_freq_{i,j} * inverse\_doc\_freq_i \tag{2}$$

3.3.3 Parts-of-Speech (POS) Tagging

POS tagging assigns tags to each word in the requirement, such as noun, verb, adjective, etc. [3, 25]. The number of each POS in a requirement is used as a feature to find differences in sentence structure in different classes of requirement [5].

3.4 Feature Selection

Finally, before the models can run on the feature sets, features must be chosen to increase classification speed and reduce complexity. BoW and TF-IDF both produce very many features, as there are almost an uncountable number of distinct words in the requirement corpus. There are copious ways to select features for a machine-learning model. Some studies, like [9], take the most informative features up to 500 or 1000 by hundreds and see where the trend levels out to find what features to select.

Another well-known method of feature selection is by using the Chi-Squared method. Chi-Squared is a statistical test used to determine if two variables are dependent on each other or not [23]. A threshold is set and if the measure is higher than the threshold, the feature is not significantly impacting the classification. Equation (3) is as follows:

$$chi\_sq(t, c) = \frac{N * (AD - CB)^2}{(A + C)(B + D)(A + D)(C + D)} \tag{3}$$

In (3), N is the total number of requirements. As shown in Table 2, A is the number of times t and c both occur, B is the number of times t occurs and c does not, C is the number of times c occurs and t does not, and D is the number of times neither occurs [10]. In addition to taking the top 100, 200, or 500 values, Chi-Squared may also take any number of values with a certain significance level.

With the multiple types of requirements and their levels of distinction, it becomes useful to find what words are distinct from specific class labels and use those. Reference [18] proposed Extensive Feature Selector (EFS), which defines the significance of a term based on both class-based and corpus-based probabilities. This feature selection model is used to find the words that are the most distinguished within the corpus. As shown in (6), each term has two parts calculated for each class label, j, in the corpus, which are multiplied together. The products are added together to obtain the value for feature selection, which is limited to the range of 0–1 [18].

$$EFS_{class\_based}(t) = \sum_{j=1}^{M} \frac{P(t|C_j)}{P(\neg t|C_j)P(t|\neg C_j) + 1} \tag{4}$$

$$EFS_{corpus\_based}(t) = \frac{P(C_j|t)}{P(\neg C_j|t)P(C_j|\neg t) + 1} \tag{5}$$

$$EFS(t) = \sum_{j=1}^{M} \left(EFS_{class\_based}(t) * EFS_{corpus\_based}(t)\right) \tag{6}$$

One issue with this method is that unbalanced classes, like in the problem of the PROMISE dataset, may have terms that are distinct and not marked as such due to low occurrences in the overall corpus. Following the development of EFS, Class-Index Corpus-Index (CICI) [19] was developed to work with imbalanced class issues. It is defined in (7) using the terms in Table 2.

$$CICI(t) = \sum_{j=1}^{M} \frac{(AD - BC)^2}{(A + C) * (B + D) + N^2} \tag{7}$$

Our proposed method is one that can be applied to either of these two algorithms to enhance multi-class feature selection. Instead of summing the products of CICI or EFS, we listed each score for each word for each class label to see which words were the most distinguishable for each class label. Following that, we used both a score and a minimum list length threshold to determine the most distinct words in the corpus. We take every word that scores higher than a threshold in each class. To get equal representation in the case of a list having significantly fewer words than the others, we provide a minimum length for each class and add the next highest-ranking words until that length threshold is met.

Table 2. Case table for term t and class c

	Requirement containing term t	Requirement not containing term t
In class c	A	C
Not in class c	B	D

3.5 Machine Learning Algorithms

Machine learning can be split mainly into two different categories: unsupervised learning and supervised learning. Unsupervised learning is conducted when the material is not labeled so the algorithm must group similar instances. Supervised learning is con- ducted when the data used to train the classifier is labeled, so it learns the connection between what it is given and what it is supposed to be [20]. In this research, supervised machine learning is the employed process. The following algorithms were used.

3.5.1 K Nearest Neighbors

K Nearest Neighbors (KNN) is a majority voting algorithm that works based on the assumption that points of the same class label are near each other. The algorithm knows the class label of a set amount of points and assigns the class label of new points based on the majority label of K nearest points [22]. K is chosen manually and is usually the square root of the number of instances in the dataset.

3.5.2 Decision Tree

Decision Tree is an algorithm that models the feature set as a hierarchy of nodes using features to make decisions. Each leaf node is a conclusion on the class label and each root node is a decision that leads to either another decision or the leaf node.

3.5.3 Random Forest

One step further from the decision tree is the random forest, which adds in multiple decision trees that are all trained with slightly different groups of the training data to produce different trees that work with majority rules.

3.5.4 Multinomial Naive Bayes

The Multinomial Naïve Bayes is a statistical method based on Bayes theorem that computes the predicted class. It also assumes that features are independent of one another [20]. By training on the data set, it finds the probability of seeing a feature given the class label. That is then used along with the probability of seeing the class label to find the probability of the class label given a new record without a class label. It calculates a probability for each class label and assigns the one with the highest probability [27].

3.5.5 Logistic Regression

The logistic regression algorithm is similar to linear regression, but it is used instead for discrete, finite values rather than continuous variables. Just like linear regression, the inputs and outputs are known, so the algorithm finds the weights for the variables and fits them into the following equation where Y is the output, X is the set of all input features, and β is the set of all constants:

$$Y = \frac{e^{\beta_0 * x_0 + \beta_1 * x_1 \dots}}{1 + e^{\beta_0 * x_0 + \beta_1 * x_1 \dots}}. \tag{8}$$

3.5.6 Support Vector Machine

The SVM is very popular for this application as it is very effective with high dimensional data. The SVM will look for points of data that are close to alternate classes and then use those points to draw informed lines of separation between classes in the feature space. These lines can be linear, polynomial and more. It works quite well and has high performance without becoming too complicated and over-fitting on the training data.

4   Results and Discussion

4.1 Dataset

One of the most popular datasets is the requirement dataset from the PROMISE Repository, used in many of the studies read for this literature review. It has 625 total requirements, 255 of which are functional requirements. The rest of the requirements are split among the nonfunctional requirement variety, with the specific classes as follows: availability, fault tolerance, legal, look and feel, maintainability, operational, performance, portability, scalability, security, and usability.

With the PROMISE data set, some of the nonfunctional requirement classes are severely underrepresented, such as fault tolerance having only 10 occurrences and portability only having 1 occurrence. There are a few ways to combat this issue. One method taken by [9] was to focus on fewer broader nonfunctional requirement categories regarding that data set. In addition, they also obtained a data set made from user comments to oversample the minority class. Another option that was accomplished by [10, 13] was to use an expanded version of the PROMISE data set. The expanded version contains a total of over 950 requirements, 525 of those being nonfunctional requirements.

As a result of the review, it is clear to see that the PROMISE data set and its expansion are the most popular data sets to use for requirement classification. The most innovative idea from these was to combine it with several others or to train it on PROMISE and to test its effectiveness on other requirement-based data sets. An open access version of the PROMISE set was found at [7]. It seems plausible that it was uploaded to make it more accessible; following that, the repository gained popularity and it became a source studies may cite when using PROMISE.

Since the PROMISE dataset is smaller and has a significant amount of imbalance, we also tried the PROMISE exp dataset [11]. The PROMISE exp dataset provides more representation for some categories, such as Portability and Fault Tolerance, but still is very imbalanced. The class distribution of PROMISE and PROMISE exp is shown in Table 3, highlighting the imbalance in these datasets. In practice, there are more functional requirements than any single category of non-functional requirements, but it becomes difficult for a model to correctly classify requirements without the proper representation.

We used Leave One Out Cross Validation (LOOCV) for our training and testing split. We had less than 1000 instances in our datasets and it removes the randomness of splitting data into testing and training [22]. The increased consistency also increased the confidence in our results, showing that it was not luck of the draw that resulted in our scores.

4.2 Evaluation Metrics

Once the model is constructed using a feature and an algorithm, its performance must be evaluated by some metric. The confusion matrix allows one to see all the guesses for class 1 that are correct, the guesses of class 1 which are incorrect, the guesses for class 0 that are correct, and the guesses for class 0 that is incorrect. These are true positive, false positive, true negative, and false negative respectively [20].

There are plenty of metrics out there, but some of the more popular metrics used are precision and recall. Precision is the measure of how many nonfunctional requirements have been classified correctly compared to the number of requirements labeled as nonfunctional [20]. It is defined in (9).

$$Precision = \frac{TP}{TP + FP} \tag{9}$$

Table 3. PROMISE and PROMISE_exp breakdown.

Requirement class	PROMISE	PROMISE_exp
Functional	255	444
Availability	21	18
Fault tolerance	10	18
Legal	13	15
Look and feel	38	49
Maintainability	17	24
Operational	62	77
Performance	54	67
Portability	1	12
Scalability	21	22
Security	66	125
Usability	67	85
Total	625	969

One way to think about precision is that the higher it is, the fewer false positives there are. Recall is similar, but it looks at the percentage of nonfunctional requirements that have been classified correctly. It is defined as:

$$Recall = \frac{TP}{TP + FN} \tag{10}$$

The thought process for this metric is that the higher the recall, the fewer false negatives there are.

As summary, a high precision score makes sure that all the positive classifications are correct, and a high recall makes sure that all positive instances are classified correctly [20]. There is always a trade-off between the two, as it is the balancing act between being too careful and not careful enough, so different scenarios can optimize for either high recall or high precision. Another metric exists called the F1 score, which weights the precision and recall together and finds a metric that describes when they are both optimized to their maximum potential. It is defined as:

$$F1\_Score = 2 * \frac{(precision * recall)}{precision + recall} \tag{11}$$

When the F1 score is high, the precision and recall are balanced and high. If the F1 score is low, one or both of the two metrics is low.

Finally, another metric that was used in [12, 13] but may not have had a place with the data sets used was the accuracy metric. This metric is defined as:

$$Accuracy = \frac{TP}{Total} \tag{12}$$

This is not a good metric for unbalanced data sets [20]. Both PROMISE and PROMISE exp are considered unbalanced as some requirement types have as many as hundreds of examples and other types can have less than ten.

4.3 Model Analysis

Some of the more popular classification algorithms used in this application are: KNN, DT, RF, MNB, LR, and SVM. These were all put to the test under various configurations to determine which algorithm could perform multi-class classification with the highest marks. For these tests, The data was processed in the same way and each classifier had the same set parameters. The data preparation involved lemmatization, stop word removal, number removal, punctuation removal, and text normalization.

The KNN algorithm had the distance metric set to cosine due to its efficacy in text classification [21], and the number of neighbors was set to the square root of the number of rows of data. The decision tree and random forest classifiers used their default parameters. The Naive Bayes algorithm used was the MultinomialNB with default parameters. Logistic regression used default parameters unless the maximum number of iterations did not allow it to converge. The maximum iterations parameter was set to 2200 to ensure convergence. The SVM classifier used was the SVC with default parameters. As shown in Fig. 2, Logistic regression is the highest performer followed closely by Naive Bayes and Random Forest. Also shown in these figures is the conclusion that TF-IDF is a more effective term weighting scheme than BoW, which has been supported by [10, 13, 14].

4.4 Pre-processing Analysis

Of the aspects of pre-processing, the following choices were analyzed and tested: stop word removal, word manipulation such as stemming and lemmatization, and whether to include only alphabetic characters. Stop word removal is done for most text classification applications, but we hypothesize that a generic list of stop words may still have an impact when classifying requirements. As shown in Fig 3, removing stop words leads to a slight decrease in performance. Looking at how stop words appear in the corpus, we see that certain stop words appear within certain classes more than others. For example, in the Performance class, the words "no", "more", and "than" appear at a higher frequency compared to the other classes. Another example of this occurrence is with the Availability class. The words "during", "between", and "up" appear frequently in the Availability class and not nearly as much in other classes.

Furthermore, Fig. 4 shows the improvement that stemming makes on no manipulation and the improvement that lemmatization makes on stemming. Both lemmatization and stemming reduce the feature space by combining the same word with different endings into one single feature, which helps reduce overfitting of the model [9, 10, 13, 16].

4.5 Feature Selection Analysis

To find out if our proposed method is more effective than EFS and CICI, we ran the LR classifier on each feature set using the pre-processing configurations that were determined to be optimal through experimentation. The corpus had numbers and punctuation

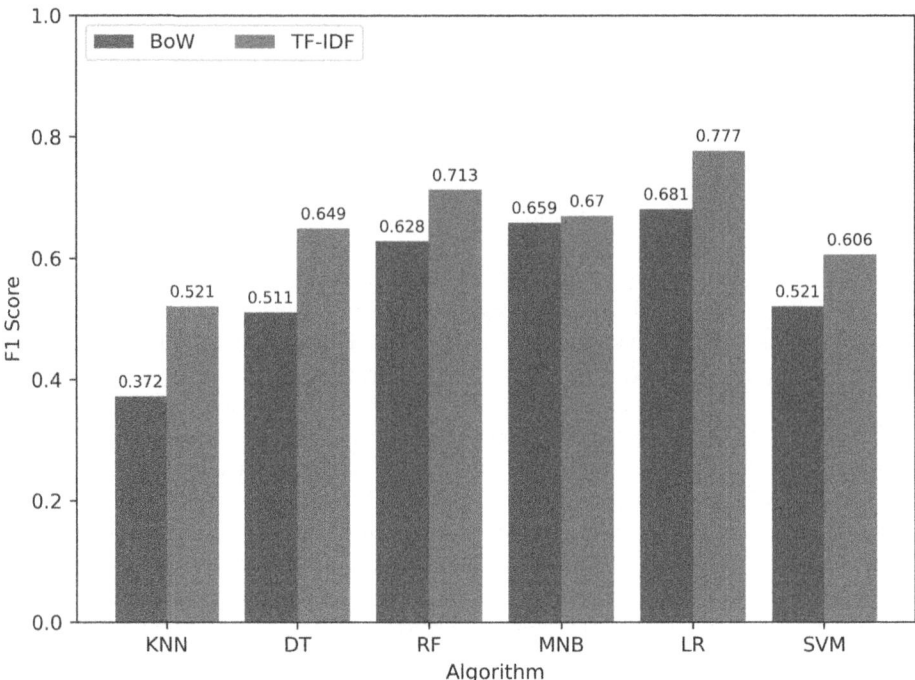

Fig. 2. Model analysis using BoW and TF-IDF.

removed, was lemmatized, and was vectorized using TF-IDF. The feature selection algorithms were limited to the top 295 words. For our proposed method, we used a score threshold of 0.014 and a minimum length of 22. The top 295 words using EFS obtained an F1 score of 0.763. The CICI top 295 words made a slight improvement with an F1 score of 0.768. Finally, Using our proposed method of combining the discriminatory terms from each class to improve representation obtained an F1 score of 0.776, beating both of the reviewed algorithms.

There is a trade-off between the amount of features used and the performance of the classifier. The best result obtained was done by using only the score threshold of 0.013, which provided a word list of 341 words and obtained an F1 score of 0.787.

4.6 Testing on Expanded PROMISE

After testing on the PROMISE dataset, we decided to see how our machine-learning model worked on the expanded PROMISE exp. Our first experiment was to see the performance with absolutely no feature selection, which yielded 1587 word features in total. The second test was to compare EFS, CICI, and our MEFS to see which gave the best result. Our MEFS had the best result, as shown in Table 4. The performances all around were worse for PROMISE exp compared to PROMISE, but the improvements in feature selection algorithms are still present.

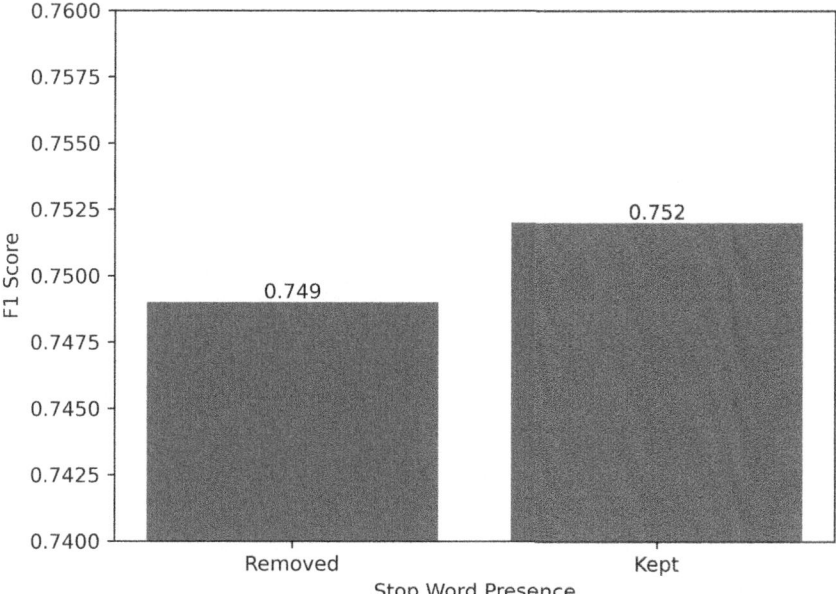

Fig. 3. Stop word removal analysis.

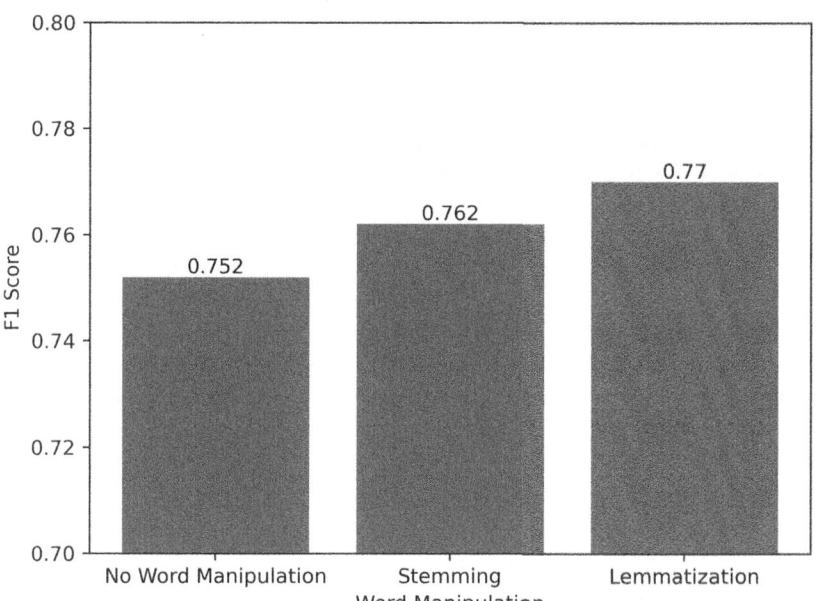

Fig. 4. Word manipulation analysis.

5   Conclusion

In this work, we combined several techniques for improving the quality of software requirement classification. We analyzed the performance of six different classifiers, natural language processing techniques such as lemmatization and stop word removal, two different feature extraction methods, and two different feature selection methods.

Table 4. Feature selection comparison results.

Selection method	F1 score	# Features
PROMISE		
None	0.790	1261
EFS	0.761	341
CICI	0.780	341
MEFS	0.787	341
PROMISE_exp		
None	0.764	1587
EFS	0.737	386
CICI	0.751	386
MEFS	0.756	386

In addition, we proposed our own method of selecting features based on lists of discriminatory words from each class. These methods were tested on both the PROMISE dataset as well as its expansion, PROMISE exp.

We gathered data on the F1 scores of the different configurations and found that the combination of lemmatization, normalization, TF-IDF, LR has the highest F1 score of all the configurations, being 0.790 and 0.764 for PROMISE and PROMISE exp respectively. However, with the copious number of features in each set, we employed feature selection to achieve a feature set with fewer features. We obtained F1 scores of 0.787 and 0.756 with around a quarter of the feature set using our new configuration, losing less than one percent on our score while dropping hundreds of features. We compared our method with existing methods, one targeting imbalanced class problems, and our method had the highest F1 scores than other methods with the same number of features.

References

1. Pfleeger, S.L., Atlee, J.M.: Software Engineering: Theory and Practice, 4th edn. Dorling Kindersley, New Delhi (2011)
2. Laplante, P.A., Kassab, M.: Requirements Engineering for Software and Systems, 4th edn. Auerbach, Boca Raton (2022)

3. Casamayor, A., Godoy, D., Campo, M.: Identification of non-functional requirements in textual specifications: a semi-supervised learning approach. Inf. Softw. Technol. **52**(4), 436–445 (2010). https://doi.org/10.1016/j.infsof.2009.10.010

4. Binkhonain, M., Zhao, L.: A review of machine learning algorithms for identification and classification of non-functional requirements. Expert Syst. Appl.: X **1** (2019). https://doi.org/10.1016/j.eswax.2019.100001

5. Sarkar, D.: Text Analytics with Python: A Practitioner's Guide to Natural Language Processing, 2nd edn. Apress, Berkeley, CA (2019)

6. Sonbol, R., Rebdawi, G., Ghneim, N.: The use of NLP-based text representation techniques to support requirement engineering tasks: a systematic mapping review. IEEE Access **10**, 62811–62830 (2022). https://doi.org/10.1109/access.2022.3182372

7. Souvik: "Software Requirements Dataset." Kaggle (2023)

8. Dalpiaz, F., Dell'Anna, D., Aydemir, F.B., Evikol, S.C,.: Requirements classification with interpretable machine learning and dependency parsing. In: 2019 IEEE 27th International Requirements Engineering Conference (RE), Jeju, Korea (South), 2019, pp. 142–152. https://doi.org/10.1109/RE.2019.00025

9. Kurtanovi´c, Z., Maalej, W.: Automatically classifying functional and non-functional requirements using supervised machine learning. In: 2017 IEEE 25th International Requirements Engineering Conference (RE) , pp. 490–495. Lisbon, Portugal (2017). https://doi.org/10.1109/RE.2017.82

10. Dias Canedo, E., Cordeiro Mendes, B.: Software requirements classification using machine learning algorithms. Entropy **22**(9), 1057 (2020). https://doi.org/10.3390/e22091057

11. Lima, M., Valle, V., Costa, E., Lira, F., Gadelha, B.: Software engineering repositories: expanding the PROMISE database. Proceedings of the XXXIII Brazilian Symposium on Software Engineering (2019). https://doi.org/10.1145/3350768.3350776

12. Mir Khatian, V., Ali Arain, Q., Alenezi, M., Owais Raza, M., Shaikh, F., Farah, I.: Comparative analysis for predicting non-functional requirements using supervised machine learning. In: 2021 1st International Conference on Artificial Intelligence and Data Analytics (CAIDA) , pp. 7–12. Riyadh, Saudi Arabia (2021). https://doi.org/10.1109/CAIDA51941.2021.9425236

13. Khurshid, I., et al.: Classification of non-functional requirements from IOT oriented healthcare requirement document. Front. Public Health **10** (2022). https://doi.org/10.3389/fpubh.2022.860536

14. Chen, L., Jiang, L., Li, C.: Using modified term frequency to improve term weighting for text classification. Eng. Appl. Artif. Intell. **101** (2021). https://doi.org/10.1016/j.engappai.2021.104215

15. Bird, S., Klein, E., Loper, E.: Natural Language Processing with Python. O'Reilly Media Inc., Beijing (2009)

16. Jivani, A.G.: A comparative study of stemming algorithms. Int. J. Comput. Appl. Technol. **2**(6), 1930–1938 (2011)

17. Salton, G., Buckley, C.: "Term-weighting approaches in automatic text retrieval. Inf. Process. Manage. **24**(5), 513–523 (1988). https://doi.org/10.1016/0306-4573(88)90021-0

18. Parlak, B., Uysal, A.K.: A novel filter feature selection method for text classification: extensive feature selector. J. Inf. Sci. **49**(1), 59–78 (2021). https://doi.org/10.1177/0165551521991037

19. Parlak, B.: Class-Index corpus-index measure: a novel feature selection method for imbalanced text data. Concurrency and Computation: Practice and Experience, vol. 34, no. 21 (2022). https://doi.org/10.1002/cpe.7140

20. Alpaydin, E.: Introduction to Machine Learning, 4th edn. The MIT Press, Cambridge, MA (2020)

21. Li, B., Han, L.: Distance weighted cosine similarity measure for text classification. Intell. Data Eng. Autom. Learn.—IDEAL 611–618 (2013). https://doi.org/10.1007/978-3-642-41278-3

22. Wong, T.-T.: Performance evaluation of classification algorithms by K-fold and leave-one-out cross validation. Pattern Recogn. **48**(9), 2839–2846 (2015). https://doi.org/10.1016/j.patcog.2015.03.009

23. Lu, M., Liang, P.: Automatic classification of non-functional requirements from augmented app user reviews. In: Proceedings of the 21st International Conference on Evaluation and Assessment in Software Engineering (2017). https://doi.org/10.1145/3084226.3084241

24. Vijayvargiya, S., Kumar, L., Murthy, L.B., Misra, S.: Software requirements classification using deep-learning approach with various hidden layers. Ann. Comput. Sci. Inf. Syst. (2022). https://doi.org/10.15439/2022f140

25. Younas, M., Jawawi, D.N., Ghani, I., Shah, M.A.: Extraction of non-functional requirement using semantic similarity distance. Neural Comput. Appl. **32**(11), 7383–7397 (2019). https://doi.org/10.1007/s00521-019-04226-5

26. Rahman, M.A., Haque, M.A., Tawhid, M.N., Siddik, M.S.: Classifying non-functional requirements using RNN variants for quality software development. In: Proceedings of the 3rd ACM SIGSOFT International Workshop on Machine Learning Techniques for Software Quality Evaluation (2019). https://doi.org/10.1145/3340482.3342745

27. Silva-Rodr´ıguez, V., et al.: Classifying design-level requirements using machine learning for a recommender of interaction design patterns. IET Softw. **14**(5), 544–552 (2020). https://doi.org/10.1049/iet-sen.2019.0291

Embracing Residuality Theory in Software Architecture to Address Uncertainty: Key Challenges and Strategies

Aziz Fellah[✉]

School of Computer Science and Information Systems, Northwest Missouri State University,
Maryville, MO 64468, USA
afellah@nwmissouri.edu
https://www.nwmissouri.edu/csis/directory/fellah.htm

Abstract. The source of uncertainty in software architecture isn't impossible to predict, but it is certainly challenging given its inherent complexity and the dynamic environments of technology, external factors and events that can potentially impact the system's operation and stability. Residuality theory, in particular, provides a new ideology that challenges conventional approaches to software design. In this paper, we propose a Residual Dynamic Management (RDM) framework for software architecture to manage residual components and stressors that constitute a residual system. RDM ensures that the system not only remains robust and capable of thriving but also flourishes in the face of uncertainty, dynamic changes, and unpredictable conditions. Furthermore, we propose a model called Residual Finite State Machines (R-FSM) to incorporate residuality complexity into software architecture, enhancing the overall system's ability to manage unforeseen changes and effectively benefit from them through the concept of antifragility.

Keywords: Residuality theory · Software architecture · Uncertainty · Antifragility

1 Introduction

Due to the increasing size and complexity of software systems across various domains, the role of software architecture becomes a crucial part in project development. In essence, software architecture serves as the blueprint for building robust and reliable software solutions to meet the needs of users and stakeholders. A software system may consist of multiple levels of abstraction and various phases, each phase is characterized by its own particular software architecture. Thus, the consequences of a specific software architecture made during the system development can significantly influence the entire system. In the early stages of developing a software architecture, some properties of the system may be difficult to determine or can even be ambiguous. This uncertainty can stem from different factors such as evolving requirements, technological constraints, or new business objectives. As a result, there may be diverse architectural options, but

W. Feng et al. (Eds.): SEDE 2024, CCIS 2244, pp. 31–42, 2024.
https://doi.org/10.1007/978-3-031-75201-8_3

uncertainty remains with respect to which architecture will perform well in the specified environment [6, 7, 18]. This can be challenging, particularly in complex systems or in environments with diverse perspectives and stakeholders. By adhering to general principles, guidelines, and tools, software architects can work towards finding the most suitable software architecture that balances the project's requirements, scope, and constraints. There may be multiple feasible architectures, but determining which architecture performs the best is a still a challenge for software architects. Software architects still do not have a clear consensus on defining the frontiers of software architecture and deciding on the components it should contain. Software architects can explore and evaluate the quality properties of each architectural candidate model to determine the best ones. Rather than being confined to a particular phase in the software development, software architecture is a pervasive discipline that influences every stage of the development process. By carefully assessing different and flexible strategies, developers can ensure that the chosen architecture is well-suited to support the system's functionality, scalability, modularity, robustness, and other important characteristics [4, 12, 14, 17]. O'Reilly's introduction of residuality theory [4, 5] offers a novel approach to understanding and managing uncertainties in complex systems. Software architects can build systems that not only meet current needs but also remain effective and valuable in the face of uncertainties and challenges over time. This may involve adopting other software development principles to adapt to new conditions without requiring a complete overhaul of the architecture. Thus, developers can create software that not only meets current needs but also anticipates changes and challenges. For example, the software architecture of a system should not fail to adapt or respond effectively to changes in the business landscape, resulting in a failure of the system [8, 10]. Uncertainty about the software architecture itself always exists, particularly in early system design, while unpredictability may potentially arise regarding the software's execution environment. While there is a large number of references in the literature on the topic of software architecture, this paper will only address specific aspects of it. See for example, [13, 15, 16, 19].

Software architecture tools are integral part of the software development process. They provide developers with necessary support and play a crucial role in designing, visualizing, analyzing, and implementing various architectures. Such tools are categorized based on their functionalities and features. Just to name a few, modeling tools (i.e., UML, ArchiMate, Enterprise Architect), code-based tools or diagrams-as-code (i.e., Graphviz, Mermaid), automated tools (i.e., Per-Opteryx, VisualVM), and diagramming tools (i.e., Microsoft Visio, Creately). Each category of tools has its advantages and disadvantages, and the choice of tool depends on various factors such as the requirements of the project, the preferences of the development team, and the complexity of the software architecture. It's important to acknowledge the significance of such tools within the context of software architecture practices, even if they are not the primary focus of this paper. The reader can refer to various conferences that discuss tools and methods, in software architecture. Some excellent conferences include: International Conference on Software Architecture (ICSA) and European Conference on Software Architecture (ECSA).

In today's dynamic software environments, developers should create architectures that can accommodate unpredictable changes and uncertainty. This requires embracing and exploiting a combination of foresight, maintainability, redundancy flexibility, modularity, and robust design principles. Some strategies that software developers have employed to achieve these design qualities such as modular design, microservices architecture, design patterns, event-driven architecture, API-first design, service-oriented architecture (SOA), and continuous integration and deployment. Additionally, DevOps [19, 20] which is an evolution of the Agile Software Development [22] advocates frequent and small release iterations with stakeholders' feedback. While there is no universal approach for capturing design rationale in architectural decisions, employing a combination of these strategies, techniques and tools can assist software architects in effectively justifying their architectural choices in a manner aligned with project goals and requirements. There are several papers and references that discuss tools and methods for analyzing, defining, and evaluating software architecture. These resources provide insights into various approaches and frameworks. Additionally, continuous conformance and alignment between the implementation and architecture have been discussed in [9]. There is no standardized framework for dealing with uncertainty that software architects should adhere to [8, 10, 11, 17]. Additionally in this paper, we use the words *uncertainty* and *unpredictability* interchangeably in conjunction with software architecture. However, uncertainty is the preferred term within the realm of software architecture over other wording variants.

The remainder of the paper is organized as follows: In Sect. 2, we propose a framework for designing software architecture that not only withstand external and internal factors but also improve in response to them. This framework ensures resilience, adaptability, and antifragility in dynamic environments, where residuality theory models software systems as interconnected residues and stressors. In addition, this section describes some principles derived from residuality theory and related approaches to address uncertainty in software architecture. Section 3 detailed a Residual Space Exploration (RSE) framework to evaluate candidate residual models within a residual space based on divers properties. In Sect. 4, we introduce Residual Dynamic Management (RDM), a framework to integrates principles of residuality theory into software architecture to dynamically manage uncertainties and residual tasks in changing environments. In Sect. 5, we model the metric of residual complexity through various states, residual components, and stressors using Residual Finite State Machine (R-FSM). This approach allows us to visualize and understand the dynamic interactions that ensure a system's resilience, adaptability, and antifragility. Finally, in Sect. 6 we conclude the paper with a brief summary and highlight looming future work and potential research directions.

2 Embracing Residuality Theory: The Intersection of Antifragility and Resilience

Uncertainty in the context of software architecture refers to the lack of complete knowledge about the consequences of deploying a specific architecture candidate model. Various sources of uncertainty can stem from various factors such as incomplete information, evolving requirements, technological constraints, or unpredictable external factors.

Uncertainty during software development can manifest itself in various ways and at different stages of the development process. Despite the inherent uncertainty and the challenges they face, software architects can make decisions that may lead to either successful or unpredictable outcomes. Vulnerabilities to certainty within the architecture of a software system can have far-reaching unpredictable consequences, impacting its stability, resilience, security, maintainability, and adaptability. Researchers have recognized the substantial risks and impacts of uncertainty and unpredictability on various aspects of software architecture. The literature in this field have provided valuable insights into managing these challenges. See for example, [10–12, 17, 23].

O'Reilly's introduction of residuality theory [4, 5] represents a significant development in the field of designing software systems. Residuality theory offers a new ideology that challenges traditional approaches to software design and proposes innovative strategies for creating more resilient and adaptable systems. In line with the theory of residuality, software systems are viewed as dynamic entities that should not remain static over time. Instead, they should possess the capability to adapt and evolve dynamically, especially when subjected to stress or changes in their environment. Resilience and adaptability in mind. Overall, residuality theory provides valuable insights for designing resilient and adaptable software architectures that are better equipped to handle uncertainty, variability, and disruptions. Here are some principles derived from residuality theory and related approaches to address uncertainty and embrace residuality in software architecture.

Resilience: Residuality theory may emphasize the importance of designing software systems that are resilient to uncertainties, failures, and changing environments. This includes strategies for handling unexpected events, recovering from failures, and maintaining system stability under stress such as the pace of innovation and business. Resilient systems can recover quickly and maintain important system's functionalities during disruptions. The main attributes of resilience are robustness, recovery, and adaptability.

Antifragility: Residuality theory is inspired by the concept of antifragility, introduced by Taleb [21], which proposes that certain systems can thrive and improve in the face of volatility, uncertainty, and disorder. While resilient systems can withstand disturbance and maintain their stability, antifragile systems actually benefit from volatility, uncertainty, and disruptions. Antifragile systems not only withstand stressors and volatility but actually benefit from them, becoming stronger and more resilient over time as a result of exposure to stressors. Continuous response to new challenges, evolution, and improvement through stressors are important attributes in antifragile systems. Residuality theory encourages software architects to design systems that can dynamically thrive in uncertain environments. By recognizing that uncertainty is an inherent feature of complex software, architects can design architectures that are not only resilient but also adaptable and responsive to changes in requirements, technologies, and changing conditions. Adaptability adjusts systems' configurations and operations based on real-time data and environment conditions.

Iterative Design: Residuality theory emphasizes an iterative approach to architecture design, where architects continuously evolve and refine the architecture based on feedback and learning. This iterative design allows software architects to incrementally address uncertainties, refine the architecture over time to better meet evolving needs.

Self-Healing Capabilities: Self-healing capabilities are an integral part of residuality theory. By incorporating self-healing mechanisms into the software architecture, developers can enhance the system's ability to detect, diagnose, and recover from faults autonomously, ensuring continuous operation in dynamic and uncertain environments.

Risk Management: Residuality theory may incorporate principles of risk management into software design, with a focus on identifying, assessing, and mitigating risks that could impact system performance and stability.

Redundancy and Fault-Tolerance: One key aspect of redundancy in residuality theory is having multiple components within a system with similar functionalities within a system to ensure continuation in the event of failures or disruptions.

Agile Collaborations and Practices: Throughout the design process, residuality theory encourages collaborative and agile practices that foster communication, continuation, transparency, and shared feedback among stakeholders.

This is just a subset of principles where software architects can create architectures that are better equipped to handle uncertainty, embrace residuality, and thrive in dynamic and unpredictable environments. In summary, embracing residuality theory in software architecture design involves adopting a mindset of embracing uncertainty, iterating on designs, designing for adaptability and resilience, fostering experimentation and learning, implementing dynamic control mechanisms, applying resilient design principles, and embracing collaborative and agile practices. By incorporating these principles into architecture design, architects can create software systems that are better equipped to handle uncertainty, adapt to change, and deliver services to stakeholders in dynamic and uncertain environments. Software architects and developers can build systems that not only endure but also flourish in the face of the unexpected. As technology continues to permeate every aspect of life, antifragile systems will become indispensable, making the understanding of this concept as crucial for tech professionals as well as for code developers.

3   Residual Space Exploration

We propose a Residual Space Exploration (RSE) framework to evaluate and compare candidate residual models within a residual space based on specific properties. These candidate models may vary in terms of their structures, components, parameters, or other relevant attributes capable of thriving in the face of evolving challenges. In general, software architectures are static and software architects design their work entirely in a way without any possibility of being changed in the near-future. However, the dynamic and evolving nature of the operating environmental conditions of such systems, coupled with various forms of threats and cyber-attacks, as well as the unpredictable component failures and deterioration over time, necessitates a different approach to software architecture. Therefore, software architects should develop models that operates in dynamic environments. It's important to recognize that software architectures are not entirely static and rigid since some of the dynamic characteristics related to resilience, fault tolerance, and dynamic adaptation are often embedded within the code and may not be explicitly visible at the highest level of the system.

By integrating residual components, which are designed to handle uncertainty and adapt to external factors and changing requirements, software architects ensure the overall system' is better equipped with resilience and adaptability to support uncertainty. In the context of residuality theory, stressors are factors or conditions that instigate challenges or interfere in a system. Thus, in essence, stressors are seen not as threats but as opportunities for improvement within the framework of residuality theory. Residual components and stressors are integral to the system's development and enhancement in the context residuality theory. The terms, uncertainty, stressors, and residual components, are broadly explained as follows:

Uncertainty: *Uncertainty in software architectures refers to the unpredictable events, unexpected changes, and unforeseen disruptions that systems may encounter during their operation.*

Categorizing uncertainties enhance software architect's ability to manage and respond to the challenges and circumstances posed by uncertainty in various domains [18]. For instance, we only mention the most important categories and attributes of uncertainty in the context of residuality theory as briefly described below.

- *Antifragile Attribute.* In the context of residuality theory, the antifragile attribute of uncertainty is the most important. It can benefit from residual tasks, using them as opportunities for strength, improvement, growth, and innovation.
- *Risk Attribute.* This attribute refers to the potential negative impacts or adverse outcomes that may arise from uncertainly conditions within a system. Identifying and evaluating risks will help architects to develop strategies to manage the potential negative impacts of the risks.
- *Source Attribute.* This type of uncertainty can be internal or external. Source of uncertainty can arise from external environments such as changes in market, regulations, and technological advancements. Also, it may internally stem from ambiguity, lack of clarity or completeness.
- *Cause Attribute.* This attribute triggers uncertainty which includes disruptions, operational interference, and business changes that may affect the normal functioning of a system.
- *Level Attribute.* This attribute exists on a spectrum ranging from full uncertainty, high, medium, or low uncertainties.
- *Application/Domain Attribute.* This attribute is tied to the complexity's and stability's of the application or domain.
- *Prioritization Attribute.* This attribute helps software architects and developers focus their efforts on addressing critical uncertainties first which may have a significant impact on the system.
- *Evidence Attribute.* This type of attribute demonstrates the evidence of the existence of uncertainty.

- *Stakeholder/User Attribute*. This attribute of uncertainty refers to uncertainties that arise from the perspectives, needs, expectations, and behaviors of stakeholders.
- *Developer/Analyst Attribute*. These uncertainties stem from the inherent variability and unpredictability in human attitudes, preferences, and responses.
- *Opportunity Attribute*. This attribute of uncertainty in the context of residuality theory highlights the potential for software architects to find innovative solutions and gain a competitive advantage to exploring new opportunities.
- *Organization Attribute*. Organizational change is an important aspect with respect to uncertainty management.

Stressors: *Stressors are external factors, unexpected events, or conditions that challenge a software system and considered as for enhancement and improvement of the system.*

In software development, stressors can arise from various sources, both internal and external. For instance, resource constraints, security concerns, technical challenges, a server crashes, and business trends. In this paper, the word stressor(s) is not tied to the human aspects of emotional stress, psychological factors, and moral that might have an impact on software developers.

Residual components: *A residual component is an element, component, or module within a software architecture that remains functionally effective in dynamic environments and under stressors.*

By incorporating residual components and stressors, a system not only becomes more robust and resilient but is also capable of evolving and improving in the face of challenges and uncertainty. Residual components are designed to handle uncertainty and adapt to external factors and changing requirements, ensuring the overall system's resilience and adaptability. While uncertainty involves managing unpredictable and expected factors, residuality emphasises on handling the tasks and responsibilities that emerge after the post-uncertainty period. By adopting appropriate strategies for each task, software architects can build systems that not only withstand volatility but also thrive in dynamic environments. This approach ensures long-term resilience and adaptability, positioning software systems for sustained success in an unpredictable landscape.

4   Residual Dynamic Management in Software Architecture

We introduce Residual Dynamic Management (RDM) as a framework that integrates principles from residuality theory into software architecture to dynamically manage uncertainties and residual tasks effectively. We define a system to be residual when its design is expressed in terms of residual components (i.e., residues) and stressors, where the future of a system is a function of its residual components and stressors. Dynamic management continuously handle tasks that were not anticipated during the initial design, adapting and responding to new challenges as they arise. RDM ensures long-term resilience and adaptability by continually learning and evolving in response to challenges. Both uncertainty and residuality are considered as the core concept of dealing with residual tasks or uncertainties within a software development context. Antifragility goes beyond resilience and robustness. It is characterized by its ability not just to withstand volatility and uncertainty but to actually benefit from them. In fact, antifragile systems improve and become stronger when exposed to to uncertainty, volatility, and stressors. Stressors may include environmental conditions, security threats, hardware failures, software errors, or any other sources of uncertainty or that the system may encounter during its lifecycle, while residues exit in connection to stressors and represent the core functionality, structure, and behavior of the system that remains intact despite encountering various stressors. Residues exit in connection to stressors and represent the core functionality, structure, and behavior of the system that remains intact despite encountering various stressors. In software architecture, low-coupling is an important principle aimed at minimizing dependencies between different components. However, even with low-coupling designs, residual tasks and can still emerge.

Figure 1 demonstrates how different stressors can impact various residual components in a software architecture. Each stressor is connected to the residual component it affects, illustrating the complexity and interdependencies within the system. Figure 2, illustrates a set of three various stressors affecting many components. Stressors may include environmental conditions, security threats, hardware failures, software errors, market trends, or any other sources of uncertainty or that the system may encounter during its lifecycle. The following graph in Fig. 2 is a combination of my own drawing and some pre-defined icons from Canva [25].

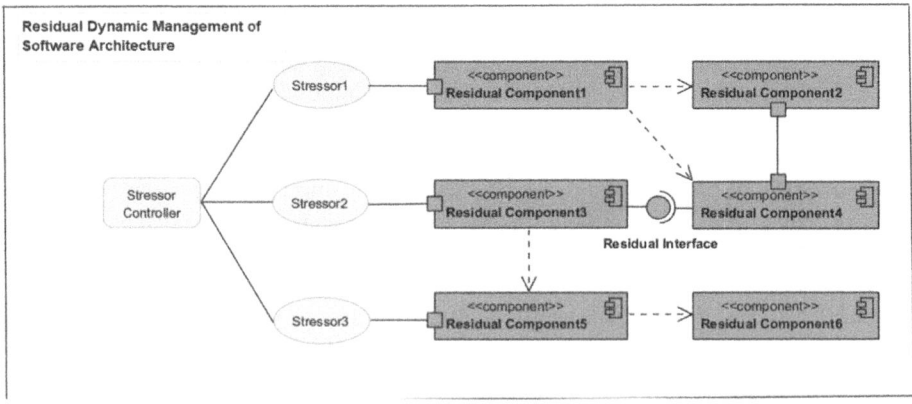

Fig. 1. A typical residual dynamic management (RDM) framework.

By explicitly modeling stressors and residues in the design process, software architects can identify potential vulnerabilities, anticipate failure modes, and implement appropriate resilience mechanisms to mitigate the impact of stressors and ensure the system's reliability and availability in the face of uncertainty. The source of predictability in software development is not impossible to predict, but it is certainly challenging given its inherent complexity and the dynamic nature of technology and business. However, a reasonable expectation of predictability can be achieved through a combination of factors, including experience, thorough analysis, and the adoption of iterative development practices like Agile. These methodologies allow teams to adapt to predictability during the development process. Residuality theory provides a valuable perspective on

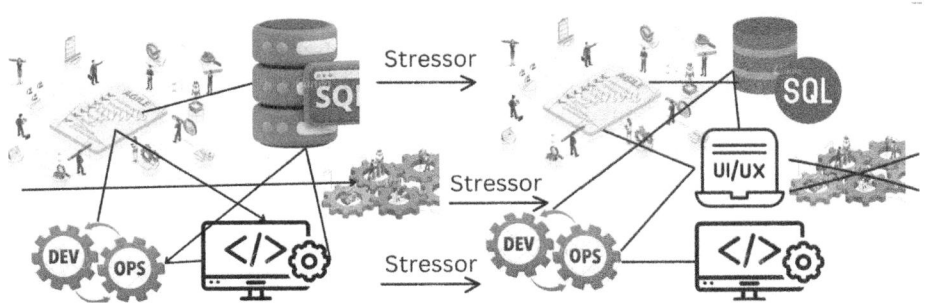

Fig. 2. An example of stressors affecting residual components.

managing unpredictability in software systems. By viewing systems as collections of residues associated with specific stressors, developers can anticipate potential challenges and design systems that are better equipped to handle uncertainty and change. Understanding residues helps in identifying critical elements of the system's design that define the future trajectory of the system. By viewing systems as collections of residues associated with specific stressors, developers can anticipate potential challenges and design systems that are better equipped to handle uncertainty and change. By identifying and analyzing these random stressors, software architects and engineers can assess the potential impact on the system and develop strategies to mitigate risks, enhance resilience, and ensure reliable operation in diverse and unpredictable environments.

Each residual component within the overall software architecture have its own state machine, reflecting its state, which is influenced by the interactions of the participating components and subsystems as each explained in the next section.

5 Modeling Residual Complexity with Residual Finite State Machines

Residual complexity [11, 24] serves as a metric for accessing and evaluating the complexity of software systems. It poses a substantial challenge in modern software development landscape and stems from relationships and interdependencies among various components within a software system. Such a complexity metric indicates how complexities persist in a system despite efforts to simplify it and streamline its software architecture. These complexities often arise due to the need to handle uncertainties, adapt to changing requirements, and manage dynamic interactions among various components. In order to manage residual complexity, residual components and stressors, which form the main constituents of a software architecture, can be effectively modeled as Finite State Machines (R-FSM). Such a modeling using R-FSM can help software architects in structuring, managing, and visualizing the dynamic interactions within a system. Moreover, R-FSM enhances understanding the system's states and transitions, which make it easier to design resilient, adaptable, and antifragile software architectures. R-FSM reflect the overall state of the system as a function of its participating subsystems, components, and stressors. The states of R-FSM represent different configurations or conditions of the system (i.e., failed, uncertain, stressors). The functions define the transition from one state to another, triggered by stressors. Stressors could be external or internal factors that trigger state changes, causing the system to adapt or evolve. Residual components maintain their functionalities and support transitions under various stressors. With several advantages such as modularity, efficiency, verification, and testing, R-FSM are a powerful tool in software development, offering a structured and manageable approach to handling system's complexity, states, and transitions. Figure 3 illustrates how the system can adapt, and improve over time, ensuring resilience, adaptability, and antifragility. In situations where state transitions in R-FSM are not deterministic, particularly when R-FSM enters an uncertain state may not knowing exactly where to move in the next transition. It is important to model this uncertainty in R-FSM to various potential states including for instance, *"failed state"*, *"recovering state"*, or *"partially functional state"*. (See dashed arrows emanating from the state labeled *"Uncertain state"*).

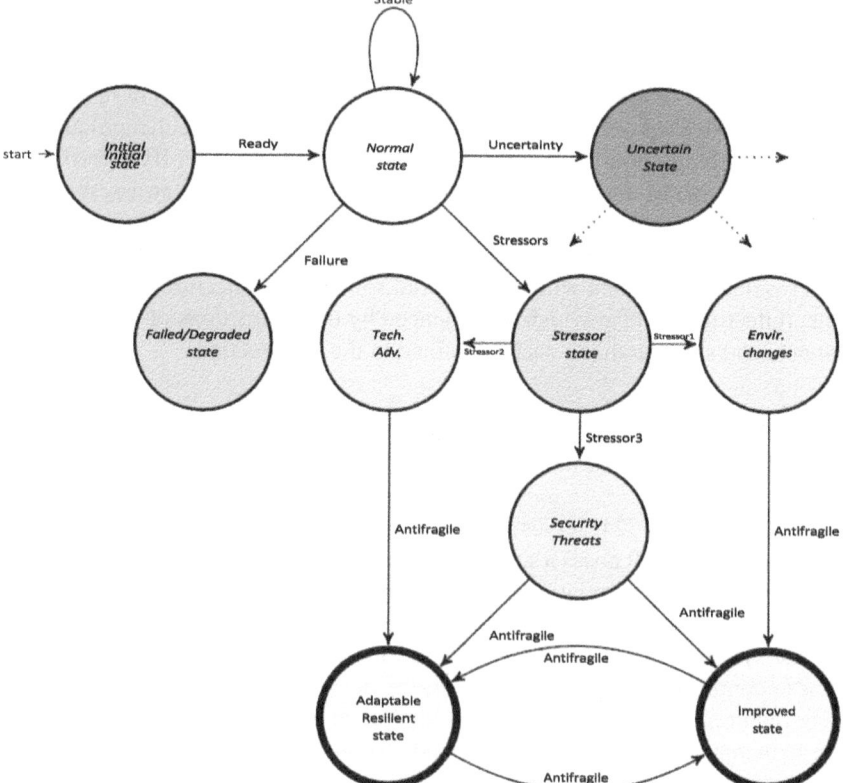

Fig. 3. A typical residual finite state machine (R-FSM) model which captures how residual components and stressors interact to ensure resilience, adaptability, and antifragility in a system.

6   Conclusion

Residuality theory presents an innovative perspective for designing and modeling software architectures by focusing on the dynamic interactions among residual components and stressors. This ideological characteristic of residual theory ensures a system's resilience, adaptability, antifragility, and leveraging principles. This paper focuses on the intersection of uncertainty and residuality theory in software architecture. We propose two frameworks, Residual Space Exploration (RSE) and Residual Dynamic Management (RDM), and a model called Residual Finite State Machine (R-FSM) for managing dynamic interactions, promote resilience, adaptability, and embrace antifragility. Through the proposed frameworks and the R-FSM model, software architects can build systems that not only endure and capable of thriving but also flourish and improve in the face of uncertainty and unexpected changes. As future work, uncertainty and residuality theory in software architecture can be enhanced by adding the dimension of time. This enhancement is currently a work in progress.

References

1. Strobel, G., Banh, L., M¨oller, F., Schoormann, T.: Exploring generative artificial intelligence: a taxonomy and types. In: Proceedings of the International Conference on System Sciences, pp. 4546–4555, HICSS 2024. Hawaii, USA (2024)
2. Teubner, T., Flath, C.M., Weinhardt, C., van der Aalst, W., Hinz, O.: Welcome to the era of ChatGPT et al.: The prospects of large language models. J. Bus. Inf. Syst. Eng. **65**, 95–101 (2023). https://doi.org/10.1007/s12599-023-00795-x
3. Banh, L., Strobel, G.: Generative artificial intelligence. J. Electron. Markets **33**(63), 1–17. Springer (2023)
4. O'Reilly, M.B.: An introduction to residuality theory: software development in heuristics for complex systems. J. Procedia Comput. Sci. **170**, 875–880 (2020). https://www.sciencedirect.com/science/article/pii/S1877050920305585
5. O'Reilly, B.M.: Residues: Time, Change, and Uncertainty in Software Architecture (2024). https://LeanPub.com/residuality
6. Rozanski, N., Woods, E.: Software Systems Architecture: Working with Stakeholders using Viewpoints and Perspectives. Addison-Wesley Professional (2005)
7. Wan, Z., Zhang, Y., Xia, X., Jiang, Y., Lo, D.: Software architecture in practice: challenges and opportunities. In: Proceedings of the 31st ACM Joint European Software Engineering Conference and Symposium on the Foundations of Software Engineering, pp. 1457–1469. arXiv:2308.09978 (2023). https://doi.org/10.1145/3611643.3616367
8. Shumaiev, K., Bhat, M., Klymenko, A., Biesdorf, A.: Uncertainty expressions in software architecture group decision making: explorative study. In: Proceedings of the 12th we European Conference on Software Architecture, pp. 1–8 (2018). https://doi.org/10.1145/3241403.3241447
9. Klein, J., Nord, R., Shull, F.: Why architecture conformance matters for software systems: In: DoD Air & Space Weapon Syst. Soft. Summit: Accelerating DoD Soft. Eng. to the Speed of Relevance, co-located with the DoD Maintenance Symposium (2022)
10. Bhat, M., Shumaiev, K., Hohenstein, U., Biesdorf, A., Matthes, F.: The evolution of Architectural decision making as a key focus area of software architecture research: a semi-systematic literature study. In: IEEE International Conference on Software Architecture (ICSA), pp. 69–80 (2020). https://doi.org/10.1109/ICSA47634.2020.00015

11. Krisper, M., Iber, J., Kreiner, C., Quaritsch, M.: A metric for evaluating residual complexity in software: In: Proceedings of European Conference on Software Process Improvement, pp. 138–149. Springer International Publishing AG. Stolfa et al. (Eds.): EuroSPI, CCIS 748, (2017). https://doi.org/10.1007/978-3-319-64218-5_11

12. Koziolek, P.: Sustainability evaluation of software architectures: a systematic review. In: Proceedings of the joint ACM SIGSOFT conference, QoSA and ACM SIGSOFT symposium, ISARCS on Quality of software architectures, QoSA and architecting critical systems, SARCS (QoSA-ISARCS '11), pp. 3–12 (2011). https://doi.org/10.1145/2000259.2000263

13. Bush, A., Fuchß, B., Koziolek A.: PerOpteryx: Automated improvement of software architectures. In: Proceedings of the 2019 IEEE International Conference on Software Architecture Companion (ICSA-C), pp. 162–165 (2019). https://doi.org/10.1109/ICSA-C.2019.00036

14. Dragomir, A., Lichter, H., Dohmen, J., Chen, H.: Run-time monitoring-based evaluation and communication integrity validation of software architectures. In: Proceedings of the 21st Asia-Pacific Software Engineering Conference, pp. 191–198 (2014)

15. Kritzinger, L.M., Krismayer, T., Vierhauser, M., Rabiser, R., Gru¨nbacher, P.: Visualization support for requirements monitoring in systems of systems. In: Proceedings of 2017 32nd IEEE/ACM International Conference on Automated Software Engineering (ASE), pp. 889–894 (2017)

16. Kritzinger, L.M., Krismayer, T., Vierhauser, M., Rabiser, R., Gru¨nbacher, P.: A user study on the usefulness of visualization support for requirements monitorings. In: Proceedings Working Conference on Software Visualization (VISSOFT), pp. 56–66 (2019)

17. Sobhy, D., Bahsoon, R., Minku L., Kazman, R.: Evaluation of software architectures under uncertainty: a systematic literature review. J. ACM Trans. Softw. Eng. Methodol. 30, 4(51), 1–50 (2021). https://doi.org/10.1145/3464305

18. Hahner, S., Seifermann, S., Heinrich, R., Reussner, R.: A Classification of software-architectural uncertainty regarding confidentiality. In: Samarati, P., van Sinderen, M., Vimercati, S.D.C.d., Wijnhoven, F. (eds.) E-Business and Telecommunications. ICETE 2021. Communications in Computer and Information Science, vol. 1795, pp. 875–880. Springer, Cham (2023). https://doi.org/10.1007/978-3-031-36840-0_8

19. Leite, L., Rocha, C., Kon, F., Milojicic, D., Meirelles, P.: A survey of DevOps concepts and challenges". J. ACM Comput. Surveys 52(6), 1–35 (2019). https://doi.org/10.1145/3359981

20. Amaro, R., Pereira, R., Mira da Silva, M.: DevOps metrics and KPIs: a multivocal literature review. J. ACM Comput. Surveys 56, 1–41 (2024). https://doi.org/10.1145/3652508

21. Taleb, N.N.: Antifragile: Things that Gain from Disorder. Random House Trade, New York (2014)

22. Bai, M., Li, D., Pei, S., Li, A., Ye D.: Continuous delivery of personalized assessment and feedback in agile software engineering projects. In: Proceedings of the 40th International Conference on Software Engineering: Software Engineering Education and Training (ICSE-SEET'18), pp. 58–67 (2028)

23. Lupafya, C.: A framework for managing uncertainty in software architecture. In: Proceedings in European Conference on Software Architecture (ECSA), pp. 1–4 (2019). https://doi.org/10.1145/3344948.3344954

24. Lavazza, L., Morasca, S., Gatto, M.: An empirical study on software understandability and its dependence on code characteristics. J. Empirical Softw. Eng. 28(155), 1–24 (2023). https://doi.org/10.1007/s10664-023-10396-7

25. https://www.canva.com/

Zoned Role-Based Approach to System Design, Implementation, and Access Control of Integrated Web Applications

Harris Wang[✉]

School of Computing and Information Systems, Athabasca University, Athabasca, Canada
harrisw@athabascau.ca

Abstract. In today's world almost all organizations heavily depend on Web-based systems or web applications for their day-to-day operations. In this paper, we will present zoned role-based (ZRB) approach to the design and implementation of integrated web-based systems for organizations and enterprises. In contrast to Role-Based Access Control (RBAC), well-known in computer security, this approach can be used throughout the entire life cycle of a web-based system, and can make the design, implementation, deployment and maintenance of integrated web system more efficient and effective for all organizations and enterprises. In this approach, areas of business, or divisions, departments or designated groups of employees for specific missions are called zones, and for each zone a set of roles are defined; for each role, some web apps, each of which consists of a set of operations, are designed and implemented for users in their respective roles to conduct their business in each associated zone; and control of user access to each operation can then be done explicitly by associating each operation with roles by inference based on the relationships between roles. Within such a zoned role-based integrated system, once a user has roles assigned in each zone he or she is affiliated, he will be able to access, precisely, all the apps and operations needed to fulfill his or her role or roles in respective zone, with only one authentication. Such integration is rather important and convenient especially when users may be affiliated with multiple zones or play multiple roles.

Keywords: Integrated web apps development · Zoned role-based system development · Zoned role-based access control · Software development methodology

1 Introduction

In today's world almost all organizations heavily depend on Web-based systems or web applications for their day-to-day operations. For big organizations like universities, governments, and corporations there can be a few divisions, departments and groups of employees within their respective organizational hierarchy. While these divisions, departments or employee groups have different functionalities and responsibilities, it is very often that they must interact and collaborate with each other by sharing information

W. Feng et al. (Eds.): SEDE 2024, CCIS 2244, pp. 43–54, 2024.
https://doi.org/10.1007/978-3-031-75201-8_4

and even sharing human resources. For example, some employees may play multiple roles within the organization, and may work for different departments. As such, to effectively support the operation of such an organization, an integrated web-based system with all functional modules or subsystems is needed to provide all its employees with precise access to the web applications needed to do their job. Unfortunately, so far in practice there is no efficient and effective way for organizations to get such an integrated web system for their needs.

In most cases organizations would get applications from different vendors to meet their various business needs through the process called vendor integration, also called third-party integration, by using Single-Sign-On (SSO) protocols [1] such as OAuth, SAML or OpenID Connect to implement authentication and access control across multiple web applications. However, SSO can only help with authentication across web applications. Once a user is authenticated for a web application, access control is up to the web application itself.

Moreover, authentication is not the only problem to be solved when an organization uses third-party web applications for its business needs. Almost for any organization, its business needs are so related to each other that data exchange, workflow automation, and seamless collaboration, and communication between web applications are required. Although an organization may use some APIs (Application Programming Interfaces) to facilitate data exchange, workflow automation, and seamless collaboration, and communication between its own web applications and third-party web applications, it has no way to implement data exchange, workflow automation, and seamless collaboration, and communication between third-party web applications, if not already implemented in individual third-party applications.

With vendor integration, potential incompatibility, risk of data breach, likelihood of miscommunication and misunderstanding of products by external vendors, as well as possibility of unforeseen costs are also challenges for the organization. It is quite common that the actual cost of integrating a third-party product far exceeded the initial budget.

In terms of incompatibility, it is quite often that the vendor product cannot fully satisfy the requirements of the business, even with some very costly customization.

In addition to vendor integration, there are also B2B (business-to-business) Integrations and Out-of-the-Box Integrations. B2B Integration involves connecting two or more organizations to enable cross-partner collaboration. For example, managed service providers (MSPs) or vendors collaborate with their customers by integrating various services and software products, whereas out-of-the-Box Integrations are done through cloud services, since many SaaS (Software as a Service) vendors offer pre-built integrations. These out-of-the-box solutions allow easy connectivity between applications. However, in case of out-of-the box integrations, organizations may sacrifice flexibility and control, as well as the ability to customize the applications for their precise needs.

Therefore, to meet the needs of an organization, the most ideal solution is to design and develop an integrated web-based system that not only has all the applications precisely and effectively for its current needs, but also can be easily scaled and maintained to meet the changing needs of the organization.

Can existing software engineering methodologies and models, including those for system analysis and design, be used to design such integrated web-based systems? In literature and software engineering practice, there are many system design and analysis methodologies, such as:

- Structured Systems Analysis and Design Method (SSADM), a well-established methodology that emphasizes a structured approach to system development. SSADM involves stages such as feasibility study, requirements analysis, logical design, physical design, and implementation.
- Flow-Service-Quality (FSQ) Systems Engineering, which focuses on developing network-centric information systems. FSQ considers flow (data and control flow), services (functional components), and quality (performance, security, and reliability) aspects.
- Agent-Oriented Systems Analysis and Design (AOSAD), which emphasizes modeling systems as a collection of interacting agents. AOSAD is particularly useful for complex, distributed systems. Agent-oriented methodologies include identifying agents, their roles, and interactions.
- Fact-Based Approach (FBA), which focuses on domain modeling for object- oriented information systems. It emphasizes capturing facts (business rules) and deriving a domain model from them.
- Agile Software Development Transition (ASDT), which emphasizes iterative development, collaboration, and responsiveness to changing requirements.
- Higher Order Software (HOS), which focuses on developing reusable software components. HOS promotes modularity, abstraction, and composability, which are essential for integrated systems.
- Hierarchy-Input-Process-Output (HIPO), which takes a top-down design methodology to break down a system into modules based on input, processing, and output. HIPO helps manage complexity and ensures a systematic approach.
- Problem Statement Language/Analyzer (PSL/PSA), which provides a structured way to define problems and analyze them. PSL/PSA aids in understanding system requirements and constraints.
- Iterative Approaches (IA), which acknowledges that requirements are evolving. In IA, cognitive processes and representational artifacts play a crucial role in iterative development.
- Domain-Specific and Implementation-Independent Software Architectures (DSI-ISA), which separates architecture from implementation details, while ensures alignment with business needs by carefully deriving and evaluating domain-specific architectures.
- Waterfall Model, which is a linear, sequential approach where each phase (requirements, design, implementation, testing, deployment) follows the previous one. It provides clear project structure and documentation, and is well-suited for small projects with stable requirements. This model is only best for straightforward projects with well-defined requirements.
- Extreme Programming (XP), which focuses on continuous testing, pair programming, and small releases. XP can lead to high code quality, rapid feedback and high customer satisfaction. It may not suit large teams and projects, and requires skilled developers.

- Rapid Application Development (RAD), which emphasizes prototyping, quick itera-tions, and user feedback. It can result in speedy development, early user involvement, iterative improvements, but may sacrifice long-term maintainability, be risk of scope creep. It is good for time-sensitive projects with evolving requirements.
- Scalable and Modular Architecture for Responsive Web Applications (SMARWA), which focuses on building responsive, modular, and scalable web applications. It provides separation of concerns, scalability, and reusability. It is suitable for large-scale, complex web applications, but with big learning curve for developers, and daunting initial setup complexity.
- DevOps and Continuous Integration/Continuous Deployment (CI/CD), which inte-grates development and operations, emphasizing automation, collaboration, and con-tinuous delivery. It has faster deployment cycles, improved collaboration and reduced manual tasks. DevOps and Continuous Integration/Continuous Deployment (CI/CD) is well suited for modern web development, especially cloud-based applications, but requires cultural shift and initial setup effort.
- Joint application development (JAD), which involves the client or end user in the design and development of a software application through a succession of collabora-tive workshops called JAD sessions. Its aim is to involve the customer (or end user) in defining the business need and developing a solution based on that need.

As can be seen, existing software engineering methodologies and models are great as general guidance for system analysis, design, development and maintenance of software systems, but none of them provides explicit and direct guidance for the design and development of integrated web applications that can sufficiently support users to play different roles in different departments or areas of business effectively, and provide precise control of access to web applications needed to fulfil their roles [7–12].

The ZRB approach is not intended to replace existing software development method-ologies. Rather, it is more as a complement and can be used together with a preferred existing software development methodology. Once web apps are determined for the orga-nization and each zone, existing software development methodologies may be applied to the analysis and design of any of the web apps if appropriate.

In the rest of this paper, we will present in detail a methodology for web applications development called zoned role based (ZRB) approach, that can be used to design and implement of an integrated web-based system for any organization, and to precisely control user's access to applications needed to play each assigned role within the system. We will first present the theoretical base of the approach, followed by system design, system implementation of integrated web systems, and then discuss how access control can be precisely done.

2 The Theoretical Base of ZRB

Role-Based Access Control (RBAC) [2–6] is widely used as an authorization model to provide a structured approach to managing access to resources in computer applications. It offers a flexible and scalable solution for enforcing fine-grained access controls based on user roles and permissions. Here we extend traditional RBAC to more effectively support the design and development of integrated web systems for organizations.

The ZRB approach is based on four important concepts: zones, apps, roles, and users. They are defined as follows:

1 – a user is an employee, a visitor or customer of the organization. We use lowercase u to denote an individual user and use uppercase U to denote a group of users.
2 - an app is a program or application that can be used by users to play their roles. We use lowercase a to denote individual app, use uppercase A to denote a set of apps.

In most cases, an app will provide a suite of operations to serve the purposes of the app. For example, an app for recruitment will provide operations for applicants to submit their job application, for HR to check applications, or add applications on behalf of applicants who submitted by email for some reasons, or for HR to view, or delete applications that don't qualify; for committee members to review and submit comments and rank the applicants, etc. Keep in mind that app operations, often classified into CRUD (Create, Read, Update and Delete), should only be accessible for users in certain role or roles. Hence, we have to identify each and every app operation. For app a, the set of operations is written as O_a, and an individual operation is written as $a.o1, a.o2, \ldots a.o_n$.

3 – a role is job title that can be assigned to a user. We use lowercase r to denote an individual role, use uppercase R to denote a set of roles. It is possible for a user to play more than one role in an organization.

Some roles in an organization are related. The most common relationship is supervision or reporting. Such relationships sometimes can be used to make inference on access permissions. For example, if role ra is the supervisor of rb in a specific zone, then users in ra may assume all the app operations accessible for rb if explicit access control rules are not set.

4 – a zone can be an organization, one of its divisions, departments or areas of business such as sale, marketing, and manufacturing, or a group of designated users for a specific mission, such as hiring. We use lowercase z to denote an individual zone, use uppercase Z to denote a list of zones. A set of zones directly under zone z are called subzones. Because a subzone may have some subzones, identified zones for an organization can be put into a tree, with the organization itself as the root.

Based on notations defined for users, apps, roles and subzones, a zone z can be either $(\text{-}, R, A, U)$, or (Z, R, A, U).

In the case of $Z = (\text{-}, R, A, U)$, the zone doesn't have any subzone; in the case of $Z = (Zs, R, A, U)$,.., Zs is a set of sub-zones of zone z, R is a set of roles that may be assigned to any user in U, A is a list of apps that may only be associated with a role in R. Moreover, $U \supseteq \cup U_i$, for all U_i in Zs.

Within the tree of zones built for a given organization, as illustrated in Fig. 1, set U on the root contains a set of all users, the roles on the root should contain least number of roles identified, which will be only authenticated and anonymous users, and minimum number of app operations that may be associated with each role.

In general, for a specific zone in the tree, the users is a superset of users in all its subzones, as specified by $U \supseteq \cup U_i$, for U_i in Zs. Roles in zone at level j will assume

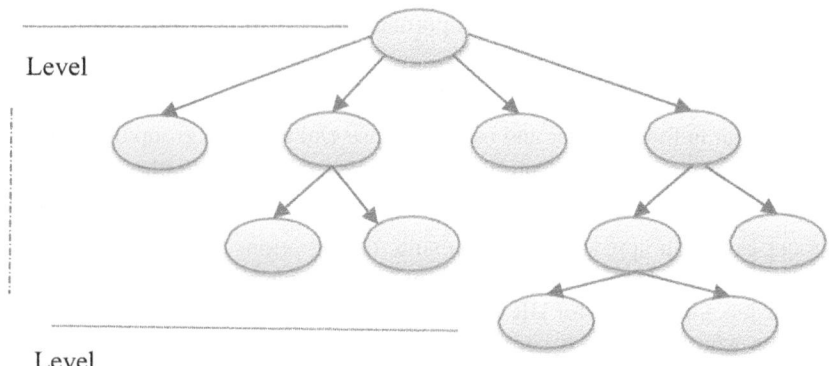

Level

Level

Fig. 1. A tree of identified zones for an organization

the actions available for roles at level $j - 1$, but only on its path from the root. This gives us some way to infer the access rules for a user in a role.

However, there can be some exceptions. For example, in a case of develop integrated web apps for a university, if a faculty established an advisory committee for its strategic planning with invited external members, the external members may or may not assume all the operations available for the regular faculty members. This really depends on the policy or practice of the organization.

To be precise in access control, we should always try our best to build a complete access control mechanism for the system.

First, we need to build a role-app matrix for each identified zone in the tree, showing details of the app operations each role can make in the zone, as illustrated in Table 1.

Table 1. Role-app matrix for zone

	a1	a2	a3	a4	a5	.....
r1	$a1.O_1$	$a2.O_1$	$a3.O_1$	$a4.O_1$		.....
r2		$a2.O_2$		$a4.O_2$	$a5.O_2$	.....
r3	$a1.O_3$		$a3.O_3$			.....
r4		$a2.O_4$	$a3.O_4$	$a4.O_4$	$a5.O_4$	.....
r5	$a1.O_5$	$a2.O_5$	$a3.O_5$		$a5.O_5$	.....
......	......	......	......	......	......	.....

In the matrix above, $ai.Oj$ is a subset of all operations of app ai that can be taken by users in role rj, and an empty cell at $\{ri, aj\}$ means app aj is not made for role ri.

For users, there will be a user-zone matrix showing what zones each user has a role or roles to play, and what role or roles the user can play in a zone, as illustrated in Table 2.

Table 2. User-zone matrix showing roles a user may play in each zone

	z1	*z2*	*z3*	*z4*	*z5*	.....
u1		*z2.R1*		*z4.R1*		.....
u2	*z1.R2*		*z3.R2*	*z4.R2*	*z5.R2*	.....
u3	*z1.R3*	*z2.R3*		*z4.R3*	*z5.R3*	.....
u4		*z2.R4*	*z3.R4*	*z4.R4*	*z5.R4*	.....
u5	*z1.R5*		*z3.R5*		*z5.R5*	.....
....	.....	.....	.....	.....	.....	.....

In the matrix above, $zi.Rj$ is a subset of all roles users may play in zone zi for user j, and an empty cell in the matrix means the user has no role to play in the zone. A row for a user is created when the user is registered, but can be changed from time to time, or deleted when the user is no longer with the organization.

The two matrices above can be used to effectively provide access control of any user in the system. Since at the any given time a user can only play a specific role in a specific zone, when the user wants to make an app operation, such as by clicking a web link, the system will check the matrix for users to see if the user is allowed to play the specific role in the specific zone, if the answer is yes, the system will then check the *role-app* matrix for the specific zone to find out if a particular app operation is allowed for the user to make.

3   ZRB in System Design of Integrated Web Applications

The ZRB methodology can be used to design an integrated web system for any organization by following the steps below:

Step 1—Identify all the organizational zones such as divisions and departments, as well as mission specific zones such as board of executives and various committees for the organization, including their relationships.

This should be done as completely as possible to include all the zones at the time because the integrated system to be developed needs to support all users to play their roles in the organization. Although the integrated system can be implemented zone by zone, at the time of system design, identifying all the zones and their relationships is crucial for correctly understanding the business logic of the organization as well as how the apps and roles in different zones are related.

Step 2—Draw a tree of zones for the organization to represent all the zones identified above as well as their relationships. This tree essentially decides the overall structure of the integrated system for the organization.

Step 3—For each zone in the tree, identify all apps needed for the zone to function for the organization, including all the operations a role player may take in each app.

Step 4—For each zone in the tree, identify all the roles a user may play. At root level, there are three special roles: super user or root user role who has the privilege to do anything within the system, authenticated user role, who has the least privilege among all registered users, and system administrator role, who can some specific system administration work within the system. All users who have not registered with the system or have not logged in are anonymous users by default, with only access to unprotected webpages and app operations.

Please note that the order of step 3 and 4 may be changed and they may be interwoven because some apps can be made for the zone to function without any role in mind, whereas some other apps may be made just for some roles.

Step 5—Build a role-app matrix for each zone to depict what app operations can be taken by what roles in the zone.

Step 6—For the entire system, design navigation UX across zones.

Step 7—For each zone, design navigation UX across roles.

Step 8—For each role, design navigation UX across apps and app operations.

Step 9—For the entire system, design the global database tables, such database table for users.

Step 10—For each app, make and choose the best possible design, including the database tables that are not global.

Please note that for a real-world organization, its zones, roles in each zone, apps needed by users to play their role or roles in each zone may change from time to time.

Moreover, users in each zone may change as well. However, such a change can be easily handled with ZRB. When a user joins in the organization, a user account is created for the user with a default role as registered user within the organization. When the user is assigned to a specific zone, the user will be added to the zone registry. When a specific role is assigned to the user, the role name or id will be added to user's profile.

The opposite action will be taken when a user is removed from a role, a zone, or the organization.

As such, there will be some system apps for super users in the root zone to manage the zones, roles, apps, and users.

4   ZRB in Implementation of Integrated Web Applications

Although the exact details of implementing an integrated web system designed for an organization using ZRB approach depend on the web technology used to implement the system, the ZRB approach can still provide some very useful common guidelines for system implementation.

Because of the nature of web-based systems and applications, the zones identified at the very beginning of system designed based on ZRB approach can and should be easily mapped into web domains, where the root zone is the root domain for the organization, whereas other zones can be mapped into subdomains.

When implementing the system, there can be a project for each zone, with the root zone being the first project, in which all shared backend databases need to be implemented and made available for other zones. The following are the steps to follow:

1. Create a web project for the root zone identified for the organization. In this project, databases to be shared by multiple zones need to be implemented, and make them sharable with other zones. Especially, the following two reg istries need to be created:

    a. A registry storing information about identified immediate subzones of the root zone, as well roles and apps identified for the root zone. We call this registry *zone registry.*

    b. A registry storing role profile about every role identified in the root zone, including information contained in the role-app matrix for the root zone, as well as the URL of the role portal, in which a role player can access all the app operations they need to fulfil the role duties. We call this registry *role registry*.

    c. A registry storing user profiles including the subzones each user works in and roles the user is assigned to play in the root zone. We call this registry *user registry*. Information about subzones is needed when a user switches from root zone to a subzone, such as from university zone to faculty zone, whereas information about the roles each user is assigned to play is needed when a user switches role in a zone, such as from professor role to tutor role, to work in a specific role portal to fulfil all his/her duties as a tutor.

       These three registries above are very important for the entire system to work and scale. They need to be created and used for all the zones identified for the organization. However, for any given zone, the registry only needs to contain information about itself, its immediate parent, if not a root zone, and all its subzones. When the organization changes its structure, the corresponding changes in the system need to be reflected in the zone registry, or ways of business operations, the corresponding changes in the system need to be reflected in the zone registry and role registry; when employees come and go, or move from one zone to another, or change their roles in the organization, corresponding changes to the system need to be reflected in the user registry.

2. Implement all the apps identified for the root zone.
3. Implement role portal for all roles providing role player with access to all needed app operations, and then implement user navigation UX across roles within the root zone.

    Repeat step 1 to step 3 for all zones identified for the organization.

4. For the entire system, implement user navigation UX across zones.
5. Register a main or root domain for the organization, which will provide access to the root of the integrated system.
6. For every subzone in the zone tree built for the organization, set a subdomain for the web project implemented for the subzone, according to its location in the zone tree.

    Normally, the initial development or future update and extension of the system will be done and tested on a development server, and then pushed onto a product server after it becomes deployable. As to how to push the initial system or new updates from development server to production, it depends on personal preferences and the web technology used. In case of using Django in Python, rsync [13] is found to be very efficient and convenient, just be sure to exclude server dependent files from the command, such as all migration files.

With ZRB approach, the development and extension can be done zone by zone, starting with the root zone. When a new app is needed for a role in a specific zone, it will be implemented under a web project for that zone; when a new role is needed for a specific zone, apps for the role need to be identified, designed and implemented for the role; when a new zone is identified and added to the zone tree, a new web project needs to be designed and implemented, a new subdomain can then be set up to provide access to the zone. Thus, the ZRB approach has made web systems very scalable and easy to maintain.

5   ZRB in Access Control of Integrated Web Applications

One of the goals of our ZRB approach is to enable precise control of users' access to app operations across zones and roles with single sign-on. In the theoretical base section, we have described the steps taken for access control. Implementation of those steps depends on what technologies are used. In this section, we assume all the apps for all zones of the integrated web system are implemented based on a MVC (Model, View and Controller) framework. To precisely control the access to all app operations, two access controllers need to be implemented for each zone: one is called n_zrbac for zoned role-based access control without inference, while the other is called i_zrbac for zoned role-based access control with inference [10]. Access control with inference in i_zrbac is done based on the relationships between roles in a zone. For example, a professor may assume the access right of his tutors, and a faculty dean may assume the access right of department chairs within the faculty. The exact inference rules must be based on the policies within the organization.

With a MVC framework, an access controller, either n_zrbac or i_zrbac, can be placed on either views or controllers. In the case of using Django in Python, n_zrbac or i_zrbac can be used as decorators of view functions for which access control is needed.

For example, when decorator @n_zrbac(['professor', 'editor', 'media producer']) is applied to a view function, only professors, editors and media producers are allowed to call the view function; when @i_zrbac(['professor', 'editor', 'media producer']) is applied, on the other hand, department chair and program directors will also be able to call the function, by inference, because department chair or program director will be the supervisor of professor, editor and media producer.

6   Conclusions and Discussions

The ZRB approach to system design, implementation and access control presented above was germinated and evolved throughout the development of KBIES, a knowledge-based integrated education system for open online education The system contains zones of schools, colleges, and universities at top level, faculties, departments, course development, course delivery, classes, tutoring groups, research and some others at lower level. The roles implemented in the system include school/college/university president, faculty dean, department chair, program director, professor, instructor, tutor, editor, media producer, student, as well as superuser, system administer, and others. The ZRB approach has been used to develop web-based systems including systems for open health, open research, and open press. The approach has been proved to be scalable, agile, efficient, and very friendly for system integration. The role portals and integrated zone and role navigation across zones and roles within an integrated system proved to be very user-friendly and effective.

Will ZRB have performance issues when applied to different organizations? Indeed, organizations may be structured differently in names, sizes, and relationships between divisions, sections, or departments. Apparently, the names won't cause any problem to system performance, but it won't change the applicability of the ZRB approach to such big organizations. In fact, since ZRB naturally takes the well-know divide-and-conquer strategy for system design, zones, roles, apps and users can be easily added or removed in response to the changes in the organization. As for system performance ZRB may affect, any call to a view function will invoke maximum one call to the n_zrbac or i_zrbac controller regardless the sizes of the organization. The size of an organization may cause performance problems when it gets very large because of the complexity of the business logic, but the issue is not unique to ZRB.

When relationships between zones and roles get very complex, it will make access control by inference more difficult. As previously mentioned, the inference rule must be designed for each relationship, and carefully reviewed against the organization's policy. This may be an area for future research.

An integrated web-based system developed with ZRB for a large organization will have many zones, roles, apps and users, which may make it more difficult to manage the matrices used by ZRB. In our practice, the solution to the problem is automation and division. Automation is to automatically generate and maintain the matrices with little or no human involvement, while division is to let each zone manage and audit their own matrices to ensure their currency, accuracy and completeness.

References

1. Nongbri, I., Hadem, P., Chettri, S.: A survey on single sign-on. Int. J. Creative Res. Thoughts. **6**(2), 595–602 (2018)
2. Warrant Blog, implementing Role Based Access Control in a Web application, https://blog. warrant.dev/implementing-role-based-access-control/. Last accessed 10 May 2024
3. Microsoft Learn, implementing Role Based Access Control in applications, https://learn. micosoft.com/en-us/entra/identity-platform/howto-implement-rbac-for-apps. Last accessed 10 May 2024
4. Indeed.com, 11 software development methodologies. https://www.indeed.com/career-adv ice/career-development/software-development-methodologies. Last accessed 17 May 2024
5. Tari, Z., Chan, S.: A role-based access control for intranet security. IEEE Internet Com put. 24–34 (1997)

6. Ferraiolo, D.F., Barkley, J.F., Kuhn, D.R.: A role-based access control model and reference implementation within a corporate intranet. ACM Trans. Info. Syst. Security **2**(1), 34–64 (1999)

7. Bammigatti, P.H., Rao, D.P.R.: GenericWA-RBAC: role based access control model for web applications. In: 9th International Conference on Information Technology (ICIT'06), pp. 237–240. Bhubaneswar, India (2006). https://doi.org/10.1109/ICIT.2006.57

8. Joshi, J.B.D., Aref, W.G., Ghafoor, A., Spafford, E.H.: Security models for Web-based applications. Commun. ACM **44**(2), 38–44 (2001)

9. Li, X., Xue, Y.: A survey on server-side approaches to securing web ap- plications. ACM Comput. Survey **46**, 4, Article 54 (2014), p. 29. https://doi.org/10.1145/2541315

10. Le, H.T., Nguyen, C.D., Briand, L., Hourte, B.: Automated inference of access control policies for web applications. In: Proceedings of the 20th ACM Symposium on Access Control Models and Technologies, pp. 27–37 (2015)

11. Bhatti, R., Bertino, E., Ghafoor, A.: A trust-based context-aware access control model for web-services. Distributed Parallel Databases **18**, 83–105 (2005). https://doi.org/10.1007/s10 619-005-1075-7

12. Coetzee, M., Eloff, J.H.: An access control framework for web services. Inf. Manage. Comput. Secur. **13**(1), 29–38 (2005)

13. Linuxize.com, rsync Command in Linux with Examples. https://linuxize.com/post/how-to-use-rsync-for-local-and-remote-data-transfer-and-synchronization/, June 9, 2024LNCS Homepage, http://www.springer.com/lncs. Last accessed 21 Nov 2016

Enhancing IoT Network Defense: A Comparative Study of Machine Learning Algorithms for Attack Classification

Alkendria McNair, Divine Precious-Esue, Soundra Newson, and Nick Rahimi[✉]

School of Computer Science and Computer Engineering, University of Southern Mississippi, Hattiesburg, MS 39401, USA
{alkendria.mcnair,devine.precious-esue,soundra.newson, nick.rahimi}@usm.edu

Abstract. As the Internet of Things (IoT) continues to expand rapidly, securing these interconnected devices and networks from cyber threats has become a critical challenge. This research investigates the application of machine learning techniques for accurately classifying IoT network traffic data to discriminate between benign activities and various types of cyber-attacks targeting IoT systems. We propose a program that employs multiple machine learning algorithms, including Decision Tree, Logistic Regression, Naive Bayes, and Random Forest, trained on a comprehensive IoT network traffic dataset the CICIoTDataset2023. Through extensive experiments, we evaluate the performance of these classification models in detecting different IoT attack categories such as web-based attacks, spoofing, denial-of-service, Mirai, reconnaissance, distributed denial-of-service, and brute force attacks. Our results demonstrate the efficacy of machine learning approaches, with the Random Forest algorithm emerging as the top performer, achieving an overall accuracy of 98.41%. We also address challenges like class imbalance through hybrid sampling techniques and implement strategies like regularization and hyperparameter tuning to mitigate overfitting and enhance model generalization. Additionally, we conduct a performance analysis of the classification models on different IoT attack categories to gain insights into their specific strengths and weaknesses. By leveraging machine learning for accurate IoT attack classification, this research contributes to developing robust security solutions that can proactively identify and mitigate cyber threats, enabling a more secure IoT ecosystem. The findings pave the way for safeguarding interconnected devices, protecting user privacy, and fostering confidence in the widespread adoption of IoT technologies.

Keywords: Internet of Things (IoT) · Machine Learning · Data Classification · Decision Tree · Logistic Regression · Naïve Bayes · Overfitting · Random Forest

1 Introduction

In the rapidly evolving landscape of cybersecurity, the integration of machine learning techniques into the classification and analysis of Internet of Things (IoT) data has emerged as a transformative approach to bolster network defenses. As our world becomes

© The Author(s), under exclusive license to Springer Nature Switzerland AG 2025
W. Feng et al. (Eds.): SEDE 2024, CCIS 2244, pp. 55–64, 2024.
https://doi.org/10.1007/978-3-031-75201-8_5

increasingly interconnected, with smart devices permeating every corner of our lives, the importance of harnessing machine learning algorithms to safeguard IoT networks cannot be overstated. This innovative strategy holds the key to detecting and mitigating cyber-attacks, ensuring the security and privacy of users in an era defined by ubiquitous connectivity. The proliferation of IoT devices has brought forth new challenges in terms of cybersecurity. These devices generate vast amounts of data that can be exploited by malicious actors. The scale and diversity of IoT devices make securing them a daunting task. Traditional security measures often struggle to keep pace with the rapid evolution of cyber threats, leaving IoT networks vulnerable. However, by leveraging machine learning algorithms, we can develop a dynamic and adaptive defense mechanism capable of identifying and responding to both known and emerging threats across the vast IoT landscape [1, 2].

Machine learning algorithms, when integrated into IoT networks, can analyze the wealth of data generated by connected devices and identify patterns indicative of malicious activities. These algorithms can distinguish between legitimate network traffic and various families of cyber-attacks, such as DDoS attacks, data exfiltration attempts, device tampering, and malware infections. By continuously learning and adapting, machine learning models provide a robust and proactive defense against the ever-evolving landscape of IoT threats. The application of machine learning for IoT data classification enables the development of targeted defense strategies tailored to specific attack families. By analyzing the unique characteristics of each attack class, machine learning algorithms can identify distinct features and implement precise countermeasures. Moreover, machine learning can help identify the origin and propagation patterns of attacks, enabling network administrators to isolate compromised devices and prevent the spread of malicious activities.

This paper proposes a program that can effectively detect and protect IoT devices from various types of attacks. To develop this program, we trained our datasets using four different machine learning algorithms. We evaluated the performance of Decision Tree (DT), Logistic Regression, Naive Bayes, and Random Forest (RF) [3, 4]. By leveraging machine learning techniques, we were able to analyze each type of attack in depth, identifying unique patterns and characteristics associated with specific attack families. This analysis allowed us to develop targeted defense strategies tailored to each type of threat, enhancing the overall effectiveness of our security solution. We also experimented with different attributes to optimize the accuracy of our results in detecting and mitigating security solution that can safeguard IoT devices from a wide range of malicious activities and ensure the safety and privacy of users in the rapidly growing IoT ecosystem. The rest of this paper is organized as follows: Sect. 2 describes the methods used in our research, including data description, data processing and training methods. Section 3 explores our results and their limitations, Sect. 4 explores each category of attacks targeting IoT devices and their detection capabilities, and Sect. 5 concludes the paper by summarizing our key findings and further implications of them in this field.

2 Methodology

Our research aims to employ machine learning algorithms to classify data within an IoT network. In this section, we will describe the process of cleaning our dataset, the algorithms, libraries, and programs used, how we resolved our problems, and the types of attacks that were found within the datasets.

2.1 Data Description

For this data classification project, we utilized the CICIoTDataset2023, which was sourced from the website of the Canadian Institute for Cybersecurity [4]. This dataset is specifically designed for research on IoT network security and includes a diverse range of IoT devices and network traffic scenarios. This dataset contains network traffic data collected from a realistic IoT network environment that simulates various IoT devices, such as smart homes, industrial IoT, and healthcare devices. The dataset encompasses both normal and malicious traffic, with a focus on IoT-specific attacks. The dataset consists of 46 columns that provide detailed information about each network flow. These features include protocol, source and destination IP addresses, port numbers, flow duration, and packet statistics. Additionally, the dataset includes derived features such as radius, covariance, magnitude, AVG, Std, and variance, which provide statistical insights into the characteristics of incoming and outgoing packets.

One of the key aspects of the CICIoTDataset2023 is the inclusion of a label column, which indicates the class of each network flow. The dataset covers a wide range of IoT-specific attacks, including:

- Web-Based Attacks: These attacks target web interfaces and APIs of IoT devices, exploiting vulnerabilities in web applications.
- Spoofing Attacks: Attackers manipulate the source IP address or other identifying information to impersonate legitimate devices or users.
- Denial-of-Service (DoS) Attacks: These attacks aim to overwhelm IoT devices or networks with a flood of traffic, rendering them unavailable to legitimate users.
- Mirai Attacks: Mirai is a notorious malware that targets IoT devices, primarily by exploiting default or weak credentials to create botnets.
- Reconnaissance (Recon) Attacks: Attackers gather information about IoT devices and networks to identify potential vulnerabilities and plan future attacks.
- Distributed Denial-of-Service (DDoS) Attacks: Similar to DoS attacks, DDoS attacks involve multiple compromised devices flooding the target with traffic, amplifying the impact.
- Brute Force Attacks: Attackers systematically attempt to guess or crack passwords or encryption keys to gain unauthorized access to IoT devices.

Figure 1 explains the different types of attacks, how they relate to each other and how they work on IoT devices CICIoTDataset2023 comprehensive and up-to-date dataset that reflects the challenges and characteristics of modern IoT networks [5, 6].

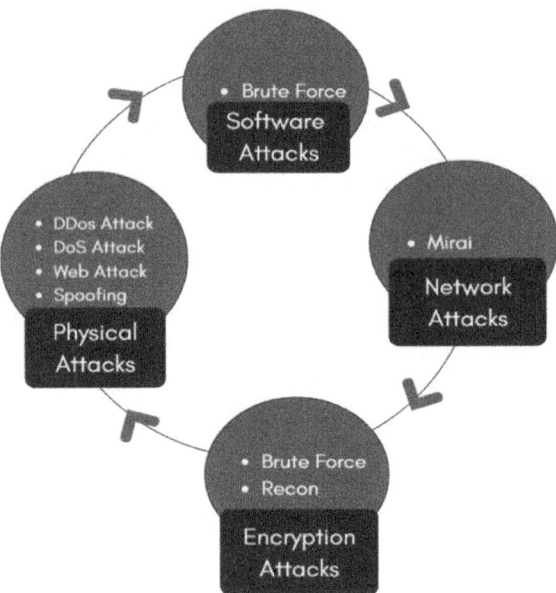

Fig. 1. Relationship between IoT attacks

2.2 Data Processing

Before training our machine learning models, we had to separate, clean, and preprocess our data to ensure its quality and suitability for analysis. The dataset required several cleaning steps to address inconsistencies and anomalies. We began by identifying and handling missing values, which can negatively impact model performance. For categorical features with missing values, we input them with the most frequent category. For numerical features, we used the median value for imputation to minimize the influence of outliers.

To enhance the performance of our models and reduce computational complexity, we employed feature selection techniques. We used the SelectKBest algorithm from the scikit learn library to identify the most informative features based on their statistical significance. This algorithm computes the ANOVA F-value between each feature and the target variable, selecting the top k features with the highest scores. By experimenting with different values of k, we found that using the top 20 features provided the best balance between model performance and computational efficiency [7].

Furthermore, we applied min-max scaling to normalize the selected features, ensuring that all values were within the range of 0–1. This normalization step was crucial to prevent features with larger magnitudes from dominating the learning process and to facilitate faster convergence of the gradient descent algorithm used in some of our models [8].

While all benign traffic was labeled as 'benign', various IoT attack types—Web-based, Spoofing, DoS, Mirai, Recon, DDoS, and Brute Force—were grouped based on their predominant classes. This distinction was crucial since the primary objective of the experiment was binary classification—that is, determining whether network data represents an assault or not.

2.3 Training Methods

Several machine learning algorithms were used in this study to train our datasets. The first algorithm that was used was Random Forest (RF), which is known for using decision trees [9] in an aggregation setting. It operates by constructing multiple decision trees during training and outputs the mode of the classes or mean prediction of the individual trees. After that, a decision tree method was used, which is a flowchart like tree structure where an internal node represents a feature, the branch represents a decision rule, and each leaf node represents the outcome.

In the following equation P1 and P2 represent the proportions of the data points that belong to each of the two possible outcomes or classes at a given node in the decision tree. These proportions are determined by the split criterion at that node, which separates the data points based on a specific feature and threshold.

$$entropy(P_1, P_2) = -P_1 \times \log_2 P_1 - P_2 \times \log_2 P_2 \qquad (1)$$

The third algorithm was Logistic Regression [6], which is a statistical method used for binary classification tasks. It models the probability of the occurrence of a binary outcome by fitting the data into a logistic curve.

In the following equation, L(x, y) represents the loss function, which quantifies the difference between the predicted values and the actual values. $\Sigma \left(y_i - h\theta(x_i) \right)^2$ is the sum of squared residuals, where:

- y_i is the actual value of the target variable for the i-th instance.
- $h\theta(x_i)$ is the predicted value of the target variable for the i th instance, calculated using the hypothesis function $h\theta(x) = \theta_0 + \theta_1 x_1 + \theta_2 x_2 + \ldots + \theta_j x_j$.
- $\left(y_i - h\theta(x_i) \right)^2$ represents the squared difference between the actual and predicted values.
- $\lambda \Sigma \theta_j^2$ is the regularization term

$$L(x, y) = \sum \left(y_i - h\theta(x_i)^2 \right) + \lambda \sum \theta_j^2 \qquad (2)$$

Finally, we used Naïve Bayes [10], which calculates the probability of each class given the input features and selects the class with the highest probability as the prediction. These algorithms were trained and tested on the dataset, which was divided into training and testing portions, with a standard 33% allocation to testing and the remainder for training.

3   Results and Discussion

To assess the efficacy of our machine learning models, we employed the scikit-learn library to compare their predictions with the ground truth labels. Figure 2 presents a comprehensive of network traffic, with a particular emphasis on discriminating between benign and malicious traffic. The table showcases precision, recall, f1-score, and support assessment metrics for each of the classifiers utilized in our research [8]. The table presents the performance of four different machine learning models: Random Forest, Decision Tree, Logistic Regression, and Naive Bayes, evaluated using metrics such as precision, recall, F1-score, and accuracy. Among these models, Random Forest emerges as the clear winner, boasting the highest accuracy of 0.9841, outperforming the second-best performer, Decision Tree, with an accuracy of 0.9735. Logistic Regression and Naive Bayes trail behind with accuracies of 0.9371 and 0.9713, respectively. The Random Forest model also excels in other metrics, achieving the highest precision, recall, and F1 scores for both the "attack" and "benign" classes, as well as the highest weighted average scores, which account for class imbalance. Notably, the dataset appears to be imbalanced, with 32813 instances of the attack class and 66000 instances of the "benign" class, potentially influencing the model's performance. To overcome this issue, we employed techniques such as oversampling the minority class and under sampling the majority class, as well as using class weights during model training to mitigate the impact of class imbalance [9]. The table in Fig. 2 provides a breakdown of the performance metrics, where the "Attack Performance" row describes the models' ability to detect malicious activity, the "Benign Performance" row highlights their accuracy in identifying acceptable network traffic, and the "General Accuracy (Overall Accuracy)" section presents the overall accuracy of the models in classifying both benign and malicious traffic in the test set.

		PRECISION	RECALL	F1-SCORE	SUPPORT
RANDOM FOREST	• ATTACK	• 0.9899	• 0.9778	• 0.9838	• 32813
	• BENIGN	• 0.9783	• 0.9901	• 0.9842	• 33187
	• ACCURACY	•	•	• 0.9840	• 66000
	• MACRO AVG	• 0.9841	• 0.9839	• 0.9840	• 66000
	• WEIGHTED AVG	• 0.9841	• 0.9840	• 0.9840	• 66000
DECISION TREE	• ATTACK	• 0.9872	• 0.9750	• 0.9811	• 32813
	• BENIGN	• 0.9756	• 0.9875	• 0.9815	• 33187
	• ACCURACY	•	•	• 0.9813	• 66000
	• MACRO AVG	• 0.9814	• 0.9813	• 0.9813	• 66000
	• WEIGHTED AV	• 0.9814	• 0.9813	• 0.9813	• 66000
LOGISTIC REGRESSION	• ATTACK	• 0.8418	• 0.9440	• 0.8900	• 32813
	• BENIGN	• 0.9371	• 0.8246	• 0.8773	• 33187
	• ACCURACY	•	•	• 0.8840	• 66000
	• MACRO AVG	• 0.8895	• 0.8843	• 0.8836	• 66000
	• WEIGHTED AV	• 0.8897	• 0.8840	• 0.8836	• 66000
NAIVE BAYES	• ATTACK	• 0.9927	• 0.9471	• 0.9693	• 32813
	• BENIGN	• 0.9499	• 0.9931	• 0.9710	• 33187
	• ACCURACY	•	•	• 0.9702	• 66000
	• MACRO AVG	• 0.9713	• 0.9701	• 0.9702	• 66000
	• WEIGHTED A\	• 0.9712	• 0.9702	• 0.9702	• 66000

Fig. 2. Performance of Classifiers

It is noteworthy that the analysis techniques we employed effectively prevented the models from overfitting the training data, a machine learning modeling error that occurs when a model performs well on training data but fails to accurately predict test data [10]. By mitigating overfitting, the models are better equipped to accurately classify test data beyond the training set, enhancing their generalizability. However, it is crucial to recognize that reducing overfitting alone does not guarantee optimal performance, as other factors such as feature selection, model complexity, and dataset characteristics also play vital roles in determining the models' effectiveness in real-world.

4 Performance Analysis of Classification Models on Different IoT Attack Categories

Securing Internet of Things (IoT) networks against a wide range of cyber threats is a critical challenge in today's interconnected world. As IoT devices continue to proliferate, it becomes increasingly important to develop robust mechanisms for detecting and classifying malicious activities targeting these devices. In our research, we employed machine learning algorithms, specifically Random Forest and Decision Tree models, to classify IoT network traffic data based on different types of attacks present in the dataset. By evaluating the performance of these models across various attack categories, we aimed to gain insights into their strengths and limitations, paving the way for more effective defense strategies against IoT specific threats. Figure 3 illustrates the classification accuracy of these models for various IoT attack categories, including Web Based, Spoofing, Reconnaissance (Recon), Mirai, Denial-of Service (DoS), Distributed Denial-of-Service (DDoS), and Brute Force attacks.

The Decision Tree model outperformed the Random Forest model in classifying Web-Based attacks, achieving an accuracy of approximately 95%, while the Random Forest model achieved an accuracy of around 92% (Fig. 3a). However, both models struggled to accurately classify Spoofing attacks, with the Decision Tree and Random Forest models achieving accuracies of only around 60 and 55%, respectively (Fig. 3b).

For Recon attacks, the models displayed relatively low classification accuracy, with the Decision Tree model performing slightly better at approximately 65% accuracy compared to the Random Forest model's accuracy of around 60% (Fig. 3c). In contrast, both models exhibited high accuracy in detecting Mirai attacks, with the Decision Tree model achieving an impressive accuracy of approximately 98% and the Random Forest model achieving an accuracy of around 97% (Fig. 3d).

The classification of DoS attacks also yielded promising results, with the Decision Tree model outperforming the Random Forest model, achieving an accuracy of approximately 95% compared to 90% for the Random Forest model (Fig. 3e). Similarly, for DDoS attacks, the Decision Tree model exhibited superior performance, with an accuracy of around 98%, while the Random Forest model achieved an accuracy of approximately 97% (Fig. 3f).

Lastly, in classifying Brute Force attacks, the Decision Tree model demonstrated higher accuracy, around 91%, compared to the Random Forest model, which achieved an accuracy of approximately 83% (Fig. 3g).

Overall, the results indicate that the Decision Tree model generally outperformed the Random Forest model in classifying most IoT attack categories, with the exception

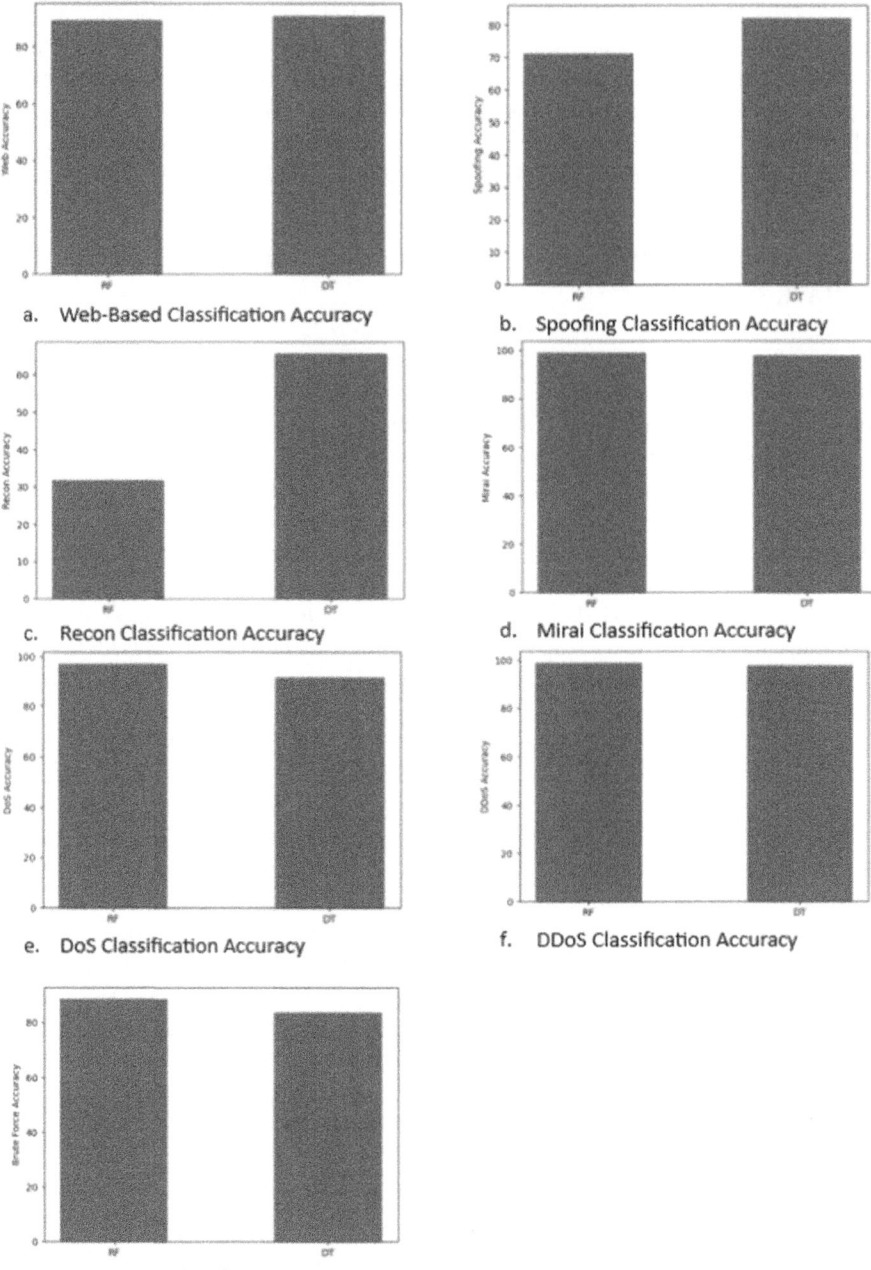

Fig. 3. Classification Accuracy of each IoT Attack

of Spoofing and Recon attacks, where both models struggled to achieve high accuracy. These findings highlight the importance of selecting appropriate machine learning algorithms and techniques for specific attack types to enhance the security of IoT networks.

5 Conclusion

In this research, we explored the critical role of machine learning in fortifying the security of Internet of Things (IoT) networks against cyber threats. By leveraging advanced algorithms to classify network data as benign or malicious, we demonstrated the potential of machine learning techniques to serve as an effective proactive defense mechanism against IoT attacks. Through rigorous experimentation and analysis, we validated the practicality and efficacy of employing Random Forest, Decision Tree, Logistic Regression, and Naive Bayes algorithms for IoT data classification.

A key challenge we addressed was the issue of imbalanced datasets, which can impede the performance of machine learning models. Our proposed hybrid sampling technique, combining under sampling of the majority class and oversampling of minority classes, proved effective in improving model accuracy in identifying different types of attacks. Furthermore, we implemented various strategies, including regularization, cost complexity pruning, and hyperparameter tuning, to mitigate overfitting and ensure the robustness and generalizability of our models across real-world scenarios.

The performance analysis of our classification models across various IoT attack categories, such as Web-Based, Spoofing, Reconnaissance, Mirai, Denial-of-Service, Distributed Denial of-Service, and Brute Force attacks, yielded valuable insights. While the Decision Tree model generally outperformed the Random Forest model in most attack categories, both models exhibited limitations in accurately classifying Spoofing and Reconnaissance attacks, highlighting areas for further improvement.

Our findings underscore the importance of adopting a comprehensive approach to model evaluation and optimization, encompassing feature engineering, algorithm selection, and hyperparameter tuning, to achieve sustainable performance in practical applications. By deepening our understanding of the synergy between machine learning and IoT security, this research contributes to the creation of a more secure and resilient digital environment.

As smart devices continue to permeate our daily lives, protecting IoT networks from cyber threats becomes increasingly paramount. By integrating machine learning algorithms, we empower users and organizations to proactively identify malicious activities, develop robust security protocols, and confidently navigate the challenges of interconnected devices. This research paves the way for a more robust digital future, where the benefits of IoT technology can be harnessed while mitigating the associated risks, fostering a safer and more secure ecosystem for all.

Acknowledgement. We sincerely appreciate the assistance and contributions provided to this research endeavor by the Louis Stokes Mississippi Alliance for Minority Participation (LSMAMP). The organization's commitment to advancing diversity and inclusion in STEM education and research has been a major factor in the success of our initiative.

References

1. Schiller, E., Aidoo, A., Fuhrer, J., Stahl, J., Ziörjen, M., Stiller, B.: Landscape of IoT security. Comput. Sci. Rev. **44**, 100467 (2022)
2. Murad, S.A., Rahimi, N.: Secure and efficient hierarchical P2P fog architecture: a novel approach for IoT. IEEE Internet Things J. (2024)
3. Rahimi, N., Gupta, B.: Security issues, vulnerabilities, and defense mechanisms in wireless sensor networks: state of the art and recommendation. In: Integration of WSNs into Internet of Things, pp. 1–15 (2021)
4. Neto, E.C.P., Dadkhah, S., Ferreira, R., Zohourian, A., Lu, R., Ghorbani, A.A.: CI-CIoT2023: a real-time dataset and benchmark for large-scale attacks in IoT environment. Sensors **23**(13), 5941 (2023)
5. Luo, C., Tan, Z., Min, G., Gan, J., Shi, W., Tian, Z.: A novel web attack detection system for internet of things via ensemble classification. IEEE Trans. Indus. Inf. **17**(8), 5810–5818 (2020)
6. Rahimi, N.: Security consideration in peer-to-peer networks with a case study application. Int. J. Netw. Secur. Appl. (IJNSA) **12** (2020)
7. Fratello, M., Tagliaferri, R.: Decision trees and random forests. In: Encyclopedia of Bioinformatics and Computational Biology: ABC of Bioinformatics, vol. 1 (2018)
8. Raju, V.G., Lakshmi, K.P., Jain, V.M., Kalidindi, A., Padma, V.: Study the influence of normalization/transformation process on the accuracy of supervised classification. In: 2020 Third International Conference on Smart Systems and Inventive Technology (ICSSIT), pp. 729–735. IEEE (2020)
9. Ramyachitra, D., Manikandan, P.: Imbalanced dataset classification and solutions: a review. Int. J. Comput. Bus. Res. (IJCBR) **5**(4), 1–29 (2014)
10. Murad, S.A., Rahimi, N., Muzahid, A.J.M.: PhishGuard: Machine learning-powered phishing URL detection. In: 2023 Congress in Computer Science, Computer Engineering, and Applied Computing (CSCE), pp. 2279–2284. IEEE (2023)
11. Broome, H., Shrestha, Y., Harrison, N., Rahimi, N.: SMS malware detection: a machine learning approach. In: 2022 International Conference on Computational Science and Computational Intelligence (CSCI), pp. 936–941. IEEE (2022)
12. Yacouby, R., Axman, D.: Probabilistic extension of precision, recall, and f1 score for more thorough evaluation of classification models. In: Proceedings of the First Workshop on Evaluation and Comparison of NLP Systems, pp. 79–91 (2020)
13. Ying, X.: An overview of overfitting and its solutions. J. Phys. Conf. Ser. **1168**, 022022. IOP Publishing (2019)

A Survey and Insights on Modern Game Development Processes for Software Engineering Education

Aakanksha Shrestha, Fei Zuo, Gang Qian, and Junghwan Rhee$^{(\boxtimes)}$

University of Central Oklahoma, Edmond, OK 73034, USA
{ashrestha51,fzuo,gqian,jrhee2}@uco.edu

Abstract. The video game industry has a fast-growing multi-billiondollar market. Due to the fast evolution of game technologies and industry, there is a pressing need to survey and analyze the current game development processes so that students who have an interest in game development can have better knowledge and skills for their projects in game software engineering education. In this paper, we present our survey and analysis of multiple aspects of modern game development and provide useful insights for students who want to work on game development. We also present a model of the common components of the game development process as well as the amount of the workload involved. This can help students, who are interested in developing their own games, craft a realistic plan for such projects.

Keywords: Software Engineering Education · Game Development Education · Survey of Game Development Processes

1 Introduction

The video game industry has a big economic and technological market that is estimated to have several hundreds of billions of dollars in revenue [16]. Along with the evolution of computing technology such as graphic processing units (GPUs), solid state disks (SSDs), and AR/VR technology as seen in recent surveys of game computers [13], the complexity and size of games have been growing fast over the years becoming challenges in software engineering [21, 34, 40, 41].

Due to its popularity and engagement with high-education students, many computer science students have an interest in the games and their underlying technologies. Some of them attempt to make games as hobbies or school projects. However, the games are complicated software not only because of their structures but also due to multiple types of resources and necessary skills to create them [45]. In addition, to achieve different game features such as cross-platform functionality, realistic 3D environments, game physics, and many more integral parts of a game [29, 33, 47], it is getting common to use a game engine instead of writing everything from scratch [1]. A lack of understanding of the nature of game development, which is different from typical computer software programming, may cause failure of program completion or frustration because of unforeseen challenges or underestimation of workload in software engineering.

In this paper, we present our survey of recent game developments, technologies, and underlying implications, from which we extract a list of takeaways for the students in higher education or novice game developers so that they can better plan their workload and have success in their school or indie projects.

Here is a list of contributions that we make in this paper.

- We analyze multiple research papers and industry articles to summarize the necessary components to understand the complexity, scope, and scale of game development.
- We present our model of common components of a game software development process, which is composed of eleven core components for the whole workflow.
- We present a list of key insights extracted from articles to guide academic students and novice game developers when they plan and execute game development projects.

This paper is organized in the following way. Section 2 presents the survey on the game development processes, current practices, and status. Based on the surveyed knowledge, Sect. 3 presents a list of key insights to be considered for projects by high-education students and/or novice game developers. Related work is discussed in Sect. 4. This paper's conclusion is given in Sect. 5.

2   Survey on the Game Development Processes

Game development projects combine multiple disciplines with coding, such as art/animation, audio/visual effects development, user-experience design, quality assurance, marketing, and management among others. In a corporate-structured game development company, usually, there are multiple departments with employees who specialize in the different fields involved in producing a game. At the same time, it is not uncommon for a single person to develop and launch a video game single-handedly. As building a game involves knowledge of different fields, there are several things that developers need to consider when building and releasing games.

2.1   Game Software Project Life Cycle

The game development life cycle can be compared to many other software development life cycles, however, in practice, most game development companies and solo developers seem to take a somewhat flexible and unstructured approach that differs from company to company [23]. Moreover, since both the technology used to build and play the games are evolving rapidly, the process of making games can vary significantly from one game to another. Even within the same company, the process/lifecycle of a game development project can be different with each game.

Even though the game development process is somewhat abstract and subject to change from one company to another, the game development life cycle (GDLC) model proposed in 2013 seems to hold up to some merit as it allows for an understanding of the iterative approach taken during the development process [45]. At the same time, the release of a game is not the end of the project for most games as games often provide new updates, features, content, and patches for fixing bugs.

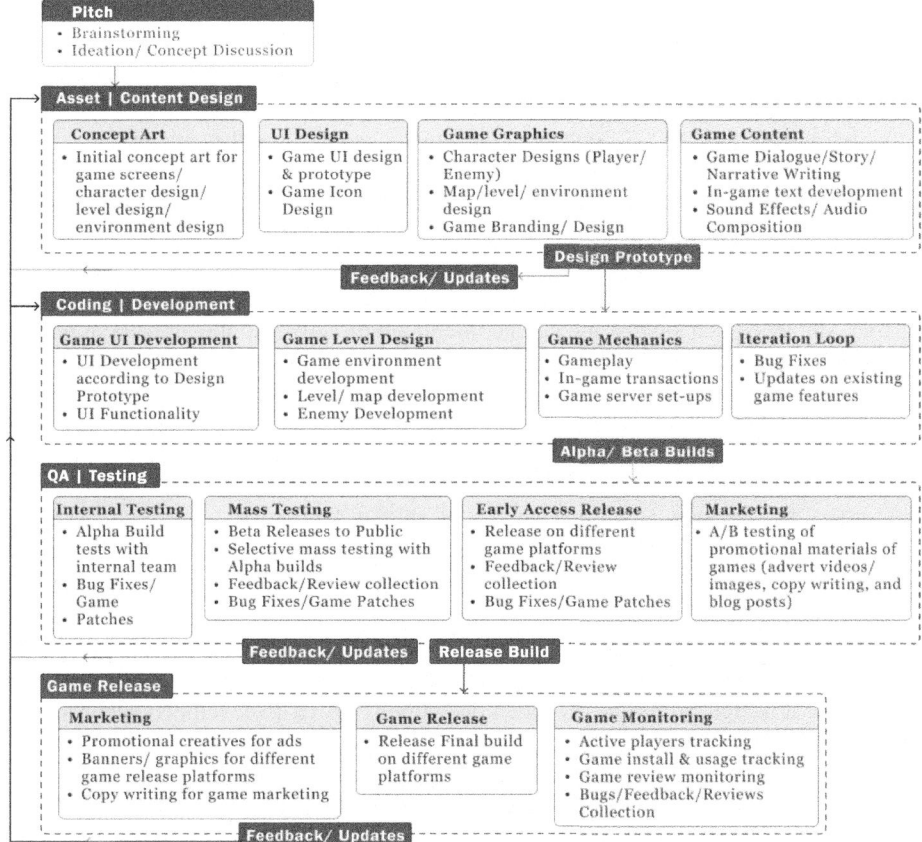

Fig. 1. Game Development Process Model.

2.2 Game Development Process Model

Figure 1 presents a closer look at the different tasks in our game development process model composed of 11 components.

1. **Pitch**: Most if not all projects start with a "pitch" stage. In the game industry, development teams might have to pitch the idea to the managers or shareholders to secure funding, while for a solo indie developer, the "pitch" is simply the initial idea of the game. Discussions on the game and different game development topics such as the scope, budget, team size, complexity, and tech stack are generally involved in this step.

2. **Asset/Content Design**: Game development involves plenty of asset and content development throughout the process. The first step is usually developing concept art, to get a feel of the game, and to figure out how the game will work. It can be the initial character sketches, environment sketches, or the game screens.

   Once the concept is approved, multiple tasks can proceed in parallel. UI and graphic designers can start building the game UI and icons for branding. Ingame graphics are developed such as characters, enemies, and environments. Likewise, the narratives, sound design, and text content of the game are developed. Depending on the type of game, these tasks might carry different weights in the process. Once the assets and content are developed, they are integrated to create a Design Prototype which solidifies the initial concept of the game, or sometimes directly integrated into the alpha/beta builds.

3. **Design Prototype**: The design prototype is like a UI mockup that is sent to the front-end developers to code the software application. Design prototypes are used to test the look and feel of the game, and improve the user experience of the game. The text content and sound effects can also be placeholders in the design prototype, as they are developed slowly and can be integrated directly into the alpha/beta builds.

4. **Design Feedback/Updates**: Design prototypes are usually shared internally among the team members to collect feedback to improve the game. There can be multiple iterations and design changes in the feedback loop from the design prototype. The game receives at least one level of refinement in this step which means fewer changes in future feedback loops.

    The design "prototype feedback design changes" loop is sometimes completely omitted by developers. Especially in a solo project, as developers might dive head-first into coding and asset implementation not giving much thought to the UI/UX design of game development in the beginning. The design aspects are then further refined on the feedback from alpha/beta builds.

5. **Coding/Development**: The coding/development stage also has multiple parallel steps. If a design prototype has been developed, the UI is developed according to the design. If the UI assets are ready then UI development proceeds with the assets otherwise proceed with temporary placeholder assets. Game mechanics and level designs can also proceed with temporary characters, environment models, and assets, which are later replaced with the assets from the design team. Another important task in this step is the iteration loop where concerns such as bugs and updates are addressed, which arise from the multiple feedback loops throughout the process.

    The project manager and the team leaders have to balance the different tasks so that either process won't be affected or slowed down while waiting for the other process to catch up.

6. **Alpha/Beta Builds**: Alpha builds are typically used for internal testing. Created early in the development process, they help shape the core gameplay. Whereas, beta builds are tested later in the process and closely resemble the finished game. Beta builds are usually shared with a larger group of testers to gather feedback and identify bugs before release.

7. **QA/Testing**: As soon as a playable build is ready, it can be used to perform internal as well as mass testing. Internal tests involve the core development team and are done early in the process. Usually, mass testing involves beta builds, and sometimes even limited access to alpha builds is provided to selective "outsiders" to receive feedback. Early access can also be a part of Testing and can be beneficial to both the players and the developers.

    Marketing materials are also developed as the game nears the release date. It involves creating different branding materials and advertisement content such as images, videos, and blog posts to be posted online. The materials can also go through

A/B testing as the performance of different creatives in the ad campaign is tested to see which one has a higher conversion rate.

8. **Build Feedback/Updates**: QA testing generally involves mass testing. Companies can sometimes hire external"game testers" who test out the beta builds. Based on the feedback received from the tests, the decision to change/iterate on different design and development choices is taken, which can then reflect back to both the coding and asset development steps. Each iteration of the test feedback changes loop brings the team one step closer to the "final" build which can be released.

9. **Release Build**: After multiple tests, a "final" build is marked for release. This release generally only happens after the development of marketing materials, as marketing is an important part of the release process.

10. **Game Release**: Game release generally involves some form of marketing or promotion, and is closely followed by game monitoring tasks. Some valuable insight can be gathered by many metrics such as active users, session length, install counts, and review collection. Game monitoring involves looking out for bugs and sending patches to fix them.

11. **Post-Release Feedback/Updates**: For many games, the moment after the release is also significant. As the game gets new users, the different features of the game are tested and the real audience finally interacts with the game which can produce even more work for the team in terms of bug fixes, patches, and adding more game content. More often than not, games require consistent updates after the release.

Observation #1

Game development has extra components compared to regular software such as visual, audio, user experience, and story production that need different skills. Their developments usually go in parallel.

2.3 Amount of Work

The workload of a game development project heavily depends on the complexity of the project, and these steps are not strictly sequential but they are components of an iterative cycle, where each step can be revisited multiple times throughout the project timeline to adapt and refine the project. The amount of work required in each of the steps is flexible and depends on the capabilities and vision of the game development team.

To understand the amount of work required for a game development project, we can divide the topic into subsequent parts including the **(1) complexity, (2) game content, (3) technology, (4) development time, (5) budget, and (6) the game release and testing**.

Observation #2

The amount of work for a game development project can be broken down into multiple components including the complexity, content, technology, development time, budget, release, and testing.

---

(1) **Game Complexity:** Most of the metrics that can be used to compare the complexity of different games such as the development timeline, development team, number of lines of code, and financial data of business are generally confidential to the public. While the number of lines of code can give us some insight into the complexity of games, it should not be an absolute way to measure the complexity of games. In addition, gaming companies do not usually release information on the number of lines of code for their games.

Since many games are built on game engines like Unity and Unreal, depending on the engine-unique tools, libraries, and packages used, the actual number of lines written by developers can change drastically. On top of that, the game assets are also a significant part of any game, from simple 2D assets to realistic 3D environments; the graphics add to a game's complexity along with the code. According to a web article by Softonic [30], AAA[1] titles like Red Dead Redemption 2 and Grand Theft Auto 5 have 60 and 36 million lines of code, respectively. Both of these games use Rockstar Advanced Game Engine (RAGE), a proprietary engine of Rockstar Games. The game engine itself would require a significant amount of code to handle all the frameworks and different features required by the game. Likewise, World of Warcraft, an MMORPG game with AAA scale, is reported to have 5.5 million lines of code, also with a proprietary game engine by Blizzard. These large numbers indicate the complexity scale of AAA games as well as the complexity of different in-game mechanics and features.

According to a blog article by ProfoundQa [44], most modern games can have around one million lines of code, which appears to be a good estimate of the average, when we consider the range of games that are currently in the market. However, it is important to note that along with the code, games also have a large amount of game assets, such as game environments, characters, dialogues, voice-overs, sound effects, and so on.

In a practical sense, the complexity of a game is directly impacted by the gameplay mechanics, which define the functionality of the game and how it is played. The approach to building an open-world, 3D exploration-style game will be significantly different from that of a 2D puzzle-solving game. The game mechanics also define how the game behaves, and how a user can interact with the game world. For instance, jumping, leveling up, and completing challenges can all be considered game mechanics.

There are some well-established gameplay mechanics that are associated with specific game genres. For example, the platformer genre has mechanics like jumping and running while the action game genre has mechanics like shooting, running, and shield mechanics. While some of these mechanics have been tried and tested for a long time, new, innovative game mechanics crop up regularly as new games are being developed.

The complexity increases for a game as more game mechanics are incorporated. For example, let us consider the different mechanics of the game Minecraft. First is Foraging-Crafting, where players need to collect resources in the game to build

---

[1] A(n) AAA (Triple-A) game title is an informal definition of a blockbuster game with a high quality often made by a major game company.

other game elements. The second mechanic can be survival, where players must be mindful of managing their health levels, their environments, and enemy creatures to survive. The third is the multi-player ability of the game, where players can join online or set up a LAN for local cooperative play.

> **Observation #3**
>
> Game complexity depends on multiple factors such as underlying game engines, gameplay mechanics, and game assets. But they should not be an absolute way to measure the complexity.

(2) **Game Content: Game playtime and the installation size:** The sheer volume of content that can be packed into a game nowadays is shocking, but perhaps such a large amount is required to keep the players engaged. The variety in the content for most games comes from the game maps or levels, the nonplayable characters (NPCs) and their dialogues, and the backstory and lore. Some story-driven games can almost be compared to an interactive movie where games have "*Easy*" modes, which have the gameplay focused more on dialogue, cut-scenes, and story exploration with minimal difficulty levels in actual combat gameplay where players engage with enemies.

From visual novels to action RPGs with cut scenes, a large emphasis is given to the game's playable characters as well as the NPCs. Baldur's Gate 3, released in 2023, has around 500 NPCs, more than 1 million words in the dialogues, and around 140 h worth of cut scenes according to IGN [26]. Some games are also known for their separate Downloadable Content (DLC) packs, which add even more to the content. Apart from DLCs, games also make new updates by adding new characters, playable maps, and new features even after the release to keep the players engaged. For instance, Overwatch released in 2014 has steadily been updated with more than 21 new maps and 11 new playable characters up till 2021, after which the game continued to evolve to a new title, Overwatch 2 [9, 10].

The gameplay content for games often depends on a player's play style. Some may prefer to stick to the main storyline while some can continue the exploration of all possible endings and side-quests, called *the completionist style*. We have compiled a graph to compare the play times of different popular modern games from the HowLongToBeat website, which has collected data from over 500 thousand players [5]. The numbers can of course change depending on the play style of different individual players, but the data does give us insight as to how long the games are being played. Figure 2 presents the number of hours of content in a game played with two different styles; main story and completionist. We can see sometimes the completionist may have ten times higher playtime compared to the main story.

As for actual game sizes for PC games, the installation size has been increasing hand-in-hand with the increasing capabilities of an average gaming PC available in the market. The Steam hardware survey [12] shows that the majority (29.8%) of Windows PC users had around 250–499 GB of total hard drive space back in July 2016. As of May 2024, more than 60% of Windows PC users have more than 1TB of total hard drive space [13]. Developers can thus take advantage of the increasing

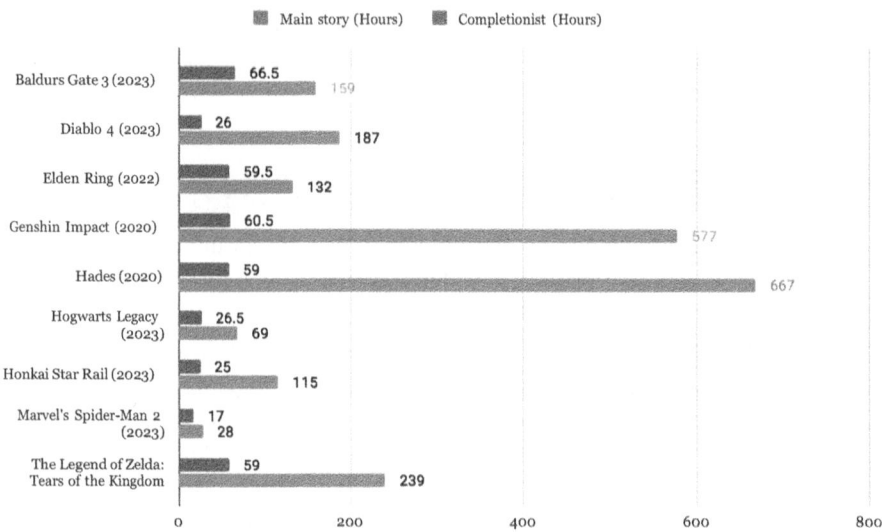

Fig. 2. A survey of game lengths (playtime) for the main story and for the completionist gameplay styles.

storage capacity of modern devices to build games with content that takes up a large amount of space.

Figure 3 presents some of the largest space-requiring games released in 2023 and 2024 [21, 41]. Generally, game optimization is a big concern both for space and performance. If it takes too long to load, players might be bored and lose interest. If the size is too big, then users might not have space to download the game; this is a more pressing issue for a mobile game. When developing 2D game assets, compression and choosing the correct size of an asset are important concerns. Whereas with 3D games, the models are often calculated as heavy or light-weight based on the polygon or triangle count, depending on the game engine. Mobile games usually use medium to low-weight polygon models.

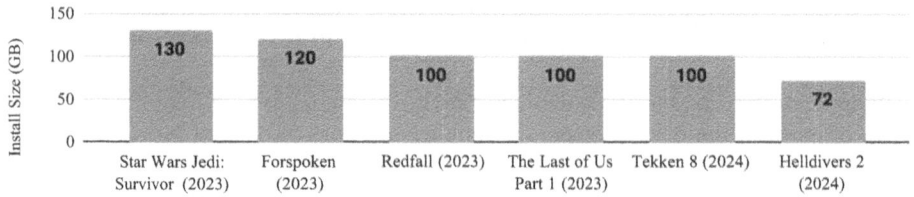

Fig. 3. The installation sizes of multiple PC games in 2023 and 2024

While most modern PC releases require somewhere around 100 GB of free space, mobile games still must be optimized for space. The base model of most mobile devices released at present has 128 GB of storage. Moreover, mobile games receive more updates and game content after release, which causes the game size to grow further. Figure 4 presents recently released Android games and their install sizes [40].

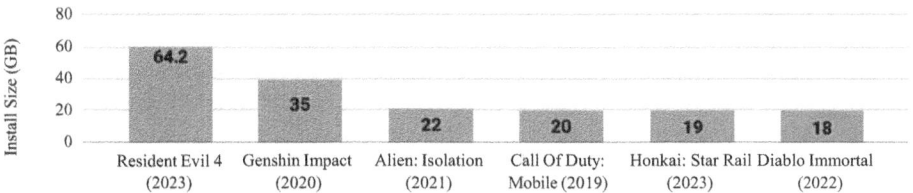

Fig. 4. Android games and their installation sizes (2019–2023).

> **Observation #4**
>
> Games released for PC have the option to push for larger game sizes, not compromising the quality of their assets. This is a freedom not yet shared by mobile games, as mobile versions of the same game have to run with low graphics settings and low-resolution assets.

(3) **Technology:** Both gaming hardware and game development software saw massive and rapid improvements in the last decade. Games have evolved as a consequence of the evolution of technology; most modern games have crossplatform functionality, massive multi-player ability, and hundreds of hours of playtime. Each new advancement in technology contributes to offer the game development industry, from processing power, graphics rendering, and storage, to new ways of interacting with the virtual game world. Newer faster graphics cards on PCs bring more realistic rendering of 3D graphics for games. Faster and larger solid-state drives (SSD) mean more scenes, levels, and downloadable content for games. Moreover, mixed-reality devices like Apple Vision Pro and Meta Quest 3 are opening the doors for the development of games with new user interfaces. According to Steam's survey [13], more than 76% of PC gamers who use Steam to play games have NVIDIA graphics cards, which support high-end computing and graphics rendering. At the time of the survey, the most popular model is the NVIDIA GeForce RTX 3060; the base model retails at present at $329.

The field of game development has already been and will likely continue to be affected by the recent wave of generative artificial intelligence which was not expected from a survey conducted in 2022 [28]. The survey found the use of machine learning very scarce in the field of game development, as game AI was mostly used for creating NPCs, real-time strategizing enemies and players, some game management features, and content creation. However, Gen-AI models seem to have found their place in the industry as the Game Engines seem to welcome the use of AI for content creation openly. Unity recently rolled out "Unity Muse" an AI assistant inside the Unity Editor in April 2024 [14]. It understands natural language prompts and helps streamline the development process by helping users understand concepts as well as generating game assets and models with animations [3]. Likewise "Unity Sentis" in beta release at present, is a neural network inference library, that can run different AI models [15].

At present, AI models can be used to create game art, write "simple" code, write scripts, dialogues, and voice-overs for the game, and even create 3D models among other game development processes. It is to be noted that while there are already AI models and services that can perform many of the game development tasks, it does require human input to use the AI services and then perform some adjustments on the AI-generated content, be it code, scripts, or art. Like with other technology, we can expect that the trend of AI-leveraged game development will continue for the foreseeable future. The 2024 State of the Game Industry Survey [1] indicates that gen-AI tools are already being used in the industry as 49% of the 3000 game developers surveyed responded that either they or their colleagues are using AI tools like ChatGPT, DALL-E, GitHub Copilot, and Adobe Generative Fill.

Observation #5

Technological advancements are always favorable to the game development industry, be it hardware or software. At present, gen-AI tools seem to be used readily by companies and developers. Using AI for art is still a controversial topic; we are still in unchartered waters trying to navigate the "proper" use of AI.

Game Engines: On the software side, game engines like Unity [47], Godot [33], and Unreal [29] in the market are developing apace, adding new features to improve the capabilities of games. While the release of Nanite, Unreal Engine's virtualized geometry system, was considered a significant advancement in terms of rendering 3D geometries back in 2022 [7], its close competitor, Unity, seems to be leaning towards building gen-AI features at present [14]. For individuals as well as companies, there isn't a "correct" answer to "Which game engine should I use?". The answer heavily depends on what the goal of the project is and which engine best suits their needs.

As an independent game developer, the decision to choose the "correct" game engine can be entirely personal. Some might choose Unreal for the relatively quick process of setting up high-definition realistic 3D graphics and its visual scripting functionality. Some might prefer Unity because of the huge community of support behind it. Yet others may prefer Godot as it is open-source and all of the profit made by the game can go straight to the developers. The GDC survey indicates that Unity and Unreal are the most popular choices among industry professionals as both have 33% of users each [1], taking more than half of the game engine market.

For all game development companies big and small, choosing the game engine and even the distribution platform can be a business decision. Most commercial game engines like Unity and Unreal, as well as game publishing platforms like Epic Games and Steam, take a cut of the revenue generated by games and may even require some form of licensing to use their applications.

As such, Unity announcing its pay-per-install pricing model last year faced heavy criticism and controversy, mostly due to the lack of clarity on the terms of "install count", and their different "license plans" [32]. This was followed by severe backlash as many popular game developers almost started a "boycott Unity" movement by planning to port their games to a different game engine [27]. Unity has since made slight changes to the initial pay-per-install pricing model and is moving ahead with the new runtime fee for Unity Pro and Enterprise licenses for Unity Engine version 6. According to the GDC survey, 35% of the developers had either considered or already switched game engines in the last year. Many developers have even pointed toward Unity's pricing policies as the reason for their switch to other game engines like Godot or Unreal [1].

(4) **Development Time of Games:** The time limit of a game development project can be a strict guide to define the scope of a game. Since a game development project goes through many testing phases, many new changes and iterations on the initial design can occur. The look and feel of a game can change drastically depending on the feedback and changes that occur once a playable version is deployed and tested. As such, it is important to have a fixed time limit for project polishing, and developers need to balance the further development of new features with the iterations and changes that need to be done on features already built. If a project is not well-planned, the development team can face work pressure. According to the Developer Satisfaction Survey 2023 by the International Game Development Association (IGDA), 63% of employees participating in the survey had experienced a time crunch more than twice in the last two years of work [2]. Therefore, as much as one can plan and use different development methodologies in a game development project, some form of work pressure or a time crunch is quite common in game development industry.

"How much time is needed to build a video game?" This question cannot be answered directly with specific numbers as it depends on a lot of different things. Everything from the level of experience of developers to the art style, sound effects, and platform of the game can impact the length of a game development project. AAA titles generally seem to have a development cycle of 5 years or longer [34]. Mobile games seem to have a shorter development time; Candy Crush is reported to have been developed in under a year [34]. Likewise, many indie games also have shorter development times when compared to AAA titles. However, since most indie game dev projects start off as passion projects, the length of the project is even more difficult to predict.

Early Access Releases are also seen in the industry, which can benefit both the company and the players. Real end-users who are interested in the game can play the game and also perform play-testing providing valuable insight to the developers. Supergiant Games, after releasing Hades I in early access for almost two years until 2020, have once again opted for an early access release for the second Hades game. According to their Steam announcement, they are collecting valuable data and feedback and sending out patches to fix the bugs identified by the early access players [4]. Figure 5 presents a snapshot of a few of the games released in 2023 and the development time in years [17–20].

Game Jams: Game jams, participated by many game developers, are events where participants try to make a video game from scratch in a limited time. Even seasoned developers participate to keep polishing and testing their skills. Game jams typically have a time limit of 24–48 h and some can run even longer. Most of the time, asset development and coding happen side by side during game jams, and the focus is usually on completing the game's core mechanics first. Different organizations host these jams and can sometimes offer monetary rewards and publishing platforms for the submitted games. Figure 6 presents a tentative timeline for a 24 h game jam project loosely based on a guide to game jam in [38].

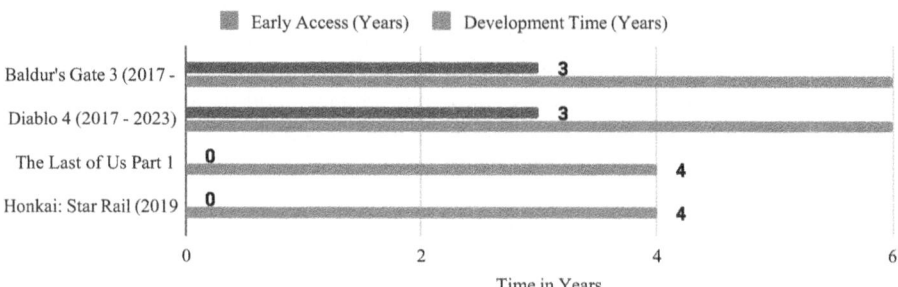

Fig. 5. Timelines of multiple game development projects. The early access time is set to zero if early access is not provided.

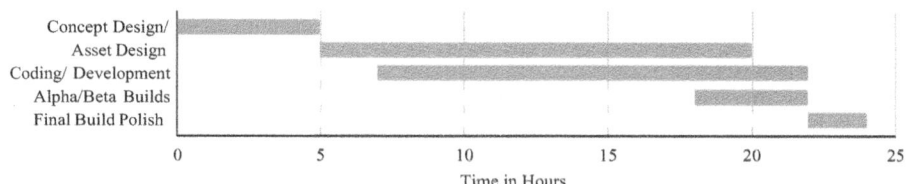

Fig. 6. A tentative timeline of a 24 h game jam project.

Observation #6

Game development time can range from a day for a game jam to multiple years for a full-blown AAA game. It could be extended or lead to time crunching due to changes in games.

---

(5) **Budget:** Other than time limitations, budget limitations can give significant weight in defining the scope of a project. Everything from the amount of time, quality of assets and game mechanics, marketing, and the size of the development content is eventually determined by the budget. Most indie games are developed by small teams or even a single developer. Budgets for games can vary depending on the game type. The budget for small indie releases can be quite small when compared

to AAA titles released by mid-sized or big companies. While it seems that a single developer can make a game for free using free game engines and free game assets, there are still hours of work put into the game, the cost of powering the computer, and other hidden costs.

The video game industry has been doing particularly well for a while now; the revenue from the worldwide gaming market in 2022 alone was estimated to be around 347 billion USD. Out of the total revenue, 70% was generated by the mobile game market, estimated at around 248 billion USD [16]. Such a large industry is bound to have a large budget invested in each project as well. While exact figures related to the budget for games are kept secret by game companies, we have some data released to the press. According to Wikipedia, the most expensive video game built to date is Genshin Impact, an open-world, action role-playing game released in 2020. It has racked up 700 million in total costs, which is expected to increase with further updates to the game. Along with regular updates of characters and maps to the game, the game will also be ported to the Nintendo Switch platform soon [8].

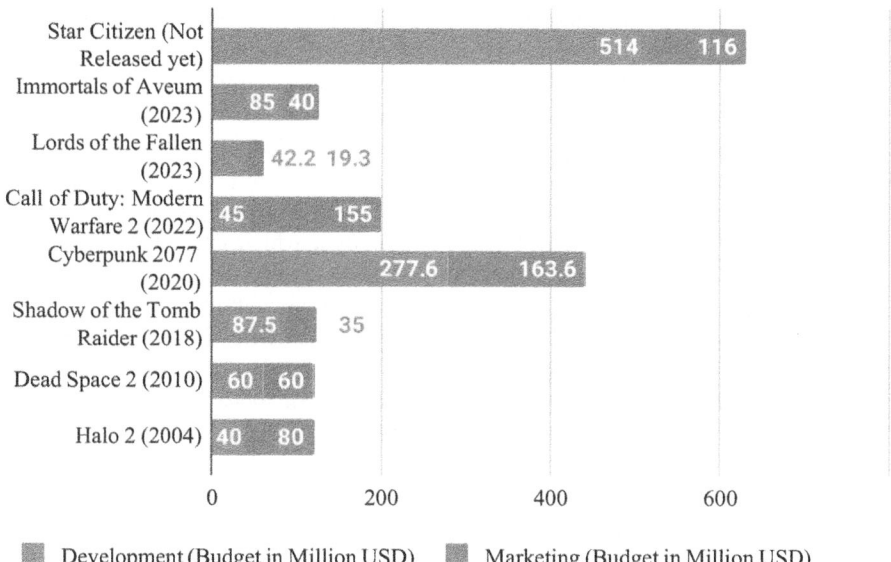

Fig. 7. Budget estimation.

With limited data available, we have compiled a graph with the known development and marketing costs of a few popular games [6]. Figure 7 presents the budget estimation for some of the games with the highest development and marketing costs.

> **Observation #7**
>
> Budget is a key to defining the scope. Recently mobile platforms grew significantly as strong platforms. Indie developers can start with less budget but need to spend a significant amount of time. Marketing costs can take up a significant part of the total budget.

(6) **Game Release and Testing:** The length of a game development project can fluctuate highly depending on how the different prototypes of the games perform. All the features of the game have to be tested and then modified according to player feedback to avoid bugs, improve the user experience of the game, and prevent unfair exploitation of gameplay. This makes the iterations go at length throughout the development phase and sometimes even post-production, as game patches and fixes are common in the industry.

Most games aimed for a commercial release need to be play-tested rigorously with quality testers, as it is not uncommon in game development projects for bugs to be present from day one and even pop up after releases [43]. In most cases, after the release developers send "patches" as updates to fix the bugs. As was the case in the release of one of the most highly anticipated game releases of 2020, Cyberpunk 2077 with a budget of more than $400 million. After its release, the game received a lot of criticism for the various bugs present in the release, which was explained by the CEO of the company as being bugs their testers didn't encounter during their tests [43]. To pacify the unsatisfied customers who had purchased the game, the company even ran a "Help Me Refund" campaign, which cost them around $51 million USD [11]. Fortunately, after multiple updates, improvements, and extension packs (Phantom Liberty), the game seems to have done well in sales by 2023.

The success of a game can be measured by many metrics in the game industry. The most common metrics are installation count, active users, session per user, in-game purchases, and reviews among others. All of these statistics are closely monitored post-release and the next steps will be to focus on sending updates and bug fixes.

3 Insights for Academic Student Projects

Many computer science students express their interest in game development as their graduation projects, special topics, or hobbies. According to the Developer Satisfaction Survey (DSS) of 2024 by the International Game Developer Association (IGDA), 10% percentage of the survey respondents are students, who are involved in game development projects academically, and 4% are teachers in the game development field [2].

Academic research activities focus on teaching students programming concepts by either teaching game development or by "gamifying" the programming concepts to foster intrinsic motivation from games [37]. Computer science students are generally exposed to games and have an interest in playing games. The intention is to build on top of this interest in games to teach them how to build games. Although playing games and developing games might be entirely different things, there is considerable merit to the idea, and has been tried out in many academic institutions.

One benefit of adopting game development projects in academia would be the opportunity for collaboration between students of different academic interests. Since a game development project requires game artists, sound designers, scriptwriters, developers, and so on, these tasks can be assigned to students whose academic interests align with the task.

Key Insights for academic student projects: We compiled a list of insights that could be helpful to consider for students and/or novice game developers who plan or run their first game projects.

– Developing a game provides a great experience and opportunity in software development to grow multiple skills.
– Careful planning on the size and scope of a game is key to an achievable goal as games have more components than other software.
– It is better to start small, and then add more functionality as you go. Gradually building the game makes it easier to manage iterations based on feedback, which prevents the team from feeling overwhelmed.
– It is important to prioritize developing the core game mechanics and functionality before polishing the smaller features and game graphics. Polishing can often take more time than anticipated. It is better to have a fully playable game with engaging mechanics than an incomplete game that looks good but cannot be played.
– As soon as a playable version is ready, it should be built and rigorously tested both internally within the development team and by external testers. Prompt feedback helps shape the project and identifies bugs and issues early in the process.
– Joining a community forum for discussions can be extremely helpful as the game development community is vast and full of passionate independent developers as well as seasoned experts in the field. It can be a good place for encouragement, feedback, support, and networking.
– Project management and teamwork are always important factors for persevering with any challenges, especially for novice game developers.

4 Related Work

Comparison of game engines: Perez et al. [42] compare the energy consumption of Unity and Unreal Engine based on three aspects of video games: physics, static meshes, and dynamic meshes. For Physics, Unity was 351% more energy-efficient than Unreal Engine. Unity was 17% more energy-efficient regarding Static Meshes. For Dynamic Meshes, Unreal Engine was 26% more energyefficient. The findings suggest proper research into choosing the correct engine can save energy equivalent to the annual energy consumption of nearly 13 million European households.

Vohera et al. [48] compare four major game engines (Unreal, Unity, CryEngine, GameMaker) based on 18 criteria. Overall, one engine cannot be suggested over another. In terms of platform deployment, Unity and Unreal are the best. For visuals and animations, Unreal and CryEngine are stronger. For advanced users, Unreal is the best option. Unreal has a steep learning curve; learning the visual.

scripting system makes it the best option for people who do not have programming experience. For novice users, Unity is the best option. It has the best documentation, the most active community, and the highest number of libraries and plug-ins.

Mohd et al. [36] compare several game engines including Cocos2D-X, CryEngine, GDevelop, Godot, Panda3D, Unity, and Unreal Engine. At present, Unity and Unreal are the most used engines due to their compatibility with all gaming platforms and ability to create both 2D and 3D games. Their popularity is also supported by a huge number of developers and communities online. CryEngine has advanced rendering tools for complex landscapes. However, it doesn't perform well in role-playing games and fast-paced games. Cocos2D-X is a great option for 2D game development and it is easy to use with the Sprite class.

Computer game education: Comber et al. taught introductory programming concepts to high school students through game development [25]. While the results were highly fruitful, the complexity of Unity as a game development platform was a big hurdle. Arnez et al. present a course plan funded by Microsoft Research to teach programming concepts through game development for undergraduate-level students. Successful results with future commercial release plans were made. However, the change in the undergrad cohort was difficult [22]. Marklund et al. [23] review 48 research papers on practices in game development to give an overview of a contemporary development process. They found that while game development procedures could vary depending on the companies, one common thing was that it was very difficult to plan a game development project in detail. They found that creativity was intrinsically involved in game development processes, which introduced democratic decision-making, informal communication, and creative autonomy among the team. Moreover, it can only be achieved through collaboration and a flexible test-driven approach as every project needs to address changes and iterations to the game project long into the development process. In fact, it was only after testing out the prototypes at various stages of development that the game would start to take shape, and as such the team had to remain open to changes. The professionals in the field have to adapt accordingly to this lack of planning and most studios have their own versions of "agile" frameworks for development; but in reality, the workflow remains just as unstructured and flexible.

Computer game development models: There are several papers in the domain of computer game development lifecycle. Ramadan et al. propose a new game development life cycle (GDLC) enhanced by guidelines addressing several research questions on game qualities [45]. Mitchell et al. conducted a correlation analysis of student experiences with peer evaluation in group game projects regarding which factors influence learning [39]. Roedavan et al. proposed a model for the games that are intended for education, business, health, and military etc. [46]. The authors' model is adapted from the game-based learning foundation. Weststar et al. discuss understanding game developers as a unique social group called an occupational community (OC) [49]. The authors characterize the game developers regarding social identity, social relations, and the evolution of the community.

Computer game developers work environments: Kasurine et al. study the game development workers' concerns on the sustainability of business [35]. Freeman et al. investigated the U.S. Indie developers' practices regarding labor, work, and technology through interviews and online reviews from people within the indie game industry. The paper draws many parallels between the established game industry and the "indie" game community. The Indie game community often views games as a cultural product and is driven by creativity and passion rather than a business, or a money generator as is often the case with the AAA game industry [31]. The indie community is known for sharing knowledge for "free" online and frequently using free tools available for game development. The community is also more accessible to everyone, which means anyone with interest in game development can join for free. These concepts of "free labor", inclusivity, and openness were found to have a significant social impact.

Borg et al. survey the video game development process in the game jam events that run for 24 or 48 h [24]. The authors have drawn a parallel between Game jams and "crunch-time", as the video game industry is known for its time crunches. They conducted a questionnaire-based opinion survey on "convenience sampling"; the participants were from the GGJ (Global Game Jam) 2017. They have 198 respondents for the survey from 51 different countries, the majority being from France and the United States, most were involved in the game development field academically or professionally. The survey is able to gather some valuable insights such as: The majority of the respondents (76%) use "Brainstorming" sessions for conceptualizing the game. Some other methods include using a whiteboard, prototyping as well as voting. For QA of the game, the popular methods were internal play testing and external play testing, while many respondents didn't have any specific form of QA testing due to the time limitation of the game jam. The most commonly used software development practices in the game jam were continuous integration, minimum viable product, and scope management.

In comparison, our paper focuses on the study of recent trends in game development processes in the past few years and the insights extracted to assist student game projects. We create and present a game development model with details of eleven components beyond what previous software development life cycle (SDLC) or game development life cycle (GDLC) discuss.

5   Conclusion

Game development is a complicated software development process that must be differentiated from typical software development in software engineering. Combined with multiple types of resource assets, such as 2D or 3D graphics, UI design, game stories, audio effects, and game music, game production requires a combination of multiple skills and project organization beyond coding. We survey multiple academic and industry articles and present our model of the game development process, which is composed of eleven components. Realistic estimation of the amount of work and successful planning requires an understanding of multiple components of the game development process, which are discussed in detail in this paper. In addition, we present a list of insights and suggestions for students and novice game developers to plan their game projects.

References

1. 2024 state of the game industry. https://web.engr.oregonstate.edu/~mjb/cs557/2024StateOfTheGameIndustry.pdf. Accessed 13 June 2024
2. Developer satisfaction survey 2023. https://igda-website.s3.us-east-2.amazonaws.com/wp-content/uploads/2024/05/01161842/2023-04-14IGSA-DSS-2023SummaryReport.pdf. Accessed 13 June 2024
3. FAQ Unity AI. https://unity.com/ai/faq. Accessed 13 June 2024
4. Hades II early access patch 1 notes. https://store.steampowered.com/news/app/1145350?emclan=103582791472836561&emgid=4175477072263852699. Accessed 13 June 2024
5. How long to beat stats. https://howlongtobeat.com/stats. Accessed 13 June 2024
6. List of most expensive games to develop. https://en.wikipedia.org/wiki/Listofmostexpensivevideogamestodevelop. Accessed 13 June 2024
7. Nanite, a revolution for virtualized geometry with unreal engine 5. https://sky-real.com/news/nanite-a-revolution-for-virtualized-geometry-with-unreal-engine-5/. Accessed 13 June 2024
8. Nintendo switch release date. https://game8.co/games/Genshin-Impact/archives/317542. Accessed 13 June 2024
9. Overwatch characters release order. https://attackofthefanboy.com/guides/overwatch-characters-release-order/. Accessed 13 June 2024
10. Overwatch list of maps by release date. https://overwatch.fandom.com/wiki/Listofmapsbyreleasedate. Accessed 13 June 2024
11. The real cost of cyberpunk 2077 refunds is $51 million, not $2.2 million. https://www.vg247.com/cyberpunk-2077-refunds-real-cost-cd-projekt. Accessed 13 June 2024
12. Steam hardware and software survey: June 2016. https://web.archive.org/web/20160731054338/, http://store.steampowered.com/hwsurvey/. Accessed 13 June 2024
13. Steam hardware and software survey: May 2024. https://web.archive.org/web/20240610084704/, https://store.steampowered.com/hwsurvey/. Accessed 13 June 2024
14. Unity AI. https://unity.com/ai. Accessed 13 June 2024
15. Unity sentis overview. https://docs.unity3d.com/Packages/com.unity.sentis@1.5/manual/index.html. Accessed 13 June 2024
16. Video game industry—statistics facts. https://www.statista.com/topics/868/video-games/#topicOverview. Accessed 3 June 2024
17. Wikipedia page for Baldur's Gate 3 (2024). https://en.wikipedia.org/wiki/Baldur%27sGate3. Accessed 15 June 2024
18. Wikipedia page for Diablo IV (2024). https://en.wikipedia.org/wiki/DiabloIV. Accessed 15 June 2024
19. Wikipedia page for Honkai: Star Rail. https://en.wikipedia.org/wiki/Honkai:StarRail (2024). Accessed 15 June 2024
20. Wikipedia page for The Last of Us Part I (2024). https://en.wikipedia.org/wiki/TheLastofUsPartI. Accessed 15 June 2024
21. Akugbe, A.: 29 of the biggest pc games by file size, ranked. https://gamerant.com/pc-games-file-size-hd-space-biggest-huge/. Accessed 13 June 2024
22. Arnez, F., Pace, J., Sung, K.: Learning while building games for teaching. Computer 47(4), 88–91 (2014)
23. Berg Marklund, B., Engstr¨omand, H., Hellkvist, M., Backlund, P.: What empirically based research tells us about game development. Comput. Game J. 8, 179–198 (2019)
24. Borg, M., Garousi, V., Mahmoud, A., Olsson, T., St°alberg, O.: Video game development in a rush: a survey of the global game jam participants. IEEE Trans. Games 12(3), 246–259 (2020)

25. Comber, O., Motschnig, R., Mayer, H., Haselberger, D.: Engaging students in computer science education through game development with unity. In: IEEE Global Engineering Education Conference, pp. 199–205 (2019)
26. Cripe, M.: Baldur's gate 3's collective dialogue has triple the word count of the lord of the rings, larian reveals. https://www.ign.com/articles/baldurs-gate-3s-collective-dialogue-has-triple-the-word-count-of-the-lord-of-the-rings-larian-reveals. Accessed 13 June 2024
27. Dawe, L.: Unity attempt to clarify new install fees as developers revolt. https://www.gamingonlinux.com/2023/09/unity-attempt-to-clarify-new-install-fees-as-developers-revolt/. Accessed 13 June 2024
28. Edwards, G., Subianto, N., Englund, D., Goh, J.W., Coughran, N., Milton, Z., Mirnateghi, N., Ali Shah, S.A.: The role of machine learning in game development domain—a review of current trends and future directions. In: Digital Image Computing: Techniques and Applications, pp. 01–07 (2021)
29. Epic Games: Unreal engine (2023). https://www.unrealengine.com/. Accessed 15 June 2023
30. Fern´andez, M.: Code by the numbers: How many lines of code in popular programs, apps, and video games? (2023). https://en.softonic.com/articles/programs-lines-code. Accessed 13 June 2024
31. Freeman, G., Bardzell, J., Bardzell, S., McNeese, N.: Mitigating exploitation: Indie game developers' reconfigurations of labor in technology. Proc. ACM Human-Comput. Interact. **4** (2020)
32. Gerblick, J.: Game devs revolt after unity reveals plan to charge them a fee based on installs: "you'll literally bankrupt me". https://www.gamesradar.com/game-devs-revolt-after-unity-reveals-plan-to-charge-them-a-fee-based-on-installs-youll-literally-bankrupt-me/. Accessed 13 June 2024
33. Godot Engine Community: Godot engine (2023). https://godotengine.org/. Accessed 15 June 2023
34. Juegoodmin: How long does it take to make a game? https://www.juegostudio.com/blog/how-long-does-it-take-to-develop-video-game. Accessed 13 June 2024
35. Kasurinen, J., Palacin-Silva, M., Vanhala, E.: What concerns game developers? a study on game development processes, sustainability and metrics. In: IEEE/ACM 8th Workshop on Emerging Trends in Software Metrics, pp. 15–21 (2017)
36. Khan Mohd, T., Bravo-Garcia, F., Love, L., Gujadhur, M., Nyadu, J.: Analyzing strengths and weaknesses of modern game engines. Int. J. Comput. Theory Eng. **15**, 54–60 (2023)
37. Laine, T.H., Lindberg, R.S.N.: Designing engaging games for education: a systematic literature review on game motivators and design principles. IEEE Trans. Learn. Technol. **13**(4), 804–821 (2020)
38. Macklin, C., Martin, J., Dikkers, S.: Planning your game jam: game design as a gateway drug. In: Mobile Media Learning, pp. 203–218 (2012)
39. Mitchell, A., Scott, M., Walton-Rivers, J., Watkins, M., New, W., Brown, D.: An exploratory analysis of student experiences with peer evaluation in group game development projects. In: Conference on United Kingdom and Ireland Computing Education Research (2022)
40. O'Connor, Q.: Mobile games with the biggest file size and how many GB they take. https://www.thegamer.com/mobile-games-big-file-size-heavy-gb/. Accessed 13 June 2024
41. Park, M.: The era of 100gb games is upon us, and the average pc gamer is underprepared. https://www.pcgamer.com/the-era-of-100gb-games-is-upon-us-and-the-average-pc-gamer-is-underprepared/. Accessed 13 June 2024
42. P´erez, C., Ver´on, J., Garc´ia, F., Moraga, M., Calero, C., Cetina, C.: A comparative analysis of energy consumption between the widespread unreal and unity video game engines (2024). arXiv:2402.06346
43. Politowski, C., Petrillo, F., Gu´eh´eneuc, Y.G.: A survey of video game testing. In: IEEE/ACM International Conference on Automation of Software Test, pp. 90–99 (2021)

44. ProfoundQa: How many lines of code does a computer game have? https://profoundqa.com/how-many-lines-of-code-does-a-computer-game-have/#HowmanylinesofcodeisWitcher3 (2022). Accessed 13 June 2024

45. Ramadan, R., Widyani, Y.: Game development life cycle guidelines. In: International Conference on Advanced Computer Science and Information Systems, pp. 95–100 (2013)

46. Roedavan, R., Pudjoatmodjo, B., Siradj, Y., Salam, S., Hardianti, B.D.: Serious game development model based on the game-based learning foundation. J. ICT Res. Appl. **15**(3), 291–305 (2021)

47. Unity Technologies: Unity real-time development platform (2023). https://unity.com/. Accessed 15 June 2023

48. Vohera, C., Chheda, H., Chouhan, D., Desai, A., Jain, V.: Game engine architecture and comparative study of different game engines. In: 12th International Conference on Computing Communication and Networking Technologies, pp. 1–6 (2021)

49. Weststar, J.: Understanding video game developers as an occupational community. Inf. Commun. Soc.Commun. Soc. **18**(10), 1238–1252 (2015)

Evaluating the Impact of Combinatorial Interaction Testing on Test Automation: A Case Study from Industry

Feras Daoud[(✉)], Miroslav Bures, Zdenek David, and Petr Syrovatka

Czech Technical University in Prague, Prague, Czechia
daoudfer@cvut.cz, {miroslav.bures,davidzde,syrovpe6}@fel.cvut.cz

Abstract. Software testing regularly involves numerous setups and user inputs, leading to a combinatorial explosion of test cases. While Combinatorial Interaction Testing (CIT) has been theoretically investigated, its effectiveness in real-world scenarios remains unclear [1]. This research fills that gap by utilizing CIT in some live software projects. We led two studies: the first focuses on optimizing user input testing in jTrac, and the second focused on managing system configurations in Redmine, a comparative web application. We looked at CIT to customary testing strategies, breaking down components like test design time, test automation, test execution, suite size, and defect detection. The investigation gave valuable insights into enhancing CIT execution and reception. The results are promising. With CIT, the number of required test cases is significantly reduced, but at the same time, defect detection is improved. In the first study, the average time to detect a defect was 1.40 h (design, automation, execution, and evaluation) compared to 0.35 h with CIT. Similar patterns emerged in the second study. These findings have important implications for both researchers and organizations. They highlight CIT's promise for software testing, including decreasing test case burden and perhaps improving defect detection rates. This study provides practical evidence for organizations and testers looking to improve their testing procedures.

Keywords: Combinatorial Testing · Model-Based Testing · Empirical Efficiency · Automated Testing · Unified Combinatorial Interaction Testing

1 Introduction

Testing innumerable configurations for software can rapidly become overwhelming. Combinatorial Interaction Testing (CIT) has developed as a powerful approach to address this difficulty. Over the past couple decades, CIT has accumulated momentum owing to its effectiveness in handling such complex systems [15]. The fundamental principle underpinning CIT is that most software defects arise from interactions between a limited set of parameters rather than individual ones. CIT significantly decreases the amount of test cases required by focusing on these pairwise and mixed-strength interactions, as opposed to standard approaches that test every conceivable combination. While CIT has shown to be an efficient approach, it has several limits. It does not ensure that all potential interactions will be covered, which implies certain defects may remain uncovered [8]. To guarantee appropriate software testing, CIT should be used cautiously and combined with other approaches [2].

Recent empirical findings call into question long-held beliefs about test suite generating techniques. While it was previously thought that more complex algorithms were required, studies now show that Simulated Annealing (SA) and Greedy Algorithms, which are generally seen as simpler approaches, provide comparable fault detection capabilities to their more complex counterparts, particularly in the early stages of testing. This effectiveness stays true even when dealing with real-world limitations and scenarios with larger interaction levels, indicating that simpler algorithms may be more reliable than previously thought. These findings demand a rethinking of existing test suite creation approaches, perhaps opening the way for more streamlined and efficient ways [10].

Pairwise testing, a specific type of CIT, covers all possible pairs of contribution parameter values. The thinking behind pairwise testing is that most defects are initiated by interactions between sets of two parameters instead of a higher number of interactions [14]. This strategy gives an acceptable trade-off between thoroughness and the number of test cases, making it a well-known decision in practice. As per exploration, pairwise testing can uncover a huge rate of flaws with a relatively modest number of test cases looked at to exhaustive testing. This has driven its selection in different enterprise areas [4]. Researchers have found that while exhaustive testing can test each potential cooperation, it ordinarily requires an undeniably enormous number of test cases. Then again, pairwise testing drastically diminishes this number while thoroughly including two sets [9, 15].

While simulations and mutation testing have regularly demonstrated the effectiveness of CIT, there is a disturbing lack of empirical data supporting its application in real-world industrial environments. This lack of data notably affects its capacity to detect real faults discovered during software development. This substantial gap in knowledge emphasizes the crucial need for more study. Such a study should focus on confirming CIT's applicability in real-world scenarios and evaluating its potential benefits over more traditional, intuitive testing approaches now used by developers [6].

This study investigates the effectiveness of CIT techniques, focusing on how effectively the resulting test suites transfer into real-world applications. We investigate a unique CIT testing application that overcomes the limitations of standard pairwise testing. This application demonstrates CIT-generated suites' ability to discover complicated connections inside a system that extend beyond basic two-way combinations. Furthermore, we look into the utility of model based mutation testing as a technique for evaluating CIT's effectiveness. We aim to provide a more complete assessment technique for CIT-generated test suites by employing code-based mutation testing ideas [2]. This integrated method will evaluate not just the ability to identify essential interactions, but also how successfully CIT suites discover complex system behaviours.

This paper aims to contribute to the body of knowledge on CIT, emphasizing the need for comprehensive empirical evidence to better understand its effectiveness in industrial testing environments. This paper investigates the real-world effectiveness of CIT as applied to software projects. It goes beyond simulations to evaluate CIT's capacity to detect defects and provides development teams with practical advise on how to integrate CIT. The study then offers a data-driven evaluation of CIT's impact on test design, test execution, and test cases count, to determining if CIT significantly improves defect detection in real-world scenarios.

The paper is organized as follows: Sect. 2 discusses the state-of-the-art CIT evaluation using testing methods. In Sect. 3, the experiment design and methodology are presented. In Sect. 4, the results are presented, while the discussion and interpretations of our findings are covered in Sect. 5. Finally, Sect. 6 is the paper's conclusion.

2 Background

Recent studies have leveraged Combinatorial Interaction Testing (CIT) and mutation testing to enhance software testing across various domains. Techniques such as Unified Combinatorial Interaction Testing (U-CIT) have shown flexibility in addressing complex coverage criteria in configurable systems [5]. Additionally, the MERCI method evaluates CIT tools in Software Product Lines (SPL), focusing on defect detection, test coverage, and test execution length, highlighting CIT's potential in practical applications [3, 11].

Mutation-Inspired Symbolic Execution (MISE) combines Dynamic Symbolic Execution (DSE) and Mutation Testing (MT) to improve test case generation and mutation detection capabilities, offering a promising direction for future research [13].

Q-value-based Particle Swarm Optimization (Q-PSO) is a technique for efficiently generating an optimal number of test cases. The technique utilizes Q-values to evaluate particles (test cases), and the total Q-value serves as the fitness function for PSO evolution and evaluation. Studies regarding Q-PSO aim to validate the proposed approach, comparing Q-PSO results to existing metaheuristics and computation-based techniques. The findings show that Q-PSO outperforms some meta-heuristics, and the comparison includes well-known computational-based techniques to examine test case size growth over time in various inputs and development environments [7, 12].

Despite these advancements, the challenge remains in simulating complex defects accurately. Real-world defects provide a more reliable measure of CIT's effectiveness compared to artificial defects. Thus, further comprehensive research is needed to fully understand CIT's practical implications and benefits over traditional testing methods.

3 Experimental Design

Traditional testing provides extensive coverage, but it may be slow. In contrast, automation offers efficiency but may miss critical interactions between test cases. CIT addresses this gap by focusing on carefully selected combinations of inputs, therefore reducing total test suite size while maintaining high defect detection capabilities. This study seeks to quantify these possible advantages by comparing the efficacy and time efficiency of both approaches.

This research investigates how CIT may be utilized within an automated testing framework. We evaluate two scenarios: manual test design and execution with an automated method that uses CIT. We investigate the time spent on every phase (design, automation, and execution) of two studies, as well as the average time to find a defect. This will help us figure out whether CIT can streamline the testing process.

3.1 Systems Under Test (SUT)

JTrac[1] is an open-source web application that focuses on issue-tracking. All of the typical features of an issue-tracking system, including file-attachment support and email integration, are included in JTrac. The experiment was conducted on stable version 2.3.1 released in May 2023.

Redmine[2] is an open-source project management web application that facilitates efficient collaboration and organization of tasks within teams. Redmine allows users to create and manage projects, and track issues and time spent on the projects. Redmine is written using Ruby on Rails framework, and is cross-platform and cross-database. The experiment was conducted on version 5.0, which was chosen because of a considerable amount of described defects, which could have been used in the experiment.

The experiment consists of two parts, each with a distinct scope:

1. Study 1—This initial study leverages CIT to test the functionality of important forms within a SUT in the jTrac environment, possibly a bug tracking tool. It focuses on two essential forms: the Issue Tracking Form, where 8 fields are analysed for interaction effects, and the Login Form, with 2 significant fields. By applying CIT, the study attempts to test the right functionality of these forms and their interaction inside the jTrac system.
2. Study 2—This study looks into functionality in two more SUTs: the New Issue form (9 fields) and the Time Logging form (4 fields). These forms were chosen due to their diverse field sets and the availability of historical defects, which were most likely used as a testing reference. Similarly to the prior studies, CIT is used to evaluate the functioning and possible interactions between various form fields.

3.2 Test Cases, Application of CIT and the Test Plans

We prepared three different sets of tests and ran each set once. The first set had test cases created without using Combinatorial Interaction Testing (CIT). The second set was made by replacing some of the test cases and swapping them with new ones we created using CIT, specifically with a technique called a 2-way uniform strength combinatorial array. We similarly made the third set but used a different CIT technique called a mixed-strength combinatorial array.

Study 1, part 1—Login Form This is a simple login form, only 2 parameters with 4 different values were used.

The initial test set contained seven test cases, which were reduced to 6 through CIT. This reduction involved replacing 5 of the original test cases with 4 new ones, both in the 2-way uniform strength combinatorial array and the mixed-strength combinatorial array.

Study 1, part 2—Creating New Item Form

In the second part of the experiment, we used a form for creating a new item (an issue in this case) with 8 identified parameters and 20 values in total. Their numbers for individual parameters are presented in Table 1.

---

[1] http://jtrac.info/.

[2] https://www.redmine.org/.

All of the 28 test cases from the initial test set were replaced by 12 test cases after applying CIT using 2-way uniform strength. The number of test cases created was equal for the third test set with mixed-strenght.

Table 1. Number of values of each parameter in Issue create form in Study 1

Parameter Name	Number of values
Summary	2
Detail	2
Severity	6
Name	2
AssignTo	2
NotifyByEmail	2
Attachment	2
SendEmailNotifications	2
Total	20

The original test set (created by the previous test automation team) consisted of 71 test cases. Using a uniform 2-way strength array, the application of CIT reduced the number of test cases to 58. Namely, 28 test cases were identified to be replaced by CIT in the original test set, and after the CIT application, they were replaced by 15 new test cases.

Using the mixed strength array, we identified three relevant sets of two interacting parameters, and 28 original test cases that were identified to be replaced by CIT were replaced by 9 test cases. In total, the size of the test set was 52 test cases.

Study 2, part 1—New Issue Form

For the first part of the Redmine SUT, a form for creating a new issue was chosen mainly because of its many fields that can be effectively tested with CIT. The first test set was designed without the knowledge of the CIT. In the second set, CIT with 2-way uniform strength was used, and the relevant tests from the first test set were replaced. In the third set, 2-way uniform strength was replaced by a mixed-strength combinatorial array. The parameters and number of values are described in Table 2.

The original test set had 18 test cases, from which 14 were replaced by 21 test cases generated with CIT, adding to a total of 25 test cases. The third test set with mixed-strength had the same amount of test cases generated.

Study 2, part 2—Time Tracking Record Form

For the second form, which is a form used to record time spent on an issue, the same approach was taken. Compared to the first form, this one is smaller. Firstly, a test set without CIT, then CIT 2-way uniform strength, and then a mixed-strength combinatorial array. Parameters and their numbers are shown in Table 3.

Table 2. Number of values of each parameter in New Issue Form in Study 2

Parameter Name	Number of values
Subject	2
Assignee	3
Category	3
Target Version	3
File	2
Parent Task	2
Start Date	3
End Date	3
Estimated Time	4
Total	25

Table 3. Number of values of each parameter in Time Tracking Form in Study 2

Parameter Name	Number of values
Issue	2
Date	3
Hours	3
Project	2
Total	10

The original set had 12 test cases, from which 6 were replaced by CIT. Both approaches generated 9 test cases, which adds up to total of 15 test cases.

3.3 Test Automation Scripts, CIT Tool

In Studies 1 and 2, a segment (32%) of the test automation scripts was manually coded in Cypress to estimate the time required for automating the remaining parts.

Cypress is a modern end-to-end testing framework for web applications that runs on JavaScript and provides a stable, easy-to-use environment for creating, executing, and troubleshooting tests.

As a CIT tool, we used ACTS 3.2[3] as the known standard for CIT. For the generation of the combinatorial arrays, the IPOG algorithm was used, as recommended within the tool as a default option.

---

[3] https://csrc.nist.gov/projects/automated-combinatorial-testing-for-software.

The selection of a Combinatorial Interaction Testing (CIT) tool is critical to the effectiveness of the testing process. The following describes the criteria for picking a CIT tool and how it can influence results. The chosen tool needs to be compatible with software technology stack and can generate test cases that are suitable for interaction types depending on individual situations. It must be able to efficiently cope with the high volume of data sets and numerous parameters for interaction. To decrease the learning curve for testers and facilitate effective use of the tool, it should be easy to operate and have a clear document. The tool should also feature different combinatorial strategies, like pairwise and n-wise testing.

The CIT tool we choose can have a huge impact on testing outcomes. A tool with excellent capabilities to generate comprehensive tests will turn up more defects, which in practice means test generation and execution can reduce the time needed to detect defects belonging as they do to test algorithms for defect injection by simply exacerbating The Completeness of the test cases the tool generates in proportion to its ability determines the scope of testing The greater the number of interaction scenarios that any given tool ensures, the more thorough will be testing for protection. The ease of use and integration possibilities open to this lab administrative officials in selecting their own type or kind tool; with Good tools easier to use and match carefully are more likely to produce correct results, and also significantly enhance reliability.

3.4 Defects Discovery

We identified the defect types into 2 categories in these studies. The first type was historical defects, which were previously found and fixed. These defects were extracted from the public defect trackers of each application. The second type of defects were artificial defects, which were created as a modification of previously mentioned historical defects and artificial defects that were created with our previous experience with testing.

Historical defects were taken from the JTrac publicly available bugs page[4]. To process the data for the test cases, we extracted the information from the reported bugs and organized them by module.

More artificial bugs were then added, but with additional, more easily detectable bugs to compensate for the system's stable version, which naturally had fewer obvious bugs.

As well as in the previous study, in this study, artificial and historical defects were introduced since the version used was almost defect-free. Historical defects were taken from the Redmine Repository[5]. Artificial defects were modeled using experience gained with software development and with regard to what types of defects can be detected using previously described techniques.

---

[4] https://sourceforge.net/p/j-trac/bugs/.

[5] https://www.redmine.org/projects/redmine/issues.

3.5 Time Harvesting and Defects Detection

For both of these studies, we have tracked the time spent designing and programming the test manually and kept track of it using an Excel table. For each test set, we have designed and programmed at least a quarter of the tests, using an average of those tracked times as an estimate for designing and programming the whole test sets. In addition, we have separated the preparation time to setup the testing frameworks to further increase the precision.

4 Results

In our experiments, we aimed to evaluate the efficacy of Combinatorial Interaction Testing (CIT)-designed tests against conventional testing methods. Through a series of tests, we evaluated the efficacy and reliability of each strategy, enabling us to provide a comprehensive comparison of their advantages and disadvantages.

4.1 Trends in Test Case Volume, Defect Detection, and Time Investment

Table 4 shows the results for Study 1. To provide more specific information, we have separated the parts about the Login and Issue create forms in this study, as they are quite different from each other. In Table 4, the term *2-way* means a 2-way uniform strength combinatorial array and *Mixed* means a combinatorial array with mixed strength. We will use these terms when we talk about the results later. The phrase *Without CIT* refers to the original test cases that were made without using the Combinatorial Interaction Testing (CIT) method.

In this study, we examined the efficiency of Combinatorial Interaction Testing (CIT) in test case creation and execution, focusing on two distinct forms: the Login form and the Issue create form. Our findings reveal significant improvements in test efficiency and defect detection when employing CIT.

For the Login form, the creation of test cases replaced by CIT showed a substantial reduction in time, dropping by 68.75% for both the 2-way and Mixed CIT methods, compared to the method without CIT. Unchanged test cases remained at a consistent duration. The execution time for replaced test cases in the Login form was notably reduced by 80% with both CIT approaches.

Regarding the Issue create form, the creation time for test cases to be replaced by CIT demonstrated a remarkable decrease of 76.39% with the 2-way and Mixed CIT approaches, respectively.

Overall, the total time for the Login form showed a decrease of 25% with both CIT approaches, while for the Issue create form, the reduction was more pronounced, at 76.26% for the 2-way and 79.86% for the Mixed CIT method.

Table 4. Study 1: Comparison of time spent, defects number, and number of test cases between with CIT and without CIT

	Without CIT	CIT - 2-way	CIT - Mixed
Time Spent (hours)			
Login form creation	0.8	0.25	0.25
Login form creation - Not changed test cases	0.5		
Issue form tests creation	7.2	1.7	1.2
Issue form tests creation - Not changed test cases	0		
Login form - Automation	0.5	0.5	0.5
Login form - Automation - Not changed test cases	1		
Issue form - Automation	1	1	1
Issue form - Automation - Not changed test cases	0.5		
Login form - Execution	0.5	0.1	0.1
Login form - Execution - Not changed test cases	0.5		
Issue form - Execution	5.2	0.1	0.1
Issue form - Execution - Not changed test cases	0		
Total for Login form	3.8	2.85	2.85
Total for Issue create form	13.9	3.3	2.8
Total	17.7	6.15	5.65
SUT defects			
Login defects (historical)	0		
Login defects (artificial)	5		
Issue create defects (historical)	1		
Issue create defects (artificial)	12		
Total	18		
Defects Detected			
Login defects (historical)	0	0	0
Login defects (artificial)	4	5	5
Issue create defects (historical)	0	0	0
Issue create defects (artificial defects)	9	11	11
Total	13	16	16

(*continued*)

Table 4. (*continued*)

	Without CIT	CIT - 2-way	CIT - Mixed
Number of Test Cases			
Login form	7	4	4
Issue create form	28	12	12
Defect Detection Effectiveness			
Defect detection time (hours)	1.4	0.4	0.35

In terms of defect detection, the number of detected defects increased with the application of CIT, from 13 without CIT to 16 with both CIT methods. This indicates an increase in defect detection of 18.75% with CIT. The number of test cases for both forms also reduced significantly with CIT, enhancing the overall efficiency of the testing process (Table 5).

Table 5. Study 2: Comparison of time spent, number of defects, and number of test cases between with CIT and without CIT

	Without CIT	CIT—2-way	CIT—Mixed
Time Spent (hours)			
New Issue tests creation	2.25	1.5	1.5
New Issue tests creation—Not changed test cases	0.75		
Time Tracking tests creation	1.25	1	1
Time Tracking tests creation—Not changed test cases	1.25		
New Issue tests—Automation	2.25	1.25	1.25
New Issue tests—Automation—Not changed test cases	1.25		
Time Tracking tests—Automation	1.75	1.5	1.5
Time Tracking tests—Automation—Not changed test cases	1.25		
New Issue tests—Execution	1.75	0.1	0.1
New Issue tests—Execution—Not changed test cases	0.5		
Time Tracking tests—Execution	1.25	0.1	0.1
Time Tracking tests—Execution—Not changed test cases	0.5		

(*continued*)

Table 5. (*continued*)

	Without CIT	CIT—2-way	CIT—Mixed
Total for New Issue form	8.75	5.6	5.6
Total for Time Tracking form	7.25	5.35	5.35
Total	16	10.95	10.95
SUT defects			
New Issue form defects (historical)	2		
New Issue form defects (artificial)	8		
Time Tracking form defects (historical)	0		
Time Tracking form defects (artificial)	4		
Total	14		
Defects Detected			
New Issue form defects (historical)	1	2	2
New Issue form defects (artificial)	3	8	8
Time Tracking form defects (historical)	0	0	0
Time Tracking form defects (artificial)	2	4	4
Total	6	14	14
Number of Test Cases			
New Issue form	18	29	29
Time Tracking form	12	15	15
Defect Detection Effectiveness			
Defect detection time (hours)	2.66	0.78	0.78

These results highlight the effectiveness of CIT in optimizing software testing, reducing the time required for test case creation and execution, and improving defect detection rates.

In the second study, where data is represented in 5, we have seen a notable increase in the efficiency of CIT testing in comparison to testing without CIT. Out of a total of 14 defects, historical and artificial, manual testing has detected only 6 out of 14 defects introduced, while 2-way and mixed strength CIT has detected all of them.

In the New Issue Form, the number of total Test Cases when using CIT in both variants, increased by 37.93%, yet the total number of hours spent decreased by 36%, and the average time to detect one defect decreased drastically from 2.1 h to 0.56 h.

In the smaller Time Tracking form, the number of Test Cases increased by 20%, the total number of hours decreased from 7.25 h to 5.35 h, and the average time to detect one defect decreased from 3.6 to 1.3 h, which is a similar result as is the previous form.

In summary, test cases prepared using CIT methods in study 2 generated more test cases, yet proved to be more time efficient and also detected all of the introduced historical and artificial defects.

Delving into the specific results from each study, in Study 1, the average time required to detect one defect decreased from 1.4 h in the original test set to 0.4 h with the CIT 2-way method and further improved to 0.35 h with the CIT Mixed method. This represents a significant reduction of 71.43% and 75% in detection time for the 2-way and Mixed CIT methods, respectively.

Similarly, in Study 2, the efficiency gains were evident. The initial average detection time of 2.66 h was substantially reduced to 0.78 h with the CIT 2-way method and remained the same with the CIT Mixed method. This corresponds to a reduction of 70.68% for both CIT approaches.

4.2   The Impact of CIT to Test Automation Structure

In addition to diminishing the average time required to identify a defect, the application of Combinatorial Interaction Testing (CIT) also contributed to a more organized method in test automation. The implementation of CIT resulted in enhanced parametrization of test data within the test cases. This improvement facilitates greater reusability of the test scripts, which can lead to reduced effort in their ongoing maintenance and future extensions.

The previously mentioned results underscore the effectiveness of CIT in streamlining the testing process. Both the 2-way and Mixed methods significantly reduced the time required to detect defects, thereby enhancing the overall efficiency of the software testing process.

5   Discussion

This study reveals that using Combinatorial Interaction Testing (CIT) leads to better detection of defects in software, which is a significant finding. CIT enhances the testing process, uncovering more hidden defects in the software under test (SUT). This effectiveness in identifying elusive defects strongly advocates for the adoption of CIT, especially in situations where uncovering such hidden issues is critical.

In our second study, the implementation of CIT did not reduce the number of test cases. However, we consider this detail to be irrelevant because we lack precise information on the effectiveness of the original test cases that were replaced by CIT-generated ones. The essential metrics that require attention are the number of defects detected by the test cases and the average time needed to detect a defect. Importantly, the average time to identify a defect was reduced. It is important to note that the average time to detect a defect remained reduced.

There could be factors that might skew the results presented, so we've examined these potential biases and have outlined measures to mitigate them. This approach ensures the credibility of our findings regarding CIT's impact on testing efficiency.

The learning effect is significant in studies like ours, especially since we are juniors with no prior testing experience. However, the oversight from experienced seniors likely lessened this impact. Despite our beginner status, this supervision helps ensure our findings' reliability. Yet, it's important to acknowledge that the effectiveness of Combinatorial Interaction Testing (CIT) could vary in a professional context without experienced supervision.

Concerns may also arise about the precision of the recorded time for each activity in the experiment. To address potential biases in this area, we meticulously tracked all time spent on specific tasks using multiple Google Docs spreadsheets, with the aggregated findings reported in this document.

Another potential issue relates to the scope of the study. Conducting empirical experiments like this one requires considerable resources, making them challenging to execute on a large scale. Therefore, to gather more comprehensive data on the effectiveness of CIT, it's necessary to aggregate the outcomes of numerous studies.

While the results offer some insights, their applicability should be approached with caution. The success of CIT can vary greatly depending on factors such as the nature and complexity of the software under test (SUT) and the experience level of the test design and automation team, among others. A thorough comparison and contextual analysis of different studies are required to draw more definitive conclusions about CIT's overall efficiency.

The findings may be applicable to more general types of software systems, particularly those with complex interaction patterns or multi-configuration settings, where CIT's combinatory approach can be used to reveal defects that other testing networks would miss entirely systematically. In such circumstances, where substantial hardware or software platforms are at stake, CIT's completeness can improve overall quality and reliability. However, the applicability of CIT may rest to some degree on its particular skillfulness and the level of expertise of the test group; these results should therefore be considered with these factors in mind.

To conclude, although our results highlight CIT's beneficial effects, a deeper insight into how it fits into various testing environments is needed. Future studies should investigate how CIT fares with systems of varying complexity, include testers with different skill levels and examine possible biases to gain a full perspective on its significance in software testing.

6 Conclusion

To evaluate the efficiency of identifying issues within software systems (SUT), our primary metric was the average duration required to detect a defect. In the initial study, encompassing test design, coding, executing automated tests, and analyzing outcomes, this duration was significantly reduced. Specifically, it decreased from 1.4 h using the conventional test suite to 0.4 h when applying Combinatorial Interaction Testing (CIT) with a 2-way uniform strength strategy and further improved to 0.35 h with a mixed-strength CIT approach. In the subsequent study, which examined the same processes in a different SUT, the time needed to uncover a defect was reduced from 2.66 h with the standard test suite to 0.78 h for both the 2-way uniform strength and mixed-strength CIT methodologies.

Diverging from earlier research that predominantly relied on mutation testing with hypothetical defects, our study incorporated actual historical defects and meticulously designed artificial defects that closely simulate the characteristics and placement of these issues within the SUT.

The use of CIT resulted in considerable improvements to the test automation framework. It allowed for more parametrization of test data within test cases, boosting the reusability of test scripts while lowering maintenance work. This revised structure highlights CIT's role in making the testing process more efficient and straightforward.

Although our research provides significant insights into CIT's efficiency, future investigations should delve into how CIT performs across varied SUT characteristics and complexities. Furthermore, assessing CIT's scalability across diverse software applications and the impact of different combinatorial strategies (considering interaction strength, uniform versus mixed strength) will enrich our understanding of CIT's comprehensive utility in the software development industry.

The results of our study provide a new approach to the application of Combinatorial Interaction Testing (CIT), as no previous research has ever considered such information and insight directly. Prior studies about CIT have mostly focused on the benefits in theory, controlled environments which make it difficult for empirical verification. By contrast, our findings come from real-world testing. This study focuses CIT's power to augment fault detection and decrease the average discovery time when detecting defects. It fills the gap between theoretical predictions and actual practice.

According to the study, the efficiency of CIT on testing tool selection and impact has made possible practical applications which were heretofore impossible. Employing methods which meticulously track the time here with great respect for task duration and address potential biases therein. While not making direct comparisons with previous studies, our results provide valuable references for CIT in different software testing environments and significantly improve its effectiveness.

In conclusion, JTrac and Redmine's testing procedures are now more effective and efficient thanks to the use of Combinatorial Interaction Testing (CIT).

The advantages of using CIT in software testing are clear when considering the reduced time required to create and execute test cases and the increased rate of defect detection.

Acknowledgment. The authors would like to acknowledge the support of the System Testing Intelligent Laboratory (STILL) of the Department of Computer Science, Faculty of Electrical Engineering at Czech Technical University in Prague, Czech Republic. Special thanks to the authors for their guidance and contributions, and heartfelt appreciation to our families for their unwavering support and encouragement throughout this study.

References

1. Bures, M., Ahmed, B.S.: On the effectiveness of combinatorial interaction testing: a case study. In: 2017 IEEE International Conference on Software Quality, Reliability and Security Companion (QRS-C), pp. 69–76. (2017)
2. Bures, M., Ahmed, B.S.: On the effectiveness of combinatorial interaction testing: a case study. In: 2017 IEEE International Conference on Software Quality, Reliability and Security Companion (QRS-C), pp. 69–76. IEEE (2017)
3. Campos, D., Neto, C.R.L., Machado, I.: Merci: A method to evaluate combinatorial interaction testing tools for software product lines. In: Proceedings of the ACM International Conference on Software Engineering (2018)
4. Cohen, D.M., Dalal, S.R., Fredman, M.L., Patton, G.C.: The aetg system: an approach to testing based on combinatorial design. IEEE Trans. Softw. Eng. **23**(7), 437–444 (1997)

5. Coşkun, G., Coşkun, C., Mercan, H., Yilmaz, C.: Using unified combinatorial interaction testing for mc/dc coverage. In: Proceedings of the IEEE International Conference on Software Testing, Verification and Validation Workshops (ICSTW) (2022)

6. Hu, L., Wong, W., Kuhn, D., Kacker, R.: How does combinatorial testing perform in the real world: an empirical study. Empirical Softw. Eng. (2020)

7. Meerza, S.I.A., Uzzal, M.M., Haq, S.E.: Q-learning based pso algorithm for tuning pid gains of uav quadcopter

8. Nie, C., Leung, H.: A survey of combinatorial testing. ACM Comput. Surv. **43**(2) (2011)

9. Nie, C., Leung, H.: A survey of combinatorial testing. ACM Comput. Surv. (CSUR) **43**(2), 1–29 (2011)

10. Petke, J., Cohen, M.B., Harman, M., Yoo, S.: Practical combinatorial interaction testing: empirical findings on efficiency and early fault detection. IEEE Trans. Softw. Eng. (2015)

11. Silva, D.D.C.C.D.: Combinatorial interaction testing tools for software product lines engineering: a comparative analysis (2021)

12. Tatale, S., Prakash, V.C.: Combinatorial test case generation using q-value based particle swarm optimization. Revue d'Intelligence Artificielle **36**(2), 319–326 (2022)

13. Valle-Gomez, K.J., García-Domínguez, A., Delgado-Pérez, P., Medina-Bulo, I.: Mutation-inspired symbolic execution for software testing. IET Software (2022)

14. Williams, A.W.: Determination of test configurations for pair-wise interaction coverage. In: Testing of Communicating Systems: Tools and Techniques. IFIP TC6/WG6. 1 13th International Conference on Testing of Communicating Systems (TestCom 2000), pp. 59–74. Springer, Ottawa, Canada (2000)

15. Yilmaz, C., Fouché, Sandro, C.M.B., Porter, A., Demiroz, G., Koc, U.: Moving forward with combinatorial interaction testing. Computer **47**(2), 37–45 (2014)

JSMBox—A Runtime Monitoring Framework for Analyzing and Classifying Malicious JavaScript

Phu H. Phung[1]([⊠]) [iD], Allen Varghese[1], Bojue Wang[2], Yu Zhao[2], and Chong Yu[2]

[1] Intelligent Systems Security Lab, Department of Computer Science, University of Dayton, 300 College Park Ave, Dayton, OH 45469, USA
phu@udayton.edu
https://isseclab-udayton.github.io/
[2] Department of Computer Science, University of Cincinnati, 2901 Woodside Drive, Cincinnati, OH 45221, USA

Abstract. In recent years, there has been a notable increase in the prevalence of malicious websites, leading to a majority of cyber-attacks and data breaches. Malicious websites often incorporate JavaScript code to execute attacks on web browsers. Despite existing methodologies documented in the literature, the analysis and detection of malicious JavaScript pose significant challenges due to the dynamic nature of JavaScript and the use of advanced evasion techniques. These challenges motivate the need for an innovative and efficient approach to comprehensively analyze the code to identify its malicious intent. In this paper, we introduce a monitoring approach for analyzing JavaScript code, which can capture all of the code's features at runtime. Our method leverages the security reference monitor technique to mediate JavaScript security-sensitive executions, including function calls and property accesses. Therefore, the proposed method can capture behaviors at runtime regardless of how the code is written, even with recent advanced evasion techniques like WebAssembly diversification. We have implemented our approach as a JavaScript dynamic analysis framework called JSMBox in a Chromium-based browser extension. Our experiments demonstrated that JSMBox is capable of effectively countering sophisticated evasion techniques found in modern malicious JavaScript code, including WebAssembly diversification. We have also evaluated the framework's ability to classify malicious behaviors based on a large-scale raw dataset comprising about 20,000 malicious and benign webpages. Our developed tool automatically launches the browser to execute these webpages, records JavaScript code execution events, and captures their execution frequency as extracted features. We have tested the extracted dataset with various machine-learning models, yielding promising experimental results that confirm the effectiveness of our approach and achieve a high accuracy rate.

Keywords: JavaScript · Dynamic Analysis · Runtime Monitoring · Maliciousness Classification

---

Phu H. Phung: Work done while the author was a Visiting Scholar in the Department of Electrical and Computer Engineering at the University of Cincinnati.

W. Feng et al. (Eds.): SEDE 2024, CCIS 2244, pp. 100–122, 2024.
https://doi.org/10.1007/978-3-031-75201-8_8

1 Introduction

The ubiquity of JavaScript in web development, as highlighted by W3Techs[1], poses both opportunities and risks. While JavaScript enhances user interaction and web functionalities, it has also become a vector for cyberattacks, particularly through malicious code on webpages. Indeed, malicious webpages with JavaScript code that launch attacks on web browsers have become increasingly problematic in recent years, carrying out threats against the user's browser, such as stealing the user's credentials or downloading additional malware. Unfortunately, the dynamic nature of the JavaScript language and its tight integration with the browser make it challenging to detect and block malicious JavaScript code. JavaScript-based attacks on webpages are a recent trend and top Internet security threats [1], which can defeat traditional signature-based approaches used in anti-virus tools [2].

Analyzing and detecting malicious JavaScript have received high attention and are still an active research direction in the literature [3], which employ static analysis, dynamic analysis, or combined static and dynamic analysis techniques [4]. Static analysis is a traditional approach that typically extracts the semantic structure of the source code, abstract syntax tree, strings, objects, and functions to provide features for detection or machine learning algorithms. However, conventional static analysis methods typically fail to deal with dynamically generated code and evasion techniques used by attackers to hide malicious code [5]. On the other hand, dynamic analysis techniques execute JavaScript code; therefore, they can capture dynamically generated code and runtime behaviors that static analysis methods might omit. Although JavaScript dynamic analysis approaches offer advantages in behavioral analysis and runtime features, their realizations suffer shortcomings [6]. For example, several methods, e.g., [7, 8], leverage platform-specific tools such as Windows-based in-browser debuggers that are not always available in other systems. Cova et al. [2] extract dynamic features from execution traces using the HtmlUnit with Rhino engine simulation environment, which attackers can bypass by leveraging the differences between the emulated environment and a real browser. Recent malicious JavaScript code employed advanced evasion techniques to detect and subvert dynamic analysis methods [6]. Notably, none of the existing work can tackle evasion techniques using WebAssembly [9, 10].

The challenges mentioned above highlight the need for a robust analysis method that can capture dynamic behaviors in potential malicious JavaScript code, especially in the presence of advanced evasion techniques. To this end, we propose a novel JavaScript runtime analysis method and framework encompassing all JavaScript executions, including traditionally on-the-fly generated code and advanced evasion techniques. Our approach mediates JavaScript's security-sensitive operations, including function calls and property accesses at runtime, by leveraging the traditional security reference monitor technique [11]. Since we monitor the code execution, our method can capture the code behaviors regard- less of the code's structure or evasion techniques. Specifically, the contributions of our work are as follows:

---

[1] According to the World Wide Web Technology Surveys in July 2024 (https://w3techs.com), 98.9% of all websites contain JavaScript code, which will be loaded and executed in a browser at the end-user.

– We introduce a novel runtime analysis method and framework by leveraging the inlined security reference monitor technique to execute JavaScript code in webpages to capture its behaviors for maliciousness classification and detection. Our framework is designed to allow customization and fine-tuning of the feature extraction process, providing the most important features for machine learning models to improve their accuracy and reliability.
– We have developed the proposed method as a JavaScript library, utilizing the language's flexibility and platform independence to create a lightweight runtime monitor. This allows us to efficiently capture all executions and their contexts, regardless of their appearances. We have implemented the framework as a browser extension, meeting the essential requirements for security reference monitors and preventing evasive code from concealing its behaviors.
– We have demonstrated that our framework is highly proficient in extracting runtime features that are crucial for machine learning models to accurately classify malicious JavaScript on large-scale raw datasets. As entailed in Sect. 4, our proposed method offers a more effective feature extraction solution than traditional static analysis techniques and advances beyond recent dynamic or hybrid analysis approaches in dealing with malicious code that employs sophisticated evasion tactics, including the latest WebAssembly obfuscation and diversification.

The remainder of this paper is structured as follows. In Sect. 2, we provide an overview of the background, review the literature, and discuss related work. Following that, Section 3 includes a running example that motivates our work, and presents our approach to developing and implementing the framework. In Sect. 4, we outline the evaluation of our proposed framework, in comparison with closely related work. Finally, we conclude our contributions and outline potential future work in Sect. 5.

2   Background and Literature Review

This section briefly describes the background of JavaScript and its analysis methods. We also discuss challenges in detecting malicious JavaScript code with evasion techniques and provide examples. Finally, we review the literature and compare related work with our JSMBox framework.

2.1   JavaScript and Malicious Webpages

JavaScript is one of the most popular versatile scripting languages primarily used for web development, enabling interactive and dynamic elements on web-pages. When a browser renders a webpage, it executes embedded JavaScript code, whether inlined, sourced from the same host, or retrieved externally. This code can access and alter the webpage's content and data stored in the browser. Furthermore, JavaScript can dynamically generate and execute new code, as well as load and run external scripts in real time. These dynamic features can be lever-aged by both developers and attackers [12]. By inserting harmful JavaScript code, attackers can craft webpages to exploit vulnerabilities in users' web browsers. These pages can contain various types of malicious content, such as malware, phishing forms, or other forms of harmful information. Despite existing detection tools, JavaScript-based attacks on webpages remain a recent prominent Internet security concern [1].

2.2   JavaScript Analysis Methods

Existing works propose solutions from several approaches, including static analysis, dynamic analysis, and hybrid analysis [4] to analyze and detect malicious JavaScript code. Specifically, static analysis is a traditional approach that typically extracts the semantic structure of the code to provide features for detection. Unlike static analysis, which analyzes code without executing it, dynamic analysis runs the code and observes its interactions with the environment in real-time [13]. By executing code, dynamic analysis can discern malicious activities that static analysis might overlook [13]. Furthermore, some existing works use a hybrid approach, combining static and dynamic analysis techniques. These works typically utilize static analysis to help identify known patterns and vulnerabilities before execution while using dynamic analysis to provide real-time insights into the actual behavior of the code during runtime execution [14]. We discuss these methods in detail in the related work sub-section (Sect. 2.4).

2.3   Evasion Techniques

Evasion techniques of malicious JavaScript code are a critical aspect of contemporary cyber threats, wherein attackers employ sophisticated strategies to evade detection mechanisms and execute malicious actions within web environments. These techniques circumvent traditional security measures, including antivirus software, intrusion detection systems, and web application firewalls, posing significant challenges to cybersecurity professionals and researchers [15]. Obfuscation is one of the commonly used evasion techniques. This technique complicates the readability and analysis of code by altering its structure and appearance to obscure its intended functionality. Techniques such as variable obfuscation, string obfuscation, property encryption, control flow flattening, dead code injection, debugging protection, self-defending, and polymorphic mutation are often utilized to impede code analysis [5, 16, 17]. Research indicates that 71% of examined malicious samples employ obfuscation techniques [18]. We describe common JavaScript evasion techniques below.

Obfuscation Techniques JavaScript obfuscation is a technique designed to make JavaScript code difficult to understand and analyze. This mechanism enhances the protection of the code and makes it more challenging to reverse engineer or replicate. The primary purpose of obfuscation is to conceal the true intent and structure of the code without altering its functionality.

Various obfuscation techniques are available for different aspects of JavaScript code. Below, we list common obfuscation methods identified in the literature, together with their code snippets to illustrate their techniques.

– *Variable and Function Renaming*: Changing the names of variables and functions to make the code more challenging to understand and analyze [15].

```
1  // Original code
2  function calculateArea(radius) {
3    const PI = 3.141592653589793;
4    return PI * radius * radius;
5  }
6  // Obfuscated code
7  function a(b) {
8    const c = 3.141592653589793;
9    return c * b * b;
10 }
```

Listing 2.1. Illustration of variable and function renaming obfuscation method

- *Code Compression (Minification)*: Compression is a technique used to reduce the size of data or code by encoding information in a more compact format. In the context of software development and obfuscation, code compression involves removing unnecessary characters, spaces, and lines from the source code to make it more concise [19].

```
1  // Original code
2  function addNumbers(a, b) {
3    return a + b;
4  }
5  // Compressed code
6  function addNumbers(a,b){return a+b;}
```

Listing 2.2. Illustration of code compression/minification obfuscation method

- *Code Transformation*: Altering the structure and form of the code, such as changing the form of conditional statements or using ternary operators [20].

```
1  // Original code
2  function isEven(num) {
3    if (num % 2 === 0) {
4      return true;
5    } else {
6      return false;
7    }
8  }
9  // Transformed code
10 function isEven(a){return 0===a%2}
```

Listing 2.3. Illustration of code transformation obfuscation method

- *Dead code injection*: Dead code injection is a technique used to inject unused or non-executing code into a program. This technique can be employed as a form of obfuscation to make the code more complex and difficult to analyze. Injecting dead code does not affect the program's functionality but can confuse and deter reverse engineers, making it more challenging for them to understand the program's logic and structure [21].

```
1  function calculateSum(a, b) {
2      // Dead code injection
3      if (false) {
4          console.log("This code will never execute.");
5      }
6      // Actual code
7      return a + b;
8  }
9  console.log(calculateSum(5, 3));
```

Listing 2.4. Example of dead code injection obfuscation method

- *String Encoding*: Converting string literals into other forms, like using Unicode encoding or Base64 encoding [22].

```
1 // Original code
2 const greating = "Hello world!"
3 // Obfuscated code
4 const encodedString = "%48%65%6C%6C%6F%2C%20%77%6F%72%6C%64%21";
5 const decodedString = unescape(encodedString);
6 console.log(decodedString); // Output: "Hello, world!"
```
Listing 2.5. Example of string encoding obfuscation method

- *Indirect method call*: Indirect method call is a programming technique that allows the determination of which method or function to call dynamically at runtime. This is typically achieved using function pointers, callback functions, or function objects. While indirect method calls enhance code flexibility, they may also increase code complexity and difficulty of understanding [23].

```
1 // Define a function
2 function greet() {
3     console.log("Hello!");
4 }
5 // Store the function name in a variable
6 var funcName = "greet";
7 // Indirectly call the function
8 window[funcName](); // Outputs: Hello!
```
Listing 2.6. Example of indirect method call obfuscation method

- *Instruction substitution*: Instruction substitution is an obfuscation technique that involves replacing original instructions in a program with equivalent instructions that have a different structure or form, thereby increasing the complexity and difficulty of understanding the code while maintaining its functionality [24].

```
1 // Original addition function
2 function add(a, b) {
3     return a + b;
4 }
5 // Obfuscated addition function
6 function add_obfuscated(x, y) {
7     return x - (-y);
8 }
```
Listing 2.7. Illustration of instruction substitution obfuscation method

- *Non-alphanumeric code*: Non-alphanumeric code is an obfuscation technique primarily used to replace alphabetic and numeric characters in code with non-alphanumeric characters, such as symbols and special characters, to increase the complexity and difficulty of understanding the code [25].

```
1 alert((+[][+[]]+[])[++[[]][+[]]]+(![]+[])[++[++[+[]][+[]]]
2 [+[]]]+(![![]][+[])[++[++[++[[]][+[]]][+[]]][+[]]]+(![!![]]+[])
3 [++[[]][+[]]]+(![!![]]+[])[+[]])//"alert"
```
Listing 2.8. Example of non-alphanumeric code obfuscation method

- *String splitting*: This method involves separating a string or function name into multiple smaller fragments and then reassembling them at runtime [5].

```
1  // Original code: alert('This could be malicious');
2  // Splited code
3  var jj = 's\')';
4  var by = 'rt(\'';
5  var dh = 's c';
6  var gf = ' ma';
7  var eu = 'oul';
8  var ii = 'iou';
9  var fg = 'd be';
10 var cg = 'Thi';
11 var ax = 'ale';
12 var hh = 'lic';
13 eval(ax + by + cg + dh + eu + fg +
14 gf + hh + ii + jj);
```

Listing 2.9. Illustration of string splitting obfuscation method

WebAssembly obfuscation and diversification WebAssembly (Wasm) is a binary instruction format that is designed to be executed in a web browser, aiming to provide a portable, high-performance for web applications that leverage existing codebases and libraries written in other common programming languages rather than JavaScript. With that design, WebAssembly has quickly become an essential part of the Web, providing a great alternative to JavaScript [26]. On the other hand, WebAssembly has also been used as a sophisticated evasion technique to conceal malicious code in webpages and evade code analysis and detection techniques. Wobfuscator [9] is a recent research tool demonstrating a WebAssembly obfuscation technique that transforms parts of the JavaScript computation into WebAssembly and evades JavaScript malware detection tools. In [10], the authors developed an automatic binary WebAssembly diversification evasion technique that can evade most of the cases in popular detectors such as VirusTotal and MINOS. The research findings motivate innovative approaches that can address the modern technology on the Web.

Browser Fingerprinting Browser fingerprinting is a technology that creates a unique identifier (fingerprint) by collecting various attributes and behaviors of the client's web browser, allowing for user identification and tracking. These attributes may include the browser's user agent string, operating system, screen resolution, and installed plugins. Browser fingerprinting is commonly used for purposes such as user tracking, personalized advertising, and security verification [27–29].

Attackers can utilize this technology to examine specific attributes or configurations of the client's web browser to determine if they meet the conditions for an attack. For example, attackers may inspect the browser's user agent string or other characteristics to determine if it is the target browser and then execute malicious code or attacks accordingly. This type of inspection may be conducted to ensure the success of an attack or to tailor different attack strategies based on the targeted browser.

Browser fingerprinting or detection helps attackers ensure that their exploit is only triggered on the intended target browsers. This technology is used not only to detect the browser's version but also can be used to detect client-side content; it also possesses strong anti-detection capabilities, making it immune analysis methods [30].

2.4 Related Work

Methods to analyze webpages and JavaScript code for classifying and detecting malicious JavaScript in the literature can be categorized into three categories: static analysis, dynamic analysis, and a hybrid combination of static and dynamic analysis [4]. In this section, we briefly discuss the static analysis approaches and review the dynamic approaches in more detail compared with our approach.

Static Analysis Traditional methods of static analysis are engineered to identify malicious JavaScript code without executing the source code. These methods extract the features of malicious code to build a malicious feature library. Subsequently, they evaluate the detected code to determine if it matches the features within this malicious feature library. More recent approaches employ machine learning and deep learning to improve the detection rate. These works typically transfer detected code into vectors using various methods, such as fixed-length vector representation, abstract syntax tree (AST), Control Flow Graph, and Program Dependency Graph [31–35]. Based on these representations, detection models are built using machine learning classifier algorithms, includ- ing Random Forest, Naive Bayes, Support Vector Machine (SVM), and Random Forest. For example, ZOZZLE [36] generates features based on the hierarchi- cal structure of the JavaScript AST and employs rapid pattern matching and Naive Bayes classifier for detection. JStap [33] is a static malicious JavaScript detector that uses lexical analysis, AST, control flow, and data flow information, utilizing a Random Forest classifier. Ren et al. [15] studies the effects of obfusca- tion on existing malicious JavaScript detectors, employing a range of classifiers. However, conventional static analysis methods typically fail to deal with dy- namically generated code and evasion techniques (e.g., obfuscation code) used by attackers to conceal malicious code [5]. In a recent study [15] of represen- tative static analysis-based approaches of detecting obfuscation code, they find "the feature spaces of existing detectors can only reflect shallow differences in code, not about the nature of benign and malicious, which can be easily affected by the differences brought by obfuscation." In other words, state-of-the-art static analysis-based approaches are still unable to detect malicious code that employs evasion techniques accurately.

Dynamic Analysis Dynamic analysis-based methods involve executing the program to uncover specific behaviors, even when the program is obfuscated, as indicated by Kim et al. [30]. Researchers employ these approaches to extract behavioral features during the execution of code for the classification of malicious code within test environments, including sandboxes [2, 7, 37, 38], honeypots [39, 40], and browsers [6]. Snyder et al. [41] investigated the usage patterns of JavaScript features in modern web browsers, revealing that most features are rarely used and are often blocked by ad and tracking blockers. Based on how third-party trackers manipulate browser state, Roesner et al. [42] developed an in-band client-side method for detecting and classifying five kinds of third-party trackers. Yagemann et al. [43] designed an offline control flow analysis method for attack detection using deep learning on hardware execution traces to model a program's behavior and detect control flow anomalies. In addition, Ratana-worabhan et al. [44] introduced a runtime heap-spraying detector that examines individual objects in the heap, interpreting them as code and performing a static analysis to detect malicious intent.

However, similar to static analysis, one limitation of these methods is their inefficiency in detecting evasion techniques.

Many studies [4, 45–49] have focused on addressing obfuscated code to overcome this aforementioned limitation. Li et al. [45] proposed a forensic engine that can efficiently record fine-grained details on the execution of JavaScript programs within the browser. Additionally, Fang et al. [46] proposed a malicious JavaScript detection model based on LSTM that extracts features from the semantic level of bytecode and optimizes the word vector. Furthermore, Song et al. [4] constructed the Program Dependency Graph to generate semantic slices. Based on this, they designed a malicious JavaScript detection model utilizing bidirectional LSTM. Neasbitt et al. [47] presented an online forensic data collection system that allows for recording enough detailed information to enable a full reconstruction of web security incidents, including phishing attacks. Moreover, Wang et al. [49] designed a deep learning framework that integrates sparse random projection, a deep learning model, and logistic regression to detect malicious JavaScript code. Rieck et al. [48] inspected web pages to block the delivery of malicious JavaScript code and collected static and dynamic code features for ma- licious pattern analysis. Besides, Jueckstock et al. [6] proposed a dynamic analysis framework hosted inside V8, the JavaScript engine of the Chrome browser, that logs native function or property accesses during any JavaScript execution to monitor browser behaviors. In comparison to others, this method proves significantly more efficient in detecting evasion techniques, as it can deal with both obfuscated code and browser fingerprinting. However, none of the existing work can address all evasion techniques discussed previously.

In contrast to the aforementioned research, our proposed method addresses the challenges of analyzing malicious JavaScript arising from dynamic JavaScript features and all advanced evasion techniques by capturing the behaviors of both static and dynamically generated code. We present our technical approach and discuss how it can tackle the challenges in the next section.

3 Technical Approach and Implementation

3.1 A Motivating Example

To present our approach, we consider the following JavaScript snippet example illustrated in Listing 3.1, providing key concepts underlying our proposed approach. The provided example highlights the code obfuscation of the HTMLCanvasElement.prototype.toDataURL method, typically used in malicious code that exploits fingerprinting attacks to identify and track users [50]. We note that actual malicious obfuscated JavaScript codes are substantially more sophisticated.

```
1  const values = [
2    72, 84, 77, 76, 67, 97, 110, 118, 97, 115, 69, 108, 101, 109, 101, 110,
       116, 46, 112, 114, 111, 116, 111, 116, 121, 112, 101, 46, 116, 111, 68,
       97, 116, 97, 85, 82, 76];
3  const code = values.map(value => String.fromCharCode(value)).join('');
4  eval(code);
```

Listing 3.1. A motivating example

Since static analysis-based techniques do not execute the code, they encounter challenges in recognizing these obfuscated scripts [5]. This limitation stems from the inadequacies of current machine-learning-based static analysis techniques to accurately identify malicious code that employs evasion strategies, as highlighted in recent empirical studies [15]. As a result, the obfuscated JavaScript is executed, activating HTMLCanvasElement.prototype.toDataURL method, which malicious actors can manipulate. To address the challenges in detecting the malicious intent of obfuscated code, various dynamic analysis strategies [2, 6, 7, 37–40] have been proposed. These strategies aim to monitor the runtime behavior of JavaScript code because obfuscated code cannot disguise its activities during execution. However, a notable gap in existing research is the lack of focus on monitoring the potentially malicious use of the HTMLCanvasElement.prototype.toDataURL method and the application of machine learning techniques to determine their maliciousness [50, 51].

3.2 Approach and the Overview of the Proposed Framework

The running example discussed above is one of many challenges in JavaScript code analysis that motivate our work. To address these challenges, we lever-age the runtime monitoring approach that executes JavaScript code to log its behaviors, regardless of their appearance or evasion techniques. Specifically, we propose JSMBox, a dynamic analysis JavaScript framework that adopts a behavioral sandbox approach [52]. Our proposed approach aims to monitor and record.

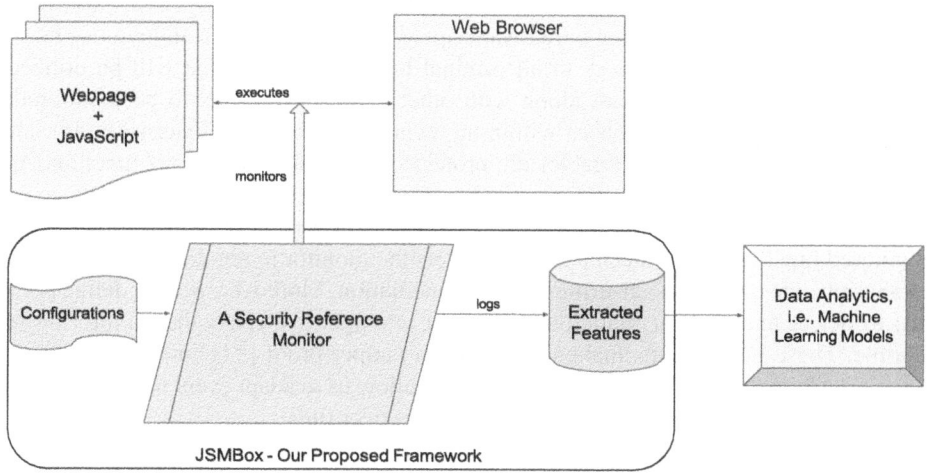

Fig. 1. Approach Overview

JavaScript code execution by intercepting its operations, such as property access and method calls, within the JavaScript execution environment. This method enables JSMBox to conduct real-time, dynamic analysis of the code, extracting its execution trace for data engineering and machine learning models. Our primary objective is to develop a robust and effective technique for analyzing malware capable of circumventing the sophisticated evasion methods employed by modern malicious webpages. In pursuit of this goal, we employ the traditional security reference monitor technique [11] to oversee code execution, implemented exclusively in JavaScript, thus providing a more dependable and holistic solution, addressing the limitations of existing static and dynamic analysis techniques. Furthermore, our approach is lightweight and platform-independent, allowing for flexible deployment and feature customization. To the best of our knowledge, no prior research has utilized the reference monitoring method in JavaScript code for dynamic malware analysis.

Figure 1 depicts the overview of our proposed framework JSMBox. Within this framework, we incorporate a reference monitor, which runs before the browser loads and executes any other JavaScript code on a given webpage. This mechanism ensures the monitor maintains a unique and original reference to the intercepted JavaScript events, i.e., function calls or property accesses, implemented in the browser. This approach effectively preserves the original functionality of the webpage while mitigating potential detection techniques employed in evasive malicious JavaScript code [53]. The monitor utilizes configuration data, defining intercepted JavaScript events and the properties of extracted features to record and retain the code execution details, such as the frequency of event execution, in a log file. This log file is then employed as input for a machine-learning algorithm to classify the maliciousness of the code. We discuss key components of our behavioral sandbox approach below.

3.3   The Monitor Initialization and Protection

We developed the monitor using pure JavaScript as a library within an anonymous function to preserve local references to all original built-in methods that will be utilized later in the monitoring process, along with other behavioral events to be monitored. By encapsulating these references within an anonymous function, external code cannot access them since local variables are protected within an anonymous function. As the library is the first code to be executed in the browser, we have the advantage of safeguarding against potential malicious attempts to subvert these built-in methods or monitored functions. This mechanism empowers the monitor to regulate all subsequent JavaScript code execution, ensuring complete mediation. Moreover, we can define policies to detect and prevent malicious code that attempts to bypass the monitoring at runtime. These mechanisms make our approach tamper-proof [54] and shielded from evasive detection methods [53]. In addition, they allow us to adapt event monitoring and policies to tackle potential new evasion techniques over time.

To make our framework more flexible and customizable, we can define JavaScript execution events, such as function calls and property accesses, as well as behaviors like the call frequency or sequence, in a configuration file. The monitor will then load this file and create wrapper functions based on the information provided. We will demonstrate the initialization steps using pseudo-code in Listing 3.2.

```
1  (()=>{
2      let $builtins = {}; $builtins.__proto__ = null;
3
4      //code to store built-in references, i.e.,:
5      $builtins.Function.apply=Function.prototype.apply;
6      // other code (not included) to store built-in references ..
7
8      //code to load the configuration file
9      let monitored_methods = loadMethods();
10     let monitored_properties = loadProperties();
11
12     //main code (not included) to intercept and log execution events
13
14 })();
```

Listing 3.2. Pseudo-code demonstrating the monitor's initialization steps

3.4 Intercepting Execution Events

We intercepted JavaScript native functions and properties of a global object, such as document, window to monitor their invocations and accesses, i.e., execution events. For every method call specified in the configuration file, we start by preserving the original reference and its aliases. This mechanism ensures that the monitor captures any existing prototype inheritance chain of the reference to prevent possible attacks in malicious code [54]. Semi-pseudo code in Listing 3.3 illustrates this interception process. For property accesses, e.g., document.cookie, we leverage the Object.defineProperty(..) standard API and define the handler functions whenever a property is accessed, i.e., read or write.

```
1  for each {object, method} in monitored_methods {
2      //... code (not included) find function corresponding to aliases
3
4      //keep the original reference:
5      var original_method = object[method];
6
7      //ensure that the stored original apply function will be invoked:
8      original_method.apply = $builtins.Function.apply;
9
10     //define the method:
11     object[method] =>() {
12         //log the event execution:
13         event_log(object,method);
14
15         //execute the event using the original reference:
16         return original_method.apply(this, arguments);
17     }
18 }
```

Listing 3.3. Semi-pseudo code illustrating the interception process

3.5 Implementation

Developed as a pure JavaScript library, our JSMBox framework can be injected into a website in multiple ways to monitor the JavaScript code execution on the site. For example, we can inject the library as the first script to be executed in a webpage using webpage instrumentation, a web proxy, or a browser extension/add-on. As a framework for JavaScript analysis, we implement JSM- Box as a browser extension so that we can effectively collect the logged data and automate the browser with our extension on a large-scale dataset. A browser extension or add-on is additional code that can be loaded into a browser to modify and enhance its capability. Major browsers, including Chromium-based browsers, such as Google Chrome, Brave, Microsoft Edge, Opera, Vivaldi, and Firefox, support browser extensions or add-ons [55]. Since our main code is written in JavaScript, it should be deployable in any browser supporting extensions/add-ons. We implement and test our code in the Chromium browser, a widely used codebase in many other browsers. As noted in [55], Chromium-based browser extensions can run in Firefox with just a few changes. To ensure that our code is executed first before the browser loads a webpage and executes its JavaScript code, we place our code in the background script of the browser extension. As discussed in Sect. 3.2, we have confirmed this mechanism by performing experimental tests.

Before loading a webpage upon request, the browser executes our code, which will intercept defined methods and properties. When a webpage is loaded in the browser, any JavaScript event that triggers these methods and properties will invoke our code, which will log the event and then invoke the original reference. This mechanism ensures that our code is set to monitor the behaviors of scripts at runtime, capturing right from the moment a page begins to load. Since we monitor the code at runtime, potential performance overhead exists. While we have not studied the overhead in this work, prior work demonstrated that the JavaScript inlined reference monitor approach poses lightweight performance overhead [52, 56, 57].

Although hundreds of commonly used JavaScript method calls exist, not all are susceptible to malicious JavaScript [58, 59]. Monitoring an excessively broad range of events can introduce noise and increase system overhead. Noises in extracted features reduce the accuracy of machine learning-based detection. In our current implementation of JSMBox, we have curated a selection of the most critical events with 59 method calls and property accesses. Benign JavaScript behaviors are selected based on the most commonly used by any website to maintain the dynamic nature of the website and keep it functioning. The malicious ones are selected based on their potential to be misused in web-based attacks, such as executing unauthorized code or scripts, e.g., eval, window.open for unwanted pop-up ads and navigator.sendBeacon can be used for unauthorized tracking. For instance, the charCodeAt(..) method of String is considered susceptible to misuse as it can be employed to encode data or generate obfuscated code that is difficult to decipher, thereby facilitating evasion techniques. These methods were identified based on analysis of human-labeled malicious JavaScript code, used in conjunction with each other [60–66]. Table 1 lists the 12 selected representative misused function calls with their descriptions implemented in JSMBox.

Our current JSMBox prototype monitors each event execution, i.e., behavior, and accumulates its frequency within a session to log the data as features. The resultant counting is transformed into a feature vector $[a_1, a_2, a_3, a_4, a_5, ..., a_{59}]$, where a_i denotes the frequency of the i-th behavior. As discussed in Sect. 3.2, our JSMBox framework supports customization of input events and features. However, we leave this implementation prototype for future work.

4   Evaluation and Experimental Results

To evaluate our approach and the proposed JSMBox framework, we consider two research questions:

Table 1. JavaScript behaviors, method calls or property accesses, and their potential misuse by malicious actors

Method/Property	Potential Misuse
charCodeAt	A method of the String object used to encode data or create obfuscated code that is not easily readable, aiding in evasion techniques
Uint8Array	To handle raw binary data which can be used in memory exploits, such as buffer overflows, or to process downloaded malicious payloads
Math.random	Domain generation algorithms (DGAs) use Math.random to generate a large number of domain names that malware can use to communicate without being easily blocked
document.cookie	A sensitive property that can accessed and manipulated to perform attacks such as session hijacking
toDataURL	A method of the HTMLCanvasElement object to capture the content of a canvas element, which can be used for browser fingerprinting or stealing information rendered on the canvas
document.write	A method to inject malicious content into a webpage, such as through XSS attacks
atob/btoa	Methods used to encode and decode base64 strings, which is commonly used in obfuscating payloads and command and control communications
document.createElement	A method used to dynamically create elements like script or iframe to load malicious code
window.location	A global property used to redirect users to malicious sites or manipulate page content for phishing or site spoofing
fromCharCode	A method of the String object likely used in obfuscation techniques to hide malicious code
eval	A global method that executes text as code, allowing for arbitrary JavaScript code execution
Image.src	A property that can be modified to exfiltrate data

RQ1 : How effective that JSMBox captures monitored behaviors in the existence of sophisticated evasion techniques in modern malicious JavaScript?

RQ2 : What is the performance of JSMBox as a dynamic analysis tool for malicious webpage classification in machine-learning models?

We present and discuss our evaluation and experimental results for each research question below.

4.1 Defeating JavaScript Evasion Techniques

To evaluate how our JSMBox framework can deal with and defeat sophisticated evasion techniques, as discussed in Sect. 2.3, to monitor defined behaviors for analysis and data extraction, we replicate these techniques in webpages. We load these webpages in the browser with our extension and observe that all behaviors hidden in obfuscation code or other advanced evasion techniques are captured by JSMBox.

For instance, we simulate the fingerprinting attack by obfuscating this method as discussed in running example in Listing 3.1, where existing analysis approaches failed to capture [50, 51]. While running this attack in the browser, our JSMBox framework can still track and log its execution.

```
1  #include <stdio.h>
2  #include <emscripten.h>
3  int main()
4  {
5    EM_ASM(alert('Alert from WebAssembly'));
6    return 0;
7  }
```

Listing 4.1. A C program invoking a JavaScript alert() method

Another notable example is the case of the WebAssembly evasion technique discussed earlier. To confirm our approach can capture this new technique, we develop a simple C program that invokes a JavaScript method, illustrated in Listing 4.1.

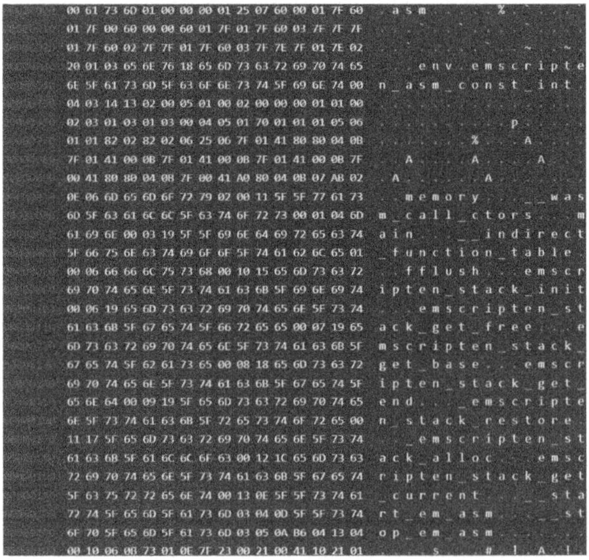

Fig. 2. WebAssembly binary code format (in a.wasm file) compiled from a C program

The C program is compiled into WebAssembly binary code (in a.wasm file, shown in Fig. 2) and embedded into a webpage. When the webpage is loaded in the browser with JSMBox, the JavaScript method invoked from WebAssembly code is executed and logged by our framework, demonstrated in Fig. 3.

Fig. 3. Test Case: A JavaScript method called from WebAssembly is captured by JSMBox

4.2 Maliciousness Classification

In this section, we will outline our experiments designed to assess the performance of our framework using machine learning models. Our experiments were conducted on a powerful CyberRange environment utilizing a virtual machine with Ubuntu 22.04 OS, 12 CPUs, 32 GB of RAM, and a 500 GB hard drive.

Dataset and feature extraction We collected a large number of malicious and benign website samples from two different datasets: the URLhaus database [67] for malicious websites, and the Tranco dataset [68] for benign websites. The URLhaus database, which is part of the Abuse.ch project, is well-known for its comprehensive collection of malicious URLs and is used by organizations such as the FBI, demonstrating its reliability. On the other hand, Tranco provides a strong website ranking by combining various data sources to ensure stability and resistance to manipulation, making it an excellent source of benign websites [68]. Our initial dataset consists of over 200,000 benign websites and over 200,000 malicious websites from these two sources. We maintain these websites in two lists to label and evaluate them separately.

For each website, we need to load it into the browser with our extension so that the JavaScript code can be executed and captured by our framework at run- time. To automate this process for large-scale datasets, we leverage Puppeteer[2], a Node.js library that allows us to control Chromium-based or Firefox browsers, which is particularly helpful for browser automation and data collection. We develop and run a script with a list of websites, launching a new browser instance for each one using Puppeteer, which is then set to load the browser extension. Once a website is fully loaded, our code checks for captured data and writes it into a CSV file labeled as malicious or benign. This process has resulted in a total of approximately 10,000 records from the malicious list, as well as a similar number of records from the benign list. The data from the two CSV files are combined to create extracted features for further analysis.

Machine-learning models We have utilized eight well-known machine learning models, which include Support Vector Machine (SVM), Logistic Regression, Naïve Bayes, K-Nearest Neighbors (KNN), Decision Tree, Random Forest, XG-Boost, and Ensemble

---

[2] https://pptr.dev/

methods [69, 70], to assess our collected dataset. Each model demonstrates different levels of accuracy in detecting malicious JavaScript, based on feature vectors extracted from the JavaScript code. Our comprehensive evaluation results enable users to choose the most suitable model for optimizing the detection process.

The metadata for our machine learning models can be found in Table 2. We have carefully fine-tuned specific hyperparameters as outlined in the second column of the table. One crucial aspect of this fine-tuning process involves optimizing model hyperparameters through the use of the GridSearchCV method [71, 72]. GridSearchCV conducts an exhaustive search over a specified parameter grid.

It trains the model on every combination of hyperparameters and selects the best combination based on cross-validation performance. This method performs a comprehensive search across a predefined grid of parameters, training the model with each parameter combination and identifying the optimal set based on cross-validation performance [71]. In addition to hyperparameter tuning, our training pipeline incorporates the Synthetic Minority Over-sampling Technique (SMOTE) [73] to address the class imbalance by generating synthetic samples within the feature space and enhancing model training effectiveness. We also use the Standard Scaler as a preprocessing step to standardize the features by removing the mean and scaling to unit variance. Additionally, we employ the Support Vector Classifier (SVC) [74, 75], an adaptation of the Support Vector Machine algorithm, for classification tasks.

Table 2. Differentiation of Machine Learning Models

Model Name	Hyperparameter Tuning	Pipeline Definition
SVM	Yes (GridSearchCV) C: 10000, gamma: 1	SMOTE, StandardScaler, SVC
Logistic Regression	Yes (GridSearchCV) C: [0.001, 0.01, 0.1, 1, 10, 100, 1000]	SMOTE, StandardScaler
GaussianNB	Yes (GridSearchCV) varsmoothing: [1e-9, 1e-8, 1e-7]	SMOTE, StandardScaler
KNN	Yes (GridSearchCV) n-neighbors: [3, 5, 7]	SMOTE, StandardScaler
Decision Tree	No	No
Random Forest	Yes (GridSearchCV) n-estimators: 300, min-samples-split: 2, max-depth: None	SMOTE
XGBoost	Yes (GridSearchCV) n-estimators: 200, max-depth: 15, learning-rate: 0.1, subsample: 1.0, colsample-bytree: 0.6	SMOTE, StandardScaler
Ensemble	Yes (GridSearchCV for individual models) same as for Random Forest and XGBoost	Voting Classifier (Random Forest and XGBoost)

JSMBox's effectiveness in classifying malicious JavaScript We have chosen specific performance metrics to directly address our research objectives, including accuracy, precision, recall, and F-scores [76, 77]. This methodology enables us to systematically categorize each JavaScript snippet, whether malicious or benign, into one of four potential outcomes. Using the classification of malicious snippets as an example: (1) Classified as malicious if it indeed contains malicious code, marking a true positive (TP) identification. (2) Classified as malicious erroneously when it is, in reality, benign, resulting in a false positive (FP). (3) Classified as benign mistakenly when it contains malicious code, leading to a false negative (FN). (4) Accurately classified as benign when it contains no malicious code, constituting a true negative (TN).

- **Accuracy:** the number of instances correctly classified over the total number of instances.

$$Accuracy = \frac{TP + TN}{TP + FP + FN + TN}$$

- **Precision:** the number of instances correctly classified as malicious codes over all instances classified as malicious codes. It indicates the model's effectiveness in correctly classifying content as malicious. A high-precision model excels in identifying malicious content.

$$P = \frac{TP}{TP + FP}$$

- **Recall:** the number of instances correctly classified as malicious codes over the total number of malicious codes. It reflects the model's ability to correctly identify the actual positives, emphasizing its capacity to detect most of the malicious content.

$$R = \frac{TP}{TP + FN}$$

- **F-Score:** a composite measure of precision and recall for malicious code detection.

$$F(b) = \frac{2 * P * R}{P + R}$$

Table 3 shows the performance of eight machine learning models, with their effectiveness in spotting malicious JavaScript code scoring between 0.77 and 0.88, and for benign code, between 0.69 and 0.88, according to the F1-score. The Ensemble model shines by pinpointing malicious code with the greatest precision, 0.89. Meanwhile, the Random Forest model is the best at catching almost all malicious codes, achieving the highest recall of 0.88. When we look at the F1-score, which balances both precision and recall, Random Forest comes out on top for identifying malicious code, with the highest score of 0.88. Similarly, when finding benign code, both Random Forest and the Ensemble models are the best choices, each with top F1-scores of 0.88. The **accuracy** column provides an over- all measure of a model's performance. High accuracy indicates that the model effectively distinguishes benign and malicious JavaScript content. As observed from the table, the Random Forest model achieved the highest accuracy of 0.88, closely followed by the Ensemble model at 0.87.

Table 3. Results of Models for Classifying JavaScript Content

Model	Benign			Malicious			Accuracy
	Precision	Recall	F1-Score	Precision	Recall	F1-Score	Score
SVM	0.97	0.64	0.77	0.73	0.98	0.84	0.81
Logistic Regression	0.985	0.57	0.72	0.70	0.99	0.82	0.78
Naïve Bayes	1.00	0.53	0.69	0.68	1.00	0.81	0.77
KNN	0.94	0.64	0.77	0.73	0.96	0.83	0.80
Decision Tree	0.97	0.68	0.80	0.76	0.98	0.85	0.83
Random Forest	0.88	0.88	0.88	0.88	0.88	0.88	0.88
XGBoost	0.92	0.78	0.84	0.81	0.93	0.87	0.86
Ensemble	0.86	0.90	0.88	0.89	0.85	0.87	0.87

5   Conclusion and Future Work

In this paper, we introduced JSMBox, a novel behavioral sandbox approach designed to address the issues of analyzing and classifying malicious JavaScript code. Our method effectively addresses the limitations of traditional static and dynamic analysis techniques by monitoring and controlling JavaScript code behavior at runtime. By leveraging an inlined security reference monitor, our approach captures the behaviors of both static and dynamically generated code, including those employing advanced evasion techniques. We implemented JSM-Box as a runtime JavaScript analysis framework, which can monitor customizable events and their behaviors. The experimental results demonstrated the effectiveness and efficacy of our method, with machine learning models trained on features extracted by the framework achieving high accuracy rates, even when advanced evasion techniques are used to conceal malicious behaviors.

Future work will focus on enhancing the range of features extracted by the framework, including more sophisticated behaviors and different behavioral patterns. We will also investigate how to extend the implementation of JSMBox to support multiple web browsers, ensuring its effectiveness and usability across different browsing environments. Additionally, we aim to develop a version of the framework that supports multiple web browsers or can be integrated directly into core browsers for more seamless and comprehensive monitoring. Experiments with a wider variety of datasets, including JavaScript files and newer web technologies like WebAssembly, will also be conducted to ensure the robustness and adaptability of our approach.

Acknowledgments. This work was partially supported by the Ohio Department of Higher Education (ODHE) through the Strategic Ohio Council for Higher Education (SOCHE) and Ohio Cyber Range Institute (OCRI) sub-awards and by the National Science Foundation (NSF) award CCF-2342355. We thank the anonymous reviewers for their insightful comments and suggestions for improving the manuscript.

References

1. Hu, C. et al.: Recent Trends in Internet Threats: Common Industries Impersonated in Phishing Attacks, Web Skimmer Analysis and More. Palo Alto Networks (2023). https://unit42.paloal tonetworks.com/internet-threats-late-2022/
2. Cova, M., Kruegel, C., Vigna, G.: Detection and analysis of drive-by-download attacks and malicious JavaScript code. In: Proceedings of the 19th International Conference on World Wide Web, pp. 281–290 (2010)
3. Aboaoja, F.A., Zainal, A., Ghaleb, F.A., Al-rimy, B.A.S., Eisa, T.A.E., Elnour, A.A.H.: Malware detection issues, challenges, and future directions: a survey. Appl. Sci. **12**(17), 8482 (2022)
4. Song, X., Chen, C., Cui, B., Fu, J.: Malicious JavaScript detection based on bidirectional LSTM model. Appl. Sci. **10**(10), 3440 (2020)
5. Xu, W., Zhang, F., Zhu, S.: The power of obfuscation techniques in malicious JavaScript code: a measurement study. In: 2012 7th International Conference on Malicious and Unwanted Software (MALWARE), pp. 9–16. IEEE (2012)
6. Jueckstock, J., Kapravelos, A.: VisibleV8: In-browser monitoring of javascript in the wild. In: Proceedings of the Internet Measurement Conference, pp. 393–405. IMC '19, Association for Computing Machinery, New York, NY, USA (2019)
7. Kim, H.C., Choi, Y.H., Lee, D.H.: Jssandbox: a framework for analyzing the behavior of malicious javascript code using internal function hooking. KSII Trans. Internet Inf. Syst. (TIIS) **6**(2), 766–783 (2012)
8. Gorji, A., Abadi, M.: Detecting obfuscated javascript malware using sequences of internal function calls. In: Proceedings of the 2014 ACM Southeast Regional Conference, pp. 1–6 (2014)
9. Romano, A., Lehmann, D., Pradel, M., Wang, W.: Wobfuscator: Obfuscating JavaScript Malware via Opportunistic Translation to WebAssembly. In: 2022 IEEE Symposium on Security and Privacy (SP), pp. 1574–1589 (2022)
10. Cabrera-Arteaga, J., Monperrus, M., Toady, T., Baudry, B.: WebAssembly diversification for malware evasion. Comput. Secur. **131**, 103296 (2023)
11. Anderson, J.P.: Computer security technology planning study. Technical report, ESDTR-73–51. Anderson (James P) And Co Fort Washington Pa Fort Washington (1972)
12. Crockford, D.: JavaScript: The Good Parts. O'Reilly Media, Inc (2008)
13. Fang, Y., Huang, C., Su, Y., Qiu, Y.: Detecting malicious javascript code based on semantic analysis. Comput. Secur. **93**, 101764 (2020)
14. Wang, R., Zhu, Y., Tan, J., Zhou, B.: Detection of malicious web pages based on hybrid analysis. J. Inf. Secur. Appl. **35**, 68–74 (2017)
15. Ren, K., Qiang, W., Wu, Y., Zhou, Y., Zou, D., Jin, H.: An empirical study on the effects of obfuscation on static machine learning-based malicious javascript detectors. In: Proceedings of the 32nd ACM SIGSOFT International Symposium on Software Testing and Analysis, pp. 1420–1432 (2023)
16. Howard, F.: Malware with Your Mocha? Obfuscation and Anti Emulation Tricks in Malicious JavaScript (2023). Online: https://www.yumpu.com/s/0PX6x19R5gw0KWvt
17. Kaplan, S., Livshits, B., Zorn, B., Siefert, C., Curtsinger, C.: NOFUS: Automatically Detecting+ String. fromCharCode (32)+ ObFuSCateD. toLowerCase ()+ JavaScript Code. Technical report, MSR-TR 2011–57, Microsoft Research (2011)
18. Xu, W., Zhang, F., Zhu, S.: JStill: mostly static detection of obfuscated malicious JavaScript code. In: Proceedings of the Third ACM Conference on Data and Application Security and Privacy, pp. 117–128 (2013)
19. Malware, B.: Obfuscation: The Hidden Malware. IEEE Security & Privacy (2011)

20. Cimitile, A., Martinelli, F., Mercaldo, F., Nardone, V., Santone, A.: Formal methods meet mobile code obfuscation identification of code reordering technique. In: 2017 IEEE 26th International Conference on Enabling Technologies: Infrastructure for Collaborative Enterprises (WETICE), pp. 263–268. IEEE (2017)

21. Wang, X., Zhang, Y., Zhao, L., Chen, X.: Dead code detection method based on program slicing. In: 2017 International Conference on Cyber-Enabled Distributed Computing and Knowledge Discovery (CyberC), pp. 155–158. IEEE (2017)

22. Kılıç, H., Katal, N.S., Selçuk, A.A.: Evasion techniques efficiency over the ips/ids technology. In: 2019 4th International Conference on Computer Science and Engineering (UBMK), pp. 542–547. IEEE (2019)

23. Luoma-aho, M.: Analysis of Modern Malware: obfuscation techniques. Master's thesis, JAMK University of Applied Sciences (2023)

24. You, I., Yim, K.: Malware obfuscation techniques: a brief survey. In: 2010 International Conference on Broadband, Wireless Computing, Communication and Applications, pp. 297–300. IEEE (2010)

25. Heiderich, M., Nava, E.A.V., Heyes, G., Lindsay, D.: Web Application Obfuscation:'-/WAFs.. evasion.. filters//alert (/obfuscation/)-'. Elsevier (2010)

26. Zhang, Y., Liu, M., Wang, H., Ma, Y., Huang, G., Liu, X.: Research on webassembly runtimes: a survey (2024). arXiv:2404.12621

27. Laperdrix, P., Bielova, N., Baudry, B., Avoine, G.: Browser fingerprinting: a survey. ACM Trans. Web (TWEB) 14(2), 1–33 (2020)

28. Zhang, D., Zhang, J., Bu, Y., Chen, B., Sun, C., Wang, T., et al.: A survey of browser fingerprint research and application. Wirel. Commun. Mobile Comput. 2022 (2022)

29. Iqbal, U., Englehardt, S., Shafiq, Z.: Fingerprinting the fingerprinters: Learning to detect browser fingerprinting behaviors. In: 2021 IEEE Symposium on Security and Privacy (SP), pp. 1143–1161. IEEE (2021)

30. Kim, K., Kim, I.L., Kim, C.H., Kwon, Y., Zheng, Y., Zhang, X., Xu, D.: J-force: forced execution on javascript. In: Proceedings of the 26th international conference on World Wide Web, pp. 897–906 (2017)

31. Fass, A., Krawczyk, R.P., Backes, M., Stock, B.: JaSt: Fully syntactic detection of malicious (obfuscated) JavaScript. In: Detection of Intrusions and Malware, and Vulnerability Assessment: 15th International Conference, DIMVA 2018, Saclay, France, Proceedings 15, pp. 303–325. Springer (2018)

32. Ndichu, S., Kim, S., Ozawa, S., Misu, T., Makishima, K.: A machine learning approach to detection of javascript-based attacks using ast features and paragraph vectors. Appl. Soft Comput. 84, 105721 (2019)

33. Fass, A., Backes, M., Stock, B.: JStap: a static pre-filter for malicious JavaScript detection. In: Proceedings of the 35th Annual Computer Security Applications Conference, pp. 257–269 (2019)

34. Fang, Y., Huang, C., Zeng, M., Zhao, Z., Huang, C.: JStrong: malicious JavaScript detection based on code semantic representation and graph neural network. Comput. Secur. 118, 102715 (2022)

35. Tellenbach, B., Paganoni, S., Rennhard, M.: Detecting obfuscated javascripts from known and unknown obfuscators using machine learning. Int. J. Adv. Secur. 9(3/4), 196–206 (2016)

36. Curtsinger, C., Livshits, B., Zorn, B.G., Seifert, C.: ZOZZLE: fast and precise in-browser javascript malware detection. In: USENIX Security Symposium, pp. 33–48. San Francisco (2011)

37. Jagpal, N., Dingle, E., Gravel, J.P., Mavrommatis, P., Provos, N., Rajab, M.A., Thomas, K.: Trends and lessons from three years fighting malicious extensions. In: 24th USENIX Security Symposium (USENIX Security 15), pp. 579–593 (2015)

38. Xue, Y., Wang, J., Liu, Y., Xiao, H., Sun, J., Chandramohan, M.: Detection and classification of malicious JavaScript via attack behavior modelling. In: Proceedings of the 2015 International Symposium on Software Testing and Analysis, pp. 48–59 (2015)
39. Kim, H.G., Kim, D.J., Cho, S.J., Park, M., Park, M.: Efficient detection of malicious web pages using high-interaction client honeypots. J. Inf. Sci. Eng. **28**(5), 911–924 (2012)
40. Alosefer, Y., Rana, O.: Honeyware: a web-based low interaction client honeypot. In: 2010 Third International Conference on Software Testing, Verification, and Validation Workshops, pp. 410–417. IEEE (2010)
41. Snyder, P., Ansari, L., Taylor, C., Kanich, C.: Browser feature usage on the modern web. In: Proceedings of the 2016 Internet Measurement Conference, pp. 97–110 (2016)
42. Roesner, F., Kohno, T., Wetherall, D.: Detecting and defending against third-party tracking on the web. In: 9th USENIX Symposium on Networked Systems Design and Implementation (NSDI 12), pp. 155–168 (2012)
43. Yagemann, C., Sultana, S., Chen, L., Lee, W.: Barnum: Detecting document malware via control flow anomalies in hardware traces. In: Proceedings of 22nd International Information Security Conference (ISC 2019), pp. 341–359. Springer, Berlin, Heidelberg (2019)
44. Ratanaworabhan, P., Livshits, V.B., Zorn, B.G.: Nozzle: A defense against heap spraying code injection attacks. In: USENIX Security Symposium, pp. 169–186 (2009)
45. Li, B., Vadrevu, P., Lee, K.H., Perdisci, R., Liu, J., Rahbarinia, B., Li, K., Antonakakis, M.: JSgraph: Enabling reconstruction of web attacks via efficient tracking of live in-browser javascript executions. In: Network and Distributed Systems Security (NDSS) Symposium (2018)
46. Fang, Y., Huang, C., Liu, L., Xue, M.: Research on malicious JavaScript detection technology based on LSTM. IEEE Access **6**, 59118–59125 (2018)
47. Neasbitt, C., Li, B., Perdisci, R., Lu, L., Singh, K., Li, K.: WebCapsule: towards a lightweight forensic engine for web browsers. In: Proceedings of the 22nd ACM SIGSAC Conference on Computer and Communications Security, pp. 133–145. CCS '15, Association for Computing Machinery, New York, NY, USA (2015)
48. Rieck, K., Krueger, T., Dewald, A.: Cujo: efficient detection and prevention of drive-by-download attacks. In: Proceedings of the 26th Annual Computer Security Applications Conference, pp. 31–39 (2010)
49. Wang, Y., Cai, W.d., Wei, P.C.: A deep learning approach for detecting malicious JavaScript code. Secur. Commun. Netw. **9**(11), 1520–1534 (2016)
50. Obidat, M.A., Obeidat, S., Holst, J., Lee, T.: Canvas deceiver–a new defense mechanism against canvas fingerprinting. J. Syst. Cybern. Inf. **18**(6) (2020)
51. Canvas fingerprinting: What is it and how to bypass it (2023). Online: https://www.zenrows.com/blog/canvas-fingerprinting#what-is
52. Phung, P.H., Sands, D., Chudnov, A.: Lightweight self-protecting javascript. In: Proceedings of the 4th International Symposium on Information, Computer, and Communications Security, pp. 47–60 (2009)
53. Sarker, S., Jueckstock, J., Kapravelos, A.: Hiding in plain site: detecting javascript obfuscation through concealed browser API usage. In: Proceedings of the ACM Internet Measurement Conference (IMC) (2020)
54. Magazinius, J., Phung, P.H., Sands, D.: Safe wrappers and sane policies for self-protecting JavaScript. In: Information Security Technology for Applications: 15th Nordic Conference on Secure IT Systems, NordSec 2010, pp. 239–255. Springer, Espoo, Finland
55. Mozilla: Browser extensions (2024). Online: https://developer.mozilla.org/en-US/docs/Mozilla/Add-ons/WebExtensions
56. Phung, P.H., Monshizadeh, M., Sridhar, M., Hamlen, K.W., Venkatakrishnan, V.: Between worlds: securing mixed javascript/actionscript multi-party web content. IEEE Trans. Dependable Secure Comput. **12**(4), 443–457 (2015)

57. Phung, P.H., Pham, H.D., Armentrout, J., Hiremath, P.N., Tran-Minh, Q.: A user-oriented approach and tool for security and privacy protection on the web. SN Comput. Sci. **1**(4) (2020)
58. MDN contributors: Web APIs (2023). Online: https://developer.mozilla.org/en-US/docs/Web/API
59. Shehoze Farooqi, Billy Melicher, B.K., Starov, A.: Malicious JavaScript Injection Campaign Infects 51k Websites (2023). https://unit42.paloaltonetworks.com/malicious-javascript-injection/
60. Breaking down NOBELIUM's latest early-stage toolset (2021). Online: https://www.microsoft.com/en-us/security/blog/2021/05/28/breaking-down-nobeliums-latest-early-stage-toolset/
61. HTML smuggling explained (2018). Online: https://www.outflank.nl/blog/2018/08/14/html-smuggling-explained/
62. Dynamic resolution: Domain generation algorithms (2022). Online https://www.attack.mitre.org/techniques/T1568/002/
63. HTML Smuggling: Recent observations of threat actor techniques (2023). Online on https://blog.delivr.to, shorthen URL: https://tinyurl.com/yck279xb
64. Attackers Turn to SVG Files to Distribute QBot Malware (2022). Online on https://www.tanium.com, shorthen URL: https://tinyurl.com/mrx2udtr
65. JavaScript invokes ms-appinstaller handler from malicious landing page at time of user click (2023). Online: https://www.microsoft.com/en-us/security/blog/2023/12/28/financially-motivated-threat-actors-misusing-app-installer/
66. Windows malware categories and families (2024). Online: https://portal.av-atlas.org/malware/statistics
67. URLhaus database-malicious URLs that are being used for malware distribution (2024). Online: https://urlhaus.abuse.ch/
68. Pochat, V.L., Van Goethem, T., Tajalizadehkhoob, S., Korczyn´ski, M., Joosen, W.: Tranco: A research-oriented top sites ranking hardened against manipulation (2018). arXiv:1806.01156
69. Likarish, P., Jung, E., Jo, I.: Obfuscated malicious JavaScript detection using classification techniques. In: 2009 4th International Conference on Malicious and Unwanted Software (MALWARE), pp. 47–54 (2009)
70. Liu, Q., Li, P., Zhao, W., Cai, W., Yu, S., Leung, V.C.M.: A survey on security threats and defensive techniques of machine learning: a data driven view. IEEE Access **6**, 12103–12117 (2018)
71. GridSearchCV (2023). Online: https://www.analyticsvidhya.com/blog/2021/06/tune-hyperparameters-with-gridsearchcv/
72. Manan, W.N.W., Han, C.Y.: Detection of distributed denial-of-service (ddos) attack with hyperparameter tuning based on machine learning approach. In: 2023 7th International Symposium on Innovative Approaches in Smart Technologies (ISAS), pp. 1–8 (2023)
73. Chawla, N.V., Bowyer, K.W., Hall, L.O., Kegelmeyer, W.P.: Smote: synthetic minority over-sampling technique. J. Artif. Intell. Res. **16**, 321–357 (2002)
74. Support vector classification (2023). Online: https://scikit-learn.org/stable/modules/generated/sklearn.svm.SVC.html#sklearn.svm.SVC
75. Support vector machines (SVMs) (2024). Online: https://scikit-learn.org/stable/modules/svm.html
76. Wang, W.H., Lv, Y.J., Chen, H.B., Fang, Z.L.: A static malicious javascript detection using SVM. In: Proceedings of the 2nd International Conference on Computer Science and Electronics Engineering (ICCSEE 2013), pp. 214–217. Atlantis Press (2013)
77. Zhu, N., Zhao, G., Yang, Y., Yang, H., Liu, Z.: AEC GAN: unbalanced data processing decision-making in network attacks based on ACGAN and machine learning. IEEE Access **11**, 52452–52465 (2023)

Securing Wireless Sensor Network from Rank Attack Using Fast Sensor Data Encryption and Decryption Protocol

Eden Teshome Hunde[1,2]([⊠])

[1] Department of Electronics and Informatics (ETRO), Vrije Universiteit Brussel, Pleinlaan 2, 1050 Brussels, Belgium
eden.teshome.hunde@vub.be, eden.teshome@ju.edu.et
[2] Department of Electrical and Computer Engineering (ECE), Jimma Institute of Technology, Jimma University, 378 Jimma, Ethiopia

Abstract. Wireless sensor and actuator networks (WSANs) are of great significance in the realm of industrial automation systems. However, the aspect of security in WSANs has been somewhat overlooked. One particular security concern is the rank attack, where malicious actors actively manipulate the transmission of messages from neighboring nodes. This undermines the entire network's data collection and routing operations, resulting in a significant degradation of network performance. This attack adversely affects crucial metrics such as packet delivery ratio (PDR), latency, and power consumption, ultimately reducing the network's overall lifespan. In order to foster trust among nodes, ensure accurate delivery of data to end users, safeguard shared data in the cloud from security breaches, and prevent rank attacks within the network, it is crucial to protect the network against such malicious activities. This research paper aims to introduce an enhanced version of the Routing Protocol for Low-Power and Lossy Networks (RPL) protocol, specifically tailored to identify and eliminate rank attacks within existing WSANs. The effectiveness of the new protocol will be assessed through experimentation using Zolertia (Z1) sensors in the Cooja network simulator. To minimize network overhead on the sensors' side, the proposed scheme limits cryptographic operations to symmetric key-based mechanisms such as XORing, hash functions, and encryption. These operations will be implemented using a C-compiler and verified through the ModelSIM Altera SE edition 11.0 simulator.

Keywords: ModelSIM Altera SE · RPL · WSANs

1 Introduction

Wireless Sensor and Actuator Networks (WSANs) are an increasingly popular research field, with a wide range of applications being explored [1–3]. These include traffic monitoring, military operations, home automation, automated agriculture, as well as environmental and health monitoring. WSANs consist of sensors that collect various data about the surroundings and actuators, like servos and motors that regulate or adjust the environment in response to the collected data.

© The Author(s), under exclusive license to Springer Nature Switzerland AG 2025
W. Feng et al. (Eds.): SEDE 2024, CCIS 2244, pp. 123–135, 2024.
https://doi.org/10.1007/978-3-031-75201-8_9

One of the popular routing protocols tailored for resource- constrained WSANs is the Routing Protocol for Low-Power and Lossy Networks (RPL) [4], established in 2012. Nonetheless, the data packet routing in this protocol is susceptible to insider attacks, like rank attacks, which can disrupt regular routing functions and reduce the network's overall performance. These attacks can severely impact networks by quickly depleting the batteries of the nodes, thus affecting their engagement in the network. The RPL rank attack is a serious threat in WSANs, where malicious nodes create inefficient paths during routing operation, especially when it is launched near to the RPL root node. Existing security measures in [5, 6] may not be effective in preventing this attack, as they do not focus enough on securing the network from this specific threat. In this study, we propose a new security approach for RPL-based WSANs to identify and discard malicious nodes, with the main goal of protecting the network. Additionally, the research also aims to ensure that data coming from small constrained devices that are store in the cloud server are totally protected from any security breaks. To the best of our knowledge, this research introduces a novel intrusion detection and prevention system with minimal communication overhead, while maintaining the integrity of the standard RPL operation in WSANs.

Section 2 offers a detailed summary of previous studies on the security challenges of RPL and the solutions offered. Section 3 outlines RPL protocol and the attacker model. Section 4 introduces the proposed new distributed RC5 (NDRC5) design aimed at identifying and preventing RPL's rank attacks. Moreover, Sect. 5 presents details on the developed security schemes. Section 6 delves into thorough simulations and the findings from experiments. Section 7 provides a detail analysis of the performance evaluation of the proposed protocol. The final section concludes with closing remarks and outlines future research directions.

2 Literature Review

A new Intrusion Detection System (IDS) for RPL-Based Internet of Things was introduced in [5], aiming to identify specific attacks like version number, worst parent, and hello food within RPL networks. This IDS utilized neural networks and gathered network features from routing and link layers for training a machine learning system. However, the study noted that the centralized IDS did not effectively utilize link layer feature extraction to detect rank attacks, particularly focusing on the worst parent or rank attacks. Furthermore, in scenarios with large network topologies and a small number of attacker nodes, such as in rank attacks, the proposed IDS exhibited suboptimal performance.

The researchers in [7] have introduced a new method for selecting parent nodes in multi-path RPL networks called Alternative Parent (AP) selection. This approach combines elements from the Triangular Pattern [8], Leap Frog Collaboration (LFC) [9, 10], and Soft Common Ancestor (CA) algorithms. In this new method, the Packet Replication and Elimination (PRE) mechanism is utilized to create multiple copies of a single data packet, increasing the likelihood of successful delivery to the destination nodes. Each copy of the transmitted packet takes a different parallel route to reach the destination, providing redundancy in case of transmission failures. By using PRE, the proposed algorithm achieves a Packet Delivery Ratio (PDR) of 95% and ensures minimal Jitter, which is crucial for high-priority data packets. However, it should be noted that the overall power consumption of the network is higher with this approach compared to traditional single-path algorithms.

The authors in [11] devised a method to detect and counter RPL rank and version number attacks in IoT networks. They introduced a Secure RPL Routing Protocol (SRPL-RP) for this purpose. In SRPL-RP, the legitimacy of the sending node is confirmed through a timestamp threshold, which tracks the time difference between exchanged DIO control messages. If the time difference exceeds a set threshold, indicating a potential attack, the DIO message is discarded. Nodes in the RPL network can monitor and captures all information about its neighboring nodes and update a blacklist if any suspicious activity is detected, preventing malicious nodes from joining the network. SRPL-RP is adaptable to various network topologies. Experimental results demonstrated an enhanced PDR of 98.48% and an average energy consumption of 1231.75 joules. Despite the improvements in PDR, the proposed system may lead to high memory consumption by storing malicious node's information in a black list table.

In [12], a new sink-based intrusion detection system (SBIDS) is introduced to detect rank attacks in routing protocols for Low Power and Lossy Networks. SBIDS checks whether a minimum rank among siblings minus the parent switching threshold exceeds the node's current rank value. If the minimum rank value is less than the node's current rank value, the nodes change their preferred parent node (PPN). If not, the node is identified as a malicious node. To protect the node's integrity in SBIDS, each node encrypts and sends its IP address, preferred parent IP address, and rank in a DAO message using a shared key with intermediate nodes and the sink node. The sink node decrypts the received DAO message. SBIDS simulation shows low computational overhead as all detection processes are focused at the sink node. However, the proposed solution requires high resources, leading to a decrease in network lifetime.

The researchers in [13] introduced a Secure Parent Node Selection Scheme in Route Construction to prevent Attacking Nodes from infiltrating the RPL Network. This scheme allows each child node to carefully choose a trustworthy parent node by setting a threshold value. By assessing the rank of potential parent nodes, a child node can avoid selecting those with suspiciously low ranks. Additionally, nodes can evaluate the rank information of their neighbors to make informed decisions about parent node selection. Through this method, nodes can steer clear of connecting to malicious nodes and transmitting data to potential attackers. Simulation results demonstrate that this approach effectively minimizes the number of child nodes linked to attacking nodes. However, a more comprehensive analysis is required to evaluate the scheme's performance in terms of PDR, latency, and energy efficiency.

3 Background

In this section, we start by introducing key details about how the RPL protocol operates in WSANs and the particular attacker model associated with the RPL protocol. Following that, we delve into the proposed cryptographic security measures aimed at identifying and removing malicious nodes within RPL networks.

A. RPL Overview

RPL is a standardized routing protocol specifically designed for energy constrained WSANs [14]. RPL creates a network structure using a Direct Acyclic Graph (DAG) made up of one or more Destination-Oriented Directed Acyclic Graphs (DODAGs). Each DODAG includes multiple wireless sensor devices connected to a central node known as the DODAG root. The root node starts the process of building and managing the DODAG graph by broadcasting the DODAG Information Object (DIO) downward at regular intervals. The DIO contains essential configuration parameters like rank, objective function, and DODAG IDs, among others [15, 16]. When a node receives the DIO message and wishes to join the DODAG, it responds with a Destination Advertisement Object (DAO) control message, which is then sent upwards to one of its parents in the leaf node's DODAG parent list. If the new node does not receive a DIO message from its preferred parent, it will broadcast a DODAG Information Solicitation (DIS) message to request topology information before joining the network. A simplified representation of this network is illustrated in Fig. 1.

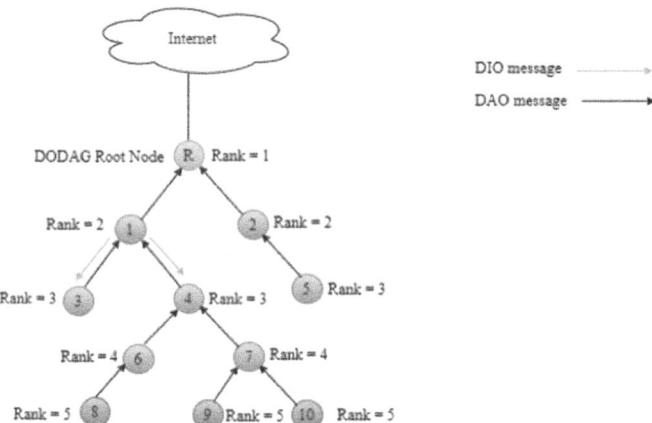

Fig. 1. A simple representation of DODAG network topology. The root of the RPL network is represented by R.

B. Attacker Model

In the attack scenario, we consider the possibility of a malicious node carrying out a rank attack within RPL-based WSANs. This type of attack involves a malicious node broadcasting false lower rank information via DIO messages to its neighboring nodes. By doing so, the malicious node aims to be chosen as a preferred parent by its neighbors and consequently be utilized as the primary path for forwarding data towards the RPL root node in the network. As a result, neighboring nodes may select this malicious node as their next hop, leading to suboptimal routing paths. This allows the malicious node to manipulate multicast data messages from neighboring nodes by altering, inserting, dropping, changing, deleting, or replying to messages. If this attack occurs in close proximity to the RPL root node, it can significantly impact network resources and disrupt the DODAG routing operation. Therefore, it is crucial to mitigate the effects of such attacks on the RPL-based WSANs. Figure 2 illustrates the rank attack on the RPL-based network. The malicious node M spreads the lowest rank value (rank 2) to nearby nodes and falsifies the relative distance to the root node in order to divert all traffic from its neighbors. Nodes 6 and 7 choose the malicious node M as their parent and start sending traffic to it. Meanwhile, the malicious node M alters the traffic it receives.

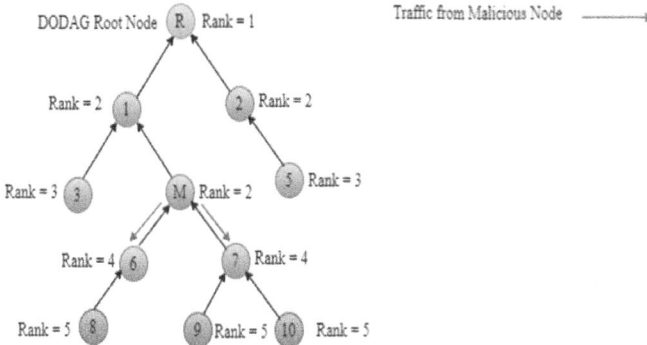

Fig. 2. An illustration of rank attack in the RPL based network.

4 Proposed Scheme

A. Cryptographic Operations

Due to the limited memory, computational resources, and minimum lifetime of sensor networks, it is crucial to minimize the network overhead required to ensure the necessary security features in RPL-based WSANs. In our proposed scheme, we focus on utilizing cryptographic operations that are efficient, such as XOR $\oplus$ operations, encryptions, and cryptographic hash functions like SHA2 and SHA3. The hash function employed in our scheme is SHAKE 256(M, d), which maps inputs of varying lengths to outputs of length d, providing security strength (i.e., in bits) of min(d/2, 256) against collision attacks and min(d, 256) against preimage, 2nd preimage attacks and rank attacks. Furthermore, the concatenation of the low cost cryptographic operations of two messages m_1 and m_2 is denoted by $m_m \parallel m_r$, and the corresponding XOR operation is represented as $m_m \oplus m_r$.

The authenticated encryption (AE) algorithm like, RC5, can be utilized. The message m sent by the multicast sender is encrypted using a symmetric key K to obtain the ciphertext C, defined as $C = E_K(m)$. Decryption using the symmetric key K is denoted as $m = D_K(C)$.

B. **Rank Verification Procedure**

We first introduce a new secure parent node selection method to ensure that every child node in the RPL-based network can choose a legitimate node as its parent. During the route construction phase, each child node in the WSANs analyzes the incoming DIO message for any signs of a rank attack within the network. In this approach, if a node receives a DIO broadcast message with a decreased rank value from its preferred parent, instead of immediately updating its routing table and sending the DAO message, it first verifies the identity of the advertised parent to check if the preferred parent node is acting maliciously. This verification process is only initiated if the node receives a reduced rank value in the incoming DIO messages from its preferred parent. When a child node receives DIO messages from its preferred parent, it checks if the rank value in the DIO message is lower than the pre-defined *threshold* (T), which is calculated as the difference between the rank values of the child node and its parent (i.e., *Threshold* $(T) = $ Child_Rank–Parent_Rank). If the rank value in the DIO message is lower than T, the child node considers the message genuine, accepts it, and updates its routing table. Conversely, if the rank value in the DIO message is higher than T, it is deemed a fake rank, and the child node rejects the message. The fake rank value is recorded in a blacklist table and excluded from the list of genuine parents, ensuring that it is not considered by the detection system in the future. This process helps identify malicious parent nodes that forward lower rank numbers than the legitimate ones, enabling each child node to avoid selecting or sending multicast traffic to such malicious nodes. The algorithm for detecting anomalies in incoming DIO messages are shown below encrypt the stored data. To authorize the user, the Owner collects the user's passcodes, such as passwords and usernames. During the decryption phase, the end user can retrieve the original sensor message. It is assumed that HTTPS is utilized for establishing secure communication between the Owner and the end user. Further details on the execution of each step by all parties involved in the scheme are explained below.

Algorithm 1: Secure parent node selection algorithm

Start: Examining the incoming DIO message to select a legitimate parent

Begin

    If (DIO-parent. Rank < T)

        {

        Accept the DIO + update routing table;

        }

    Else

        {

        Discard the DIO message + black list table;

        }

End

Stop

In the scenario depicted in Fig. 2, when nodes 6 and 7 receive a new DIO message from the malicious node M, they check whether the rank value in the message is lower than a threshold value, denoted as T. In this specific case shown in Figure 2, T is set to 2 because the rank values of nodes 6 and 7 are 4, while the rank of node M is 2. Therefore, T is calculated as 4 minus 2 equals 2. Upon receiving the rank value of node M in the DIO message, nodes 6 and 7 compare it with the threshold T, which is 2 in this case. As the received rank value of node M is not less than the specified threshold T, nodes 6 and 7 reject this rank value from the malicious node M and add it to the blacklist table. Consequently, nodes 6 and 7 remove node M from their parent list to prevent selecting a malicious node in the future.

C. Topology Setting

To meet the security requirements in WSANs, we have developed a security scheme for the suggested setup. This scheme comprises three main phases: *key initialization, authentication,* and *formal communication.* Our setup involves a WSN made up of a cloud server, sensor owner, nodes Ni (where i ranges from 1 to n), and a border router (BR) or the RPL root node. The border router connects the WSN to the end users via the internet, as depicted in Fig. 3.

During the initialization phase, the sensor Owner generates and distributes key material to the cloud server and the sensor nodes that are subscribed to the multicast group. Subscribed sensor nodes undergo a rank verification phase, as detailed in Sect. 4, before sending their encrypted multicast data m to the server. The encrypted data is then uploaded to the server. If an end user wishes to receive the multicast data, they must make a specific request to the sensor's Owner. Upon receiving the request, the Owner authorizes the user by providing a proxy re-encryption key, which is used by the server to re-encryption

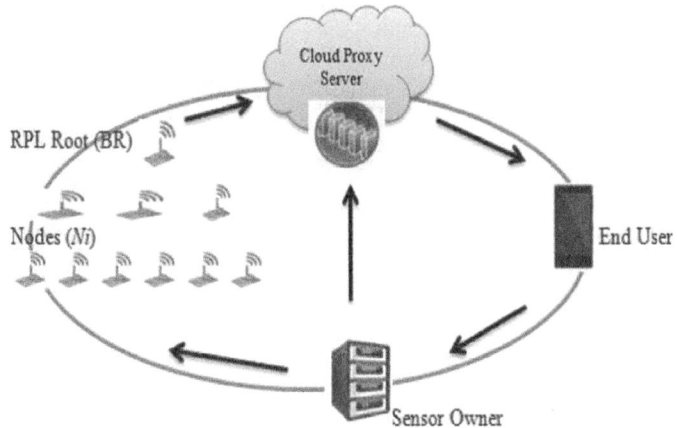

Fig. 3. A schematic overview of the message flow in the scheme

5 Security Scheme

A. **Key Initialization Phase**

In this phase, the owner creates two master keys, referred to as Y_1 and Y_2. The owner also assigns a unique identity ID_j to each sensor and calculates the keys for each sensor using the formulas $K_j = H(Y_1||ID_j)$ and $Y_j = H(Y_2||ID_j)$. The Owner shares the identity ID_j and the key K_j with the server, which provides service to the user through the HTTPS channel. A table is then created on the server side to store all sensor credentials ID_j and K_j received from the owner. A common shared key K_u is established between the Owner and the server, and this K_u, along with the IDs of various owners (ID_u), is stored in the server's storage table. The owner installs the keys K_j and Y_j in the sensor devices for each sensor identified by ID_j. The owner maintains two separate tables: one for sensor IDs and the other for user information such as passwords and usernames. Users are granted access to the collected sensor data.

B. **Data Encryption and Uploading Phase**

In this stage, when the sensor node identified as ID_j intends to transmit its multicast message m to the server, it first starts by selecting a pseudo-random number R and generating a secret key $R_k = H(R\|ID_j)$. After that, the device calculates the specified parameters.

$$K = R \oplus H\left(Y_j\|ID_j\right) \oplus H(K_j\|ID_j)$$

$$C = E_{Rk}(m)$$

$$f = H(C\|K \oplus H(K_j\|ID_j))$$

$$f_i = H(m\|R)$$

The multicast message $m_{m=}\{ID_j, K, C, f, f_i\}$ is sent to the server. When the server receives such a message, it computes $K_s = K \oplus H\left(K_j\|ID_j\right) = R \oplus H\left(Y_j\|ID_j\right)$. Then, it checks if the received f is equal to $H(C\|K_s)$. If so, the server confirms that the received message is from a legitimate sensor node with ID_j, K_j. It stores the computed parameters $D_m = \{ID_j, K_s, C, f, f_i\}$ in its table.

C. End User's Request Phase

In this process, if an end user wants to access the multicast data from the sensor node ID_j, they need to send a request to the sensor's Owner. The request is sent through a secure HTTPS connection using the user's password, known as PW_i. Once the request is verified, a pseudo-random number R_l (created by the Owner) is shared between the user and the Owner. The user then keeps a record of R_l.

D. Proxy Re-encryption Key Phase

When the end user requested to receive specific encrypted data from the Owner, the Owner granted access to the user by providing a proxy re-encryption key, which is described as follows.

$$preK = H(Y_j\|ID_j) \oplus H(PW_{i.}\|R_l) \oplus H(K_u\|H(R_l)\|ID_j)$$
$$Pe = H(H(Y_j\|ID_j) \oplus H(PW_{i.}\|R_l))$$

The multicast message $m_r = \{H(R_l), ID_j, ID_u, PreK, Pe\}$ is sent to the server. Upon receiving the message, the server checks if ID_j and ID_u are already stored in its tables. If they exist, the server retrieves the necessary key material from its tables to calculate $H(K_u\|H(R_l)\|ID_j) \oplus PreK$. The server then verifies the authenticity of the request and creates a new table with the values of $D_n = \{H(R_l), ID_j, K_r, C, f_i\}$. The value of K_r is determined as $K_r = K_s \oplus PreK \oplus H(K_u\|H(R_l)\| ID_j)$ and $K_r = R \oplus H(PW_i\|R_l)$.

E. **Decryption Key Phase**

During the decryption process, the end user must first go through authentication and authorization steps by using their own password, PW_i, and a pseudo-random number, R_l, when communicating with the Owner. Afterward, the user can log in to the server using the credential R_l, which is encrypted using the server's public key. This allows the user to access the multicast data identified by $(H(R_l), ID_j)$. This data contains the following records $\{K_r, C, f_i\}$. The user can compute $R = K_r \oplus H(PW_i\|R_l)$ using their password, and the decryption key $R_k = H(R\|ID_j)$. With the decryption key, the end user can decrypt the cipher text C and retrieve the original message m. The message's integrity is verified by checking if $H(m\|R)$ matches the stored value f_i.

6 Security Analysis

A. **Software Based Validations**

The symmetric key based encryption and decryption algorithm was developed using both the C language and Verilog HDL. In the C compilation process, when an end user wishes to receive specific multicast data, they must contact the Owner and request access using their password or pass number. These pass numbers are represented as two distinct user prime pass numbers in the simulation. Once the pass numbers are authenticated, a pseudo-random number R_l ranging from a to z is generated and shared between the user and the Owner. The Owner then grants access to the end user by providing a proxy re-encryption key. This key is utilized by the server to re-encrypt the incoming data, which in this case is the message uploaded by the sensor. Ultimately, the simulation demonstrates that the end user can successfully retrieve the original test message by employing their decryption key. In this way, the end user can securely log in to access the encrypted sensor's data stored on the server. By retrieving notifications or alerts from the sensors, the end user can make informed decisions. Sensors commonly used in home automation, like moisture detection sensors, motion sensors, and smart thermostats, are excellent examples of WSNs that offer valuable information to users. Extensive design testing was successfully conducted on simulator, and the results of the C implementation can be seen in the Fig. 4 below.

The Verilog simulation results also show that the modified RC5 encryption and decryption algorithm has been successfully implemented on ModelSIM Altera SE simulator and is ready to be deployed on a Field Programmable Gate Array (FPGA) board.

7 Perfomance Evaluation

A. **Computational Cost**

In the experiment, it is demonstrated that our proposed method is highly efficient in terms of computational cost. Specifically, when considering the limited capabilities of devices

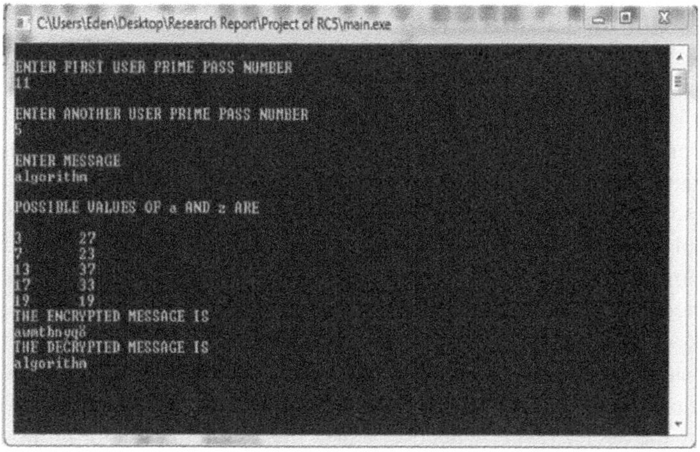

Fig. 4. Output of C implementation

in the network, one encryption and five cryptographic hash operations are utilized. For the Cooja simulated Zolertia (Z1) mote, we have incorporated an RC5 symmetric encryption and SHA256 hash function. The time required for the node to execute the necessary encryption and hashing functions is 1.052 ms and 4.089 ms, respectively. On average, a total of 2.57 ms is needed for computing m_m. The experimental results also indicate that the implemented DIO cross-checking mechanism does not add extra computational cost. We have further evaluated this for the resource-limited Zolertia platform using LooCI Contiki (LC). This platform features the core architecture of MSP430 microcontrollers and CC2420 radio transceivers. The calculated performance metric demonstrates that the implemented security protocol is suitable to be used for practical network scenarios.

B. Communication Cost

When considering the size of the node, the RC5 encryption and hash function have lengths of 64 bits and 256 bits, respectively. The total number of bits sent and received varies depending on the number of nodes in the RPL network. Specifically, a node sends a multicast message of 64 bits in length, requiring a total of 480 bits. For transmitting a 256-bit message, the node needs a total of 1920 bits.

C. Memory overhead

The experimental results shows that the total storage needed based on the network's size. It is apparent that the storage overhead for Dm and Dn of each subscriber node (s nodes) and each new end user (n users) can be calculated as $(s * D_{mx}) + (n * D_{ny})$. The number of parameters stored is directly proportional to the number of end users and subscriber nodes in the network. As the network grows larger, the memory space required to store Dm and Dn increases. For a single user, the overhead is 1632 bits, while for more than ten users, it amounts to 10150 bits.

8 Conclusion and Future Work

In this research, we introduced a robust and efficient ranking-based verification security approach to identify and eliminate malicious nodes from accessing the RPL network. The effectiveness of this approach was evaluated using Zolertia (Z1) sensors in the Cooja simulator. Additionally, the distributed RC5 (NDRC5) encryption and decryption algorithm was implemented to secure data transmitted from resource-constrained devices that are stored on the cloud server to end user. The algorithm's performance was validated using a C compiler and verified with the ModelSIM Altera SE edition 11.0 simulator.

Our strategy ensures that data is delivered accurately to end users while preventing rank attacks and safeguarding shared data in the cloud from security breaches. In our proposed system, accessing cloud-stored data securely requires an authorized end user to provide a password or passcode, along with a pseudo-random number computation performed by the device owner whenever a user makes a request. Our proposed scheme excels in terms of computational efficiency, using only one encryption and five hashes. Additionally, the communication costs are reasonable, especially in realistic scenarios.

We intend to extend the work by verifying the proposed scheme on a real hardware setup called FPGA board.

References

1. Majid, M., et al.: Applications of wireless sensor networks and internet of things frameworks in the industry revolution 4.0: a systematic literature review. Sensors **22**(6) (2022). https://doi.org/10.3390/s22062087
2. Ma, C., Zheng, M., Liang, W., Kasparick, M., Lin, Y.: Deploying hierarchical mesh networks for supporting distributed computing in industrial Internet of Things. IEEE Syst. J. **16**(3), 4433–4444 (2022)
3. Redekar, A., Deb, D., Ozana, S.: Functionality analysis of electric actuators in renewable energy systems—a review. Sensors **22**(11) (2022)
4. Winter, T., Thubert, P., Brandt, A., et al.: RPL: IPv6 Routing Protocol for Low-Power and Lossy Networks Standard (2012)
5. Wise, L.: A Cross-Layer Intrusion Detection System for RPL-Based Internet of Thing
6. Bang, A., Rao, R.P.: Performance evaluation of RPL protocol under decreased and increased rank attacks: a focus on smart home use-case. SN Comput. Sci. **4**(329) (2023). https://doi.org/10.1007/s42979-023-01799-w
7. Jenschke, T.L., Papadopoulos, G., Koutsiamanis, R.-A., Montavont, N.: Alternative parent selection for multi-path RPL networks. In: 2019 IEEE 5th World Forum on Internet of Things (WF IoT), pp. 533–538. Limerick, Ireland (2019)
8. Minet, P., Khoufi, I., Laouiti, A.: Increasing reliability of a TSCH network for the Industry 4.0. In: Proceedings of the 16th IEEE International Symposium on Network Computing and Applications (NCA). United States, Boston (2017). https://doi.org/10.1109/NCA.2017.8171344ï
9. Jenschke, T.L., Papadopoulos, G.Z., Koutsiamanis, R.-A., Montavont, N.: Alternative parent selection for multi-path RPL networks. In: 2019 IEEE 5th World Forum on Internet of Things (WF-IoT), pp. 533–538. Limerick, Ireland, 2019. https://doi.org/10.1109/WF-IoT.2019.8767236

10. Papadopoulos G.Z., Matsui, T., Thubert, P., Texier, G., Watteyne, T., Montavont, N.: Leapfrog collaboration: toward determinism and predictability in industrial-IoT applications. In: 2017 IEEE International Conference on Communications (ICC), pp. 1–6. Paris, France (2017)
11. Almusaylim, Z.A., Jhanjhi, N.Z., Alhumam, A.: Detection and mitigation of RPL rank and version number attacks in the internet of things: SRPL-RP. Sensors (Switzerland) **20**(21), 1–25 (2020). https://doi.org/10.3390/s20215997
12. Shafique, U., Khan, A., Rehman, A., Bashir, F., Alam, M.: Detection of rank attack in routing protocol for low power and lossy networks. Annales des Telecommunications/Ann. Telecommun. **73**(7–8), 429–438 (2018). https://doi.org/10.1007/s12243-018-0645-4
13. Verma, A., Ranga, V.: Security of RPL based 6LoWPAN networks in the Internet of Things: a review. IEEE Sens. J. **20**(11), 5666–5690 (2020). https://doi.org/10.1109/JSEN.2020.297 3677
14. Sobral, J.V.V., Rodrigues, J.J.P.C., Rabêlo, R.A.L., Al-Muhtadi, J., Korotaev, V.: Routing protocols for low power and lossy networks in internet of things applications. Sensors (Switzerland) **19**(9) (2019). https://doi.org/10.3390/s19092144
15. Nandhini P.S., Kuppuswami S., Malliga S., DeviPriya R.: A lightweight energy-efficient algorithm for mitigation and isolation of internal rank attackers in RPL based Internet of Things. Comput. Netw. **218** (2022). https://doi.org/10.1016/j.comnet.2022.109391
16. Diniesh, V.C., Murugesan, G., Jude, M.J., Harshini, A., Bhavataarani, S., Krishnan, R.G.: Impacts of objective function on RPL-routing protocol: a survey. In: 2021 Sixth International Conference on Wireless Communications, Signal Processing and Networking (WiSPNET), pp. 251–255. Chennai, India (2021)

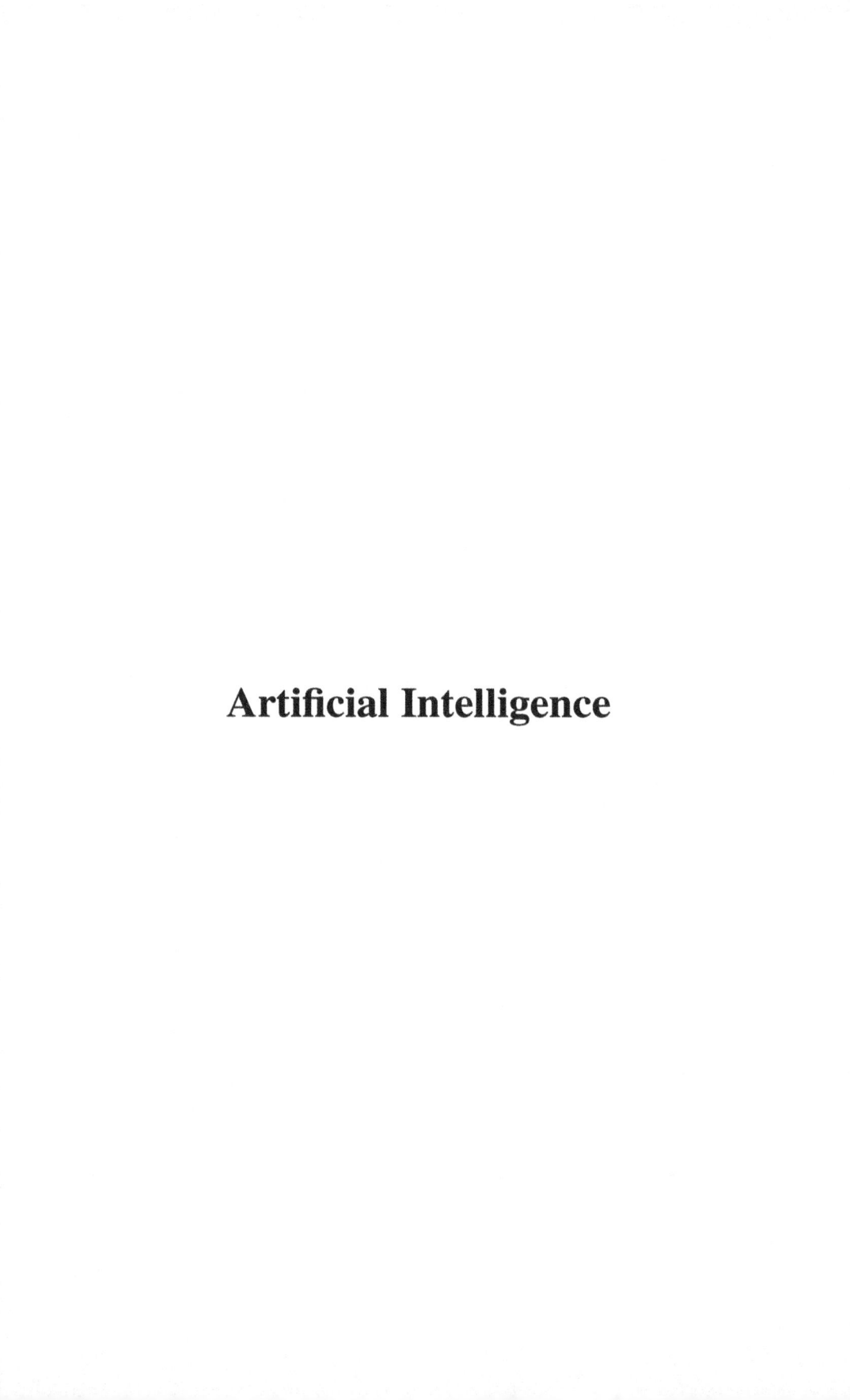

Artificial Intelligence

Enhancing Transparency and Privacy in Financial Fraud Detection: The Integration of Explainable AI and Federated Learning

Waquar Ahmad[1(✉)], Aditya Vashist[2], Neel Sinha[2], Manisha Prasad[3], Vishesh Shrivastava[4], and Junaid Hussain Muzamal[5]

[1] University of California, San Diego, US
waquarahmad5@gmail.com
[2] University of Florida, Gainesville, US
[3] The University of Texas at Dallas, Richardson, US
[4] University of Minnesota Twin Cities, Minneapolis and Saint Paul, US
[5] Fast—National University of Computer and Emerging Sciences, Lahore, Pakistan

Abstract. The pervasive issue of fraudulent transactions presents a considerable challenge for financial institutions globally. Developing innovative fraud detection systems is critical to maintaining customer confidence. However, several factors complicate the creating of effective and efficient fraud detection systems. Notably, fraudulent transactions are infrequent, resulting in imbalanced transaction datasets where legitimate transactions vastly outnumber instances of fraud. This data imbalance can concede the performance of fraud detection. Additionally, stringent data privacy regulations prevent the sharing of customer data, hindering the development of high-performing centralized models. Furthermore, fraud detection mechanisms must remain transparent to avoid impairing the user experience. This research proposes an approach utilizing Federated Learning (FL) with Explainable Artificial Intelligence (XAI) to overcome these obstacles. FL allows financial organizations to train fraud detection models collaboratively without requiring direct data sharing. So, customer confidentiality and data privacy are never compromised. Simultaneously, the incorporation of XAI guarantees that the model's predictions are interpretable by human experts. Experimental evaluations using real-time transaction datasets consistently demonstrate that the FL-based fraud detection system performs well. This study establishes the potential of FL as a reliable, privacy-preserving tool in combating fraud.

Keywords: Fraud detection systems · EAI · Federated learning · Collaborative machine learning · Data privacy · Transaction analysis · Model transparency · Anomaly detection · Imbalanced data handling · Privacy-preserving algorithms

1 Introduction

In the digital banking field, the integrity and security of financial transactions are paramount [1]. The transition to digital platforms offers convenience but exposes users to various cyber threats simultaneously. Financial fraud poses significant risks to the

© The Author(s), under exclusive license to Springer Nature Switzerland AG 2025
W. Feng et al. (Eds.): SEDE 2024, CCIS 2244, pp. 139–156, 2024.
https://doi.org/10.1007/978-3-031-75201-8_10

worldwide economy, especially in online banking and credit card transactions [2]. It affects financial institutions' credibility and individuals' financial security. According to the Alexander et al. [3] report, fraudulent activities result in the annual loss of billions of dollars, emphasizing the need for enhanced detection methods.

Financial organizations have been working continuously to develop methods of fraud identification, regardless of its form. Despite these efforts, the complexity of fraud persists due to its continuously evolving tactics and the diversity of its behaviors. A primary area of focus is bank-related fraud [4], which is the foundation for the present study. Banking fraud is distinct from other financial deception because sophisticated methods present many challenges. Bank account fraud involves account takeovers, unauthorized funds transfers, or new fake identity accounts [5]. The ramifications for victims extend beyond immediate financial loss, impacting them emotionally and enduringly. Effectively understanding these threats necessitates research supported by comprehensive methods.

In developing systems capable of detecting bank account fraud, Machine Learning (ML) is often utilized due to its efficacy in training systems to produce accurate predictions from data inputs. The selection of a particular ML algorithm depends on the data and type of fraud being targeted. Datasets comprising bank account transactions contain confidential information and are imbalanced. This means that fraudulent transactions occur less frequently than in real life. These attributes pose significant challenges in developing a mature fraud detection approach. Banks utilize their private data to train ML models to identify fraudulent activities. This approach is ubiquitous in the financial sector due to its ability to process massive data [6]. However, a notable challenge with such models is the variation in fraudulent patterns met by different banks, which may impede their capacity to detect new types of fraudulent behaviors. It is in this context that FL emerges as a significant solution.

FL stands for a cutting-edge, privacy-preserving method in decentralized ML [7, 8]. It offers a promising method to tackle prevalent challenges by allowing local devices-based model training while sharing only combined updates and, in this way, keeping data confidential. This approach differs from traditional ML methods, which are restricted to a single institution. FL facilitates collaboration across multiple banks, enhancing integrity and data protection. Within the fraud detection domain, FL is recognized as a pivotal component of a collaborative strategy to combat fraud. The importance of FL is increasingly acknowledged due to its ability to amalgamate insights from various institutions without needing direct data exchanges. Furthermore, FL emphasizes the transmission of model updates rather than extensive data sets, which expedites the process, enhances efficiency, and ensures the security of customer data.

Moreover, AI-based fraud detection techniques often operate as "black boxes" with limited transparency. AI systems must be accurate and trustworthy in critical applications like bank fraud detection. This research integrates EAI methods into the FL-based framework to tackle the issue of banking fraud. The proposed methodology preserves user privacy, provides a collaborative setup, and enhances trustworthiness. This study introduces a robust fraud detection technique that utilizes the strengths of FL and is combined with XAI. The methodology stands out for several reasons, notably its focus on user privacy preservation and increased transparency. This paper summarizes the critical contributions of the study, emphasizing the innovative integration of FL and XAI to address the dual challenges of efficacy and ethical transparency in fraud detection.

1. Implement an FL strategy within a fraud detection system to safeguard the individual data, with only model-based feature updates being centralized.
2. Develop a Convolution Neural Network (CNN) model to detect patterns indicative of fraudulent transactions across databases, ensuring privacy and accuracy.
3. Employ EAI techniques to imbue the fraud detection model with transparency, facilitating a clear understanding of decision-making processes within the system.
4. Integrate the FL-based method into a web application to demonstrate the operational efficacy of the approach, providing a tangible interface.

The rest of this paper is organized in the following manner: Sect. 2 provides a comprehensive literature review and discusses related work in the field. Section 3 outlines our methodology, detailing the approach to integrating Federated Learning and Explainable AI in fraud detection. Section 3.3 explains our detailed implementation of the proposed system. Section 5 discusses the results obtained from our experimental evaluations. Finally, the research is concluded in Sect. 6, where we summarize the findings and suggest potential directions for future research.

2   Literature Review

Fraud detection, an enduring challenge, has substantially evolved in response to technological advancements and increasingly sophisticated strategies [9]. Historically, fraud has posed a significant threat. Still, modern technologies, such as digital communication platforms and financial tools designed to offer benefits, have also inadvertently expanded opportunities for malicious entities intent on inflicting harm. This has led to novel forms of fraud, including computer security breaches and telecommunications scams. Understanding the motivations behind this behavior has been a focal point of research [10]. One of the primary focuses is the "fraud triangle," which is a conceptual framework prompting individuals to engage in fraudulent acts. This model highlights three critical elements: incentive, rationalization, and opportunity. Using this model, studies have added further layers of complexity by introducing additional elements such as the execution of the fraudulent act, the techniques used to hide it, and the change process wherein the perpetrators take advantage of their deceitful activities [11]. As financial organizations confront the challenge of managing a vast volume of fraudulent transactions, ML and deep learning (DL) have risen to prominence, offering innovative solutions to detect these risks. At this point, ML can be described as a branch of AI that combines algorithms and statistical models [12]. This integration enables software to execute tasks without being explicitly programmed. As an alternative, the system understands the training data, leveraging the empirical knowledge to make decisions. DL, a more advanced subset of ML, employs ANN, which is designed to parse complex relationships within data. The complexity of networks, exemplified by architectures such as CNNs and Restricted Boltzmann Machines (RBMs), allow them to understand intricate patterns within vast datasets, making them particularly effective in environments characterized by large-scale and complex data challenges. Many ML and DL methodologies have been investigated within the research community for fraud detection. For example, Shamsolmoali et al. [13] examined the effectiveness of Support Vector Machines, k-nearest Neighbors, and ensemble models in identifying fraudulent transactions. This research highlighted significant challenges, such as the highly unbalanced nature of transaction data—where legitimate ones vastly outnumber fraudulent instances—and the dynamic characteristics of fraud, which require ML algorithms to be regularly updated to maintain effectiveness.

Randhawa et al. [14] have explored ML algorithms such as SVM, Random Forest, and ensemble models for similar applications. Sharma et al. [15] examined the utilization of transformer-based models for fraud detection. Transformers are Auto-Encoders based neural networks aimed at data encoding before attempting to reconstruct the original input. Discrepancies in the reconstruction, especially when the model is trained exclusively on legitimate transactions, may signal potential fraud. The Restricted Boltzmann Machine (RBM), discussed in [16], is another neural network model that excels in learning a probability distribution over its inputs. The capability of RBMs to uncover complex patterns in unlabeled data renders them particularly effective for spotting unauthorized transactions within large, imbalanced datasets, where fraudulent activities constitute only a small fraction of the total transactions.

The traditional ML methods of fraud detection have predominantly employed centralized methodologies. In these systems, individual clients transmit data to a server where model training is conducted [17]. However, this approach introduces several challenges, particularly in industries dealing with sensitive information. Using confidential data entails risks associated with data security, latency, and privacy issues. Furthermore, in some scenarios, data owners may be legally constrained from sharing data, complicating the data collection. There has been a shift towards decentralized learning methodologies in response to these impediments, with FL emerging as an up-and-coming solution [18]. Initially developed for mobile devices, FL ensures data privacy by allowing end users' data to remain on their devices. Rather than transmitting raw data, this approach sends only model-generated feature maps to a server, aggregating the global model. FL is versatile and capable of managing independent and identically distributed (IID) and non-IID data. This adaptability proves advantageous when dealing with assets that exhibit varying failure modes or operate under different conditions.

Still, the decision over the preference of the abovementioned two models, centralized and decentralized, is not only a matter of data security and privacy. It is also about what ML model will ensure better fraud detection. Although Recurrent Neural Networks, namely extended short-term memory networks, are widely applied to fraud detection, they also have some main drawbacks [19]. For instance, LSTMs cannot learn from long sequences seen in earlier steps due to their sequential-based nature. Choosing between the centralized and decentralized models of the use of ML in finance and asset management is complicated. Centralized systems are easier to control and safer. However, different problems, including data confidentiality and privacy, arise in data transfer.

Conversely, decentralized systems, particularly those employing FL, offer enhanced privacy and potentially more significant efficiency. As industries progressively evolve and emphasize operational reliability and safety, the balance between these two paradigms is expected to shift. It is anticipated that innovations in decentralized learning approaches will increasingly predominate, steering the future direction of technological applications in these sectors.

Traditional centralized training methods pose a significant challenge to FL, which is well addressed by the latter. In this regard, FL ensures that ML model training is conducted on local devices, after which only the accumulated updates are shared. The principle integrates the training of one ML model from datasets of various decentralized devices or servers. In this case, these devices maintain their data samples, eliminating the need to share data, and only the updates are exchanged with the central server. The server collects and aggregates these updates to develop a global model, later disseminated to each device involved in the computation. The global model is also aggregated across many other devices, after which the resultant model is used to conduct another round of localized training. Later on, the model has aggregated again, yielding a data model that has been used and accessed without sharing through the process of FL [20]. Another related study [21] mentions the rising issue regarding the privacy of data, which makes it difficult for a bank to obtain new data sources.

Furthermore, although most fraud detection systems are primarily built from scratch, some details about the models are kept proprietary to ensure the safety of the data. We now present a federated learning arrangement concentrating on banking fraud discovery as a possible solution. We propose integrating EAI techniques in the proposed FL-based framework to enhance transparency and policy, creating a more trustworthy financial system. In addition to establishing the FL platform's theoretical groundwork, we also execute it in a browser-based structure to make it usable.

3 Proposed Methodology

3.1 System Architecture

The system architecture, depicted in Fig. 1, illustrates the operational flow of the proposed FL method for fraud detection. This architecture's core point is a central server that does the training in aggregation across multiple banks. Each participating bank is a node, keeping a local Deep Neural Network (DNN) model, M_i, trained on private data. This ensures that the data stays within the institution, thereby enhancing privacy. Periodically, these nodes communicate their model updates—precisely, the parameters θ_i of M_i—to the central server. Crucially, it is the model insights represented by θ_i, and not the raw data, which are transmitted. The server then aggregates θ_i into a global model, M_{global}, using an aggregation function, $F(\theta_1, \theta_2, ..., \theta_n)$. This process refines M_{global} and leverages the collective data from entities while prioritizing the need for data security and privacy.

This client-server architecture plays a pivotal role within the FL framework. The server initiates the process by initializing the global model, M_{global}, which is initialized using randomized weights. This global model is then provided to the participating nodes $c_i \in \{c_1, c_2, c_3, ..., c_N\}$ for local training on their local data. Each node, after completing its local training, computes updates $\Delta\theta_i$ to the model parameters and sends these back to the server. The server's responsibility is to aggregate these $\Delta\theta_i$ to fine-tune M_{global}. This aggregation involves the average of the weights, represented as

$$M_{global} = \frac{1}{N} \sum_{i=1}^{N} \Delta\theta_i \tag{1}$$

where N is the number of nodes c; however, more sophisticated aggregation algorithms may enhance the model's robustness and performance.

Following aggregation, the server confirms the updated M_{global}. A validation set compares the performance to ensure it adheres to predetermined standards. The server also ensures synchronization across all nodes, maintaining that each is working with the most recent version of M_{global}. Additionally, the server manages necessary node communications, although direct client-to-client interaction is minimal in FL setups. Nodes in this FL setup are tasked with training the global model, M_{global}, received from the central server on their local datasets. This process entails conducting multiple epochs to fine-tune the FL model using data characteristics.

This process does not involve the transfer of any private local data, thereby preserving data privacy. All data-related preprocessing is conducted in-house, upholding the confidentiality of data. This method ensures the convergence of the globally shared model and tailors the model to specific detection needs. A specialized DNN model is employed to identify patterns of fraudulent activities. This method's robustness of DNNs enables more effective identification of fraudulent activities. This approach enhances the overall efficacy of the fraud detection system within the FL framework.

Moreover, this approach integrates FL with Explainable AI (XAI) to initiate a novel method of fraud detection. FL facilitates robust model training across banks without compromising data privacy, while XAI provides the interpretability of model decisions. This integration is particularly crucial when the reasoning behind a model's decisions is vital [22]. The advantages of FL are multiple. It primarily enhances data privacy and security by ensuring that private data remains private. This minimizes the risk of data breaches during transfers to centralized servers—a critical consideration given the susceptibility of cyber-attacks [23]. Additionally, FL optimizes efficient resource utilization by enabling models to train on real-time multiple sources. This capability results in a fraud detection system that is both more comprehensive and current [24].

In this framework, the mathematical representation of the global model, M_{global}, could be enhanced by including parameters θ that are updated through an aggregation function $F(\theta_1, \theta_2, ..., \theta_n)$. These parameters are optimized to perform effectively across various data distributions and provide interpretable insights, aligning with XAI principles to elucidate the decision-making process. Thus, the system predicts and explains, enhancing trust and reliability in its outputs.

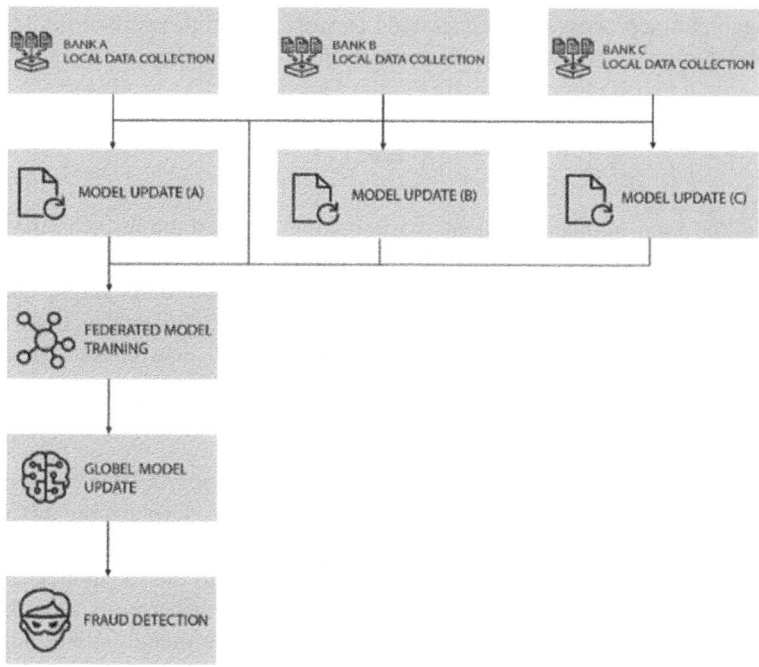

Fig. 1. Proposed federated learning architecture.

3.2   Proposed Model

The proposed method enables leveraging collective intelligence from diverse data sources while preserving the privacy of each participant's data. This approach promotes cooperative efforts among banks to combat financial fraud in a dynamic field.

In traditional centralized ML settings, an update to the model parameters using Stochastic Gradient Descent (SGD) is typically expressed as:

$$W_{k+1} = W_k - \eta \nabla L(W_k) \tag{2}$$

where:

- W_k and W_{k+1} represent the model parameters at iterations k and $k + 1$, respectively.
- η is the learning rate.
- $\nabla L(W_k)$ is the gradient of the loss function L with respect to the model parameters at iteration k.

In the context of FL, the update procedure is decentralized. Each client (e.g., a bank or financial institution) computes its update locally based on its dataset. This local update can be mathematically described as follows:

$$W_{k,c+1} = W_k - \eta \nabla L_c(W_k) \tag{3}$$

where L_c represents the local loss function computed on node c. After computing the local updates, the server combines the updates to form the new global model.

The aggregation process in the Federated Learning algorithm, proposed by McMahan et al. [23], often involves a weighted average of these local updates:

$$W_k = \frac{1}{N} \sum_{j=1}^{J} n_j W_{k,j+1} \tag{4}$$

where J is the total number of clients participating in the training, n_j is the number of data points from node c, and n is the total number of data points from all clients, $n = \sum_{j=1}^{J} n_j$. This aggregation is repeated over many epochs until the model converges. This methodology preserves data privacy by communicating only model updates (not raw data) and benefits from the localized knowledge inherent in diverse datasets. Hence, Federated Averaging provides an optimal balance between localized and centralized learning paradigms, enabling enhanced fraud detection capabilities without compromising privacy.

In the financial sector, the interpretability of ML models is crucial due to the significant real-world implications of their predictions and decisions. Explainable AI (XAI) has emerged as a critical tool to enhance transparency in complex models whose decisions were previously opaque. By integrating XAI techniques into the FL model, interested parties gain valuable insights into the model's decisions. Furthermore, identifying the importance of features assists in debugging and refining the model, addressing potential biases. A prominent XAI technique utilized for this purpose is Shapley Additive Explanations (SHAP). SHAP values offer a comprehensive understanding of feature importance and show the difference between the prediction for a particular instance and the average prediction across all the cases of each feature involved.

The calculation of SHAP values is structured as follows. For each feature j in a set of features N, the SHAP value $\phi_j(f)$ quantifies the average marginal contribution of feature j across all possible combinations of features. This is mathematically defined by:

$$\phi_j(f) = \sum_{S \subseteq N \setminus \{j\}} \frac{|S|!(|N| - |S| - 1)!}{|N|!} [f(S \cup \{j\}) - f(S)] \tag{5}$$

where N is the complete set of features, S is a subset of N excluding feature j, $f(S)$ represents the model's prediction with input features in set S, and $f(S \cup \{j\})$ represents the model's prediction with input features in set S, including feature j. This formula iteratively considers all subsets S of features that do not include j, assessing the impact of adding j to each subset. The factor $\frac{|S|!(|N|-|S|-1)!}{|N|!}$ normalizes the contributions based on the number of permutations of the features, ensuring a fair distribution of importance among all features. By applying SHAP values within the FL framework, each client can locally compute feature importances that reflect local data characteristics and the aggregated insights from the global model, enhancing both local and global understanding of the model's decision-making process.

3.3 Model Implementation

The implementation details of the proposed method are illustrated in Fig. 2. The implementation process encompasses several critical steps: conducting preliminary checks, processing data, developing the FL framework, and integrating XAI techniques. Each of these steps is crucial for ensuring the effectiveness and reliability of the proposed fraud detection system.

The dataset employed in this study is derived from reference [25], comprising realistic data modeled after a contemporary real-world dataset for fraud detection. It encompasses a total of 630,000 entries distributed across 18 distinctive features. The feature types are shown in the Fig. 3. This comprehensive dataset includes diverse data types: eighteen columns consisting of integer values, ten feature numbers, and five columns containing categorical data. This rich composition facilitates a unique analysis of fraudulent activities, providing a robust foundation for implementing and evaluating the proposed techniques. The major column characteristics are shown in Fig. 4.

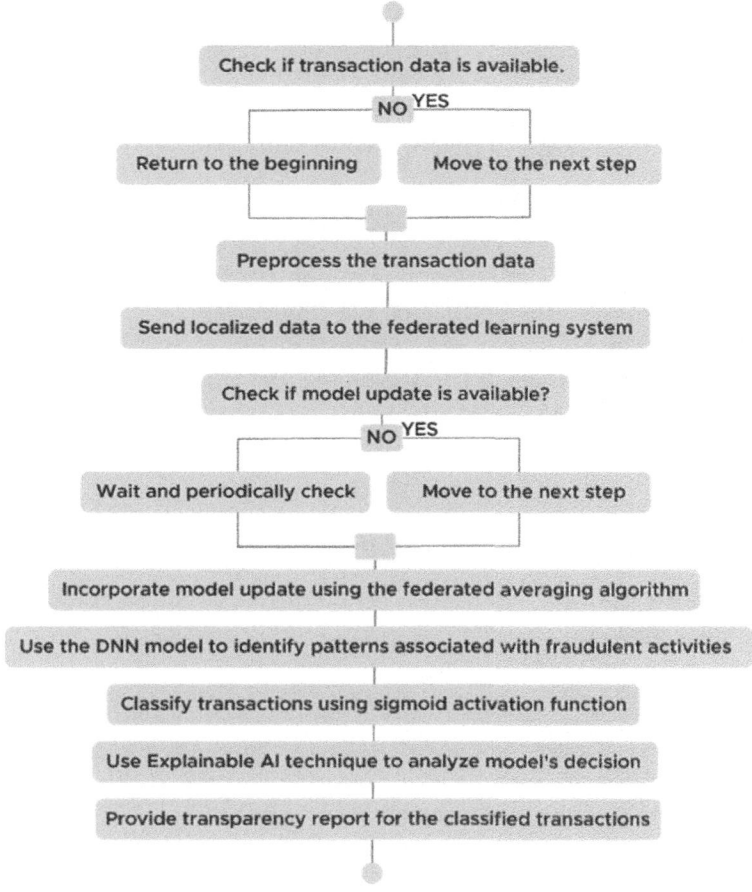

Fig. 2. Workflow of the proposed system.

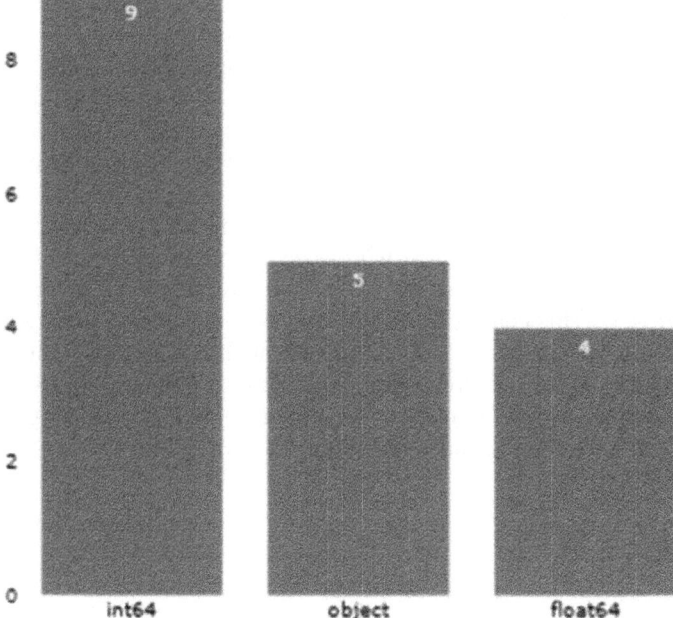

Fig. 3. Feature types from the dataset.

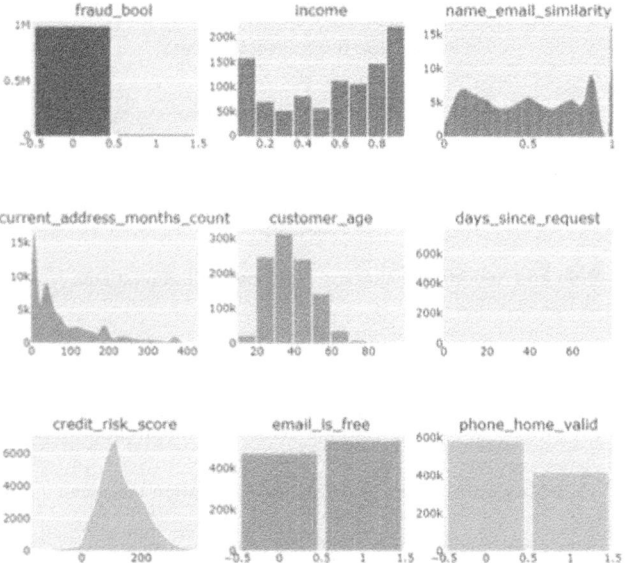

Fig. 4. Characteristics of the dataset.

3.4 Data Preprocessing

As illustrated in Fig. 5, the dataset used in this study was characterized by a significant imbalance. To address this issue, the Synthetic Minority Over-sampling Technique (SMOTE) [26] was employed. SMOTE is a widely recognized method for mitigating class imbalance within datasets by generating synthetic samples within the minority class space. This technique aims to equalize the number of samples between the majority and minority classes, thereby rectifying the imbalance in the training data and enhancing the robustness of the subsequent analytical models.

The issue of missing data management was handled according to data type. For numerical attributes, missing entries were imputed with the mean value of the respective column. Conversely, model-based imputation was utilized for categorical attributes. Outlier detection and removal were conducted for columns containing floating-point values during the data preprocessing stage. This was achieved using the Interquartile Range (IQR) method; specifically, the data points lying more than 1.5 times the IQR from Q1 or Q3 were classified as outliers and removed [27]. Subsequently, a correlation matrix was computed and visualized, as depicted in Fig. 6, to explore the relationships among the numeric attributes. This correlation was represented as a heatmap, providing the pairwise linear relationships between variables.

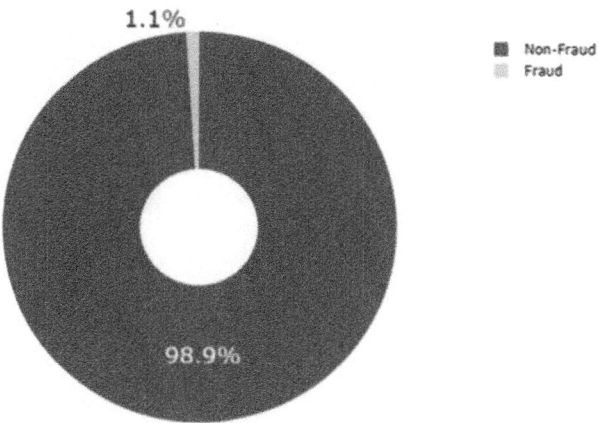

Fig. 5. Imbalanced distribution of the proposed dataset.

Feature engineering techniques were applied to improve the model's capacity to learn from the data in a structured format. The continuous variable from the income column was segmented into discrete intervals through a process known as binning. This technique transforms continuous data into bins, facilitating the model's ability to identify trends more effectively across income ranges. Specifically, the income was divided into ten discrete bins and labeled with integers [28]. Additionally, one-hot encoding was employed for categorical columns such as *housing status, employment status, payment type, device os,* and *source.* One hot encoding is a method in which variables with categorical numbers are converted into a binary format, particularly those requiring numerical input. This transformation enables the model to handle categorical data efficiently by treating each category as an independent feature.

3.5 Deep Learning Model and XAI

The DL model utilized in this study consists of a three-layer dense neural network designed for binary classification tasks. The initial layer comprises 64 neurons with a ReLU activation function, which receives its input from the feature dimensions of the validation dataset. The subsequent layer contains 32 neurons, also activated by ReLU. The final layer features a single neuron activated by a sigmoid function tailored for binary classification. The model employs the Adam optimization algorithm for weight adjustments and uses binary cross-entropy to evaluate prediction losses. Figure 6 shows the correlation metrics of the selected features.

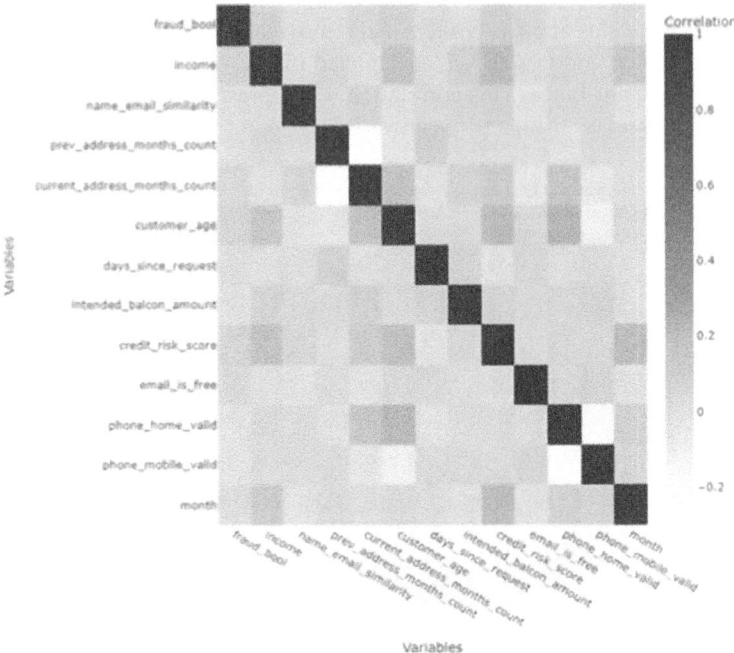

Fig. 6. Fraud dataset correlation matrix.

Data for this research was split after preprocessing, adhering to the standard practice of allocating 80% for training and 20% for testing, which ensures unbiased partitioning. The dataset was divided into three segments to integrate these datasets into the FL framework. Performance assessment of the ML model utilized a multi-pronged metric approach, applying the confusion matrix. Additional metrics included Accuracy, Precision, Recall, and F1-Score, which provides a balance between Precision and Recall, essential in addressing class imbalances. Feature importance within the model was visualized using the SHAP method, which clarifies the impact of each feature relative to a specified baseline, enhancing interpretability [24]. This setup uses modern DL frameworks, and the simulation illustrates how individual client-side models contribute to the global model's learning process. Post-training, SHAP values elucidate model decisions, enhancing their interpretability. The infrastructure was constructed using a Kaggle-based notebook. A web application framework for server-client interactions was developed using Flask and API [29], while TensorFlow supported DL operations.

4 Results and Analysis

Analyzing the performance metrics from the visual data provided in Figs. 7, 8, 9, 10, it is clear that the FL model demonstrates robust performance across several key metrics. Figure 7 shows the confusion metrics of all three models. Figure 8 illustrates that the model's accuracy increases consistently over time, reaching an impressive peak accuracy of approximately 93%.

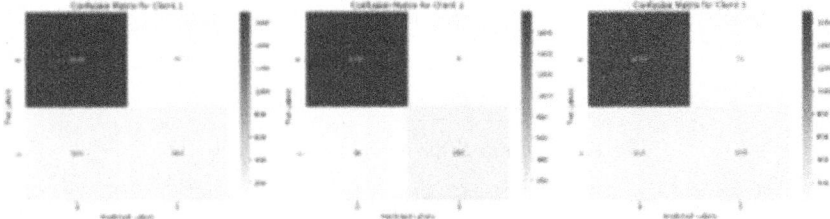

Fig. 7. The confusion metric of the proposed model.

This strong performance indicates effective model convergence and suggests that the model can correctly classify fraudulent and non-fraudulent transactions as the training progresses. Figure 8 captures the precision of the model, which increases to about 0.067. This increase, which continues linearly until approximately 40 epochs, demonstrates the model's increasing accuracy in identifying only true positive cases as fraudulent. After 40 epochs, the precision plateaus around this value, stabilizing the model's predictive accuracy regarding fraudulent transactions.

In Fig. 9, the model accuracy improves significantly, starting at approximately 0.5 and increasing to about 0.93. This improvement highlights the model's enhanced ability to detect all actual fraudulent cases, reducing the chances of false negatives. Such a high recall rate is crucial in fraud detection, ensuring fewer fraudulent activities go unnoticed. The average accuracy and accuracy of all three models, as depicted in Fig. 10, similarly show a significant upward trend from around 0.045 to about 0.12. This metric, which balances precision and recall, suggests that the model effectively harmonizes its sensitivity and specificity, providing a more balanced approach to predicting fraudulent transactions. The increase in accuracy is significant in scenarios where it is critical to maintain a balance between not missing actual fraud cases (high recall) and not mislabeling legitimate transactions as fraudulent (high precision). These metrics, derived from the FL model, underscore its capability to perform well in a real-world application like fraud detection. The high accuracy, precision, recall, and F1 score contribute to a comprehensive understanding that the model is effectively learning and adapting to the uniqueness of detecting fraudulent activities. Moreover, the FL framework enhances data privacy and security by ensuring that raw data does not leave local devices, further emphasizing the suitability of this approach for sensitive financial applications.

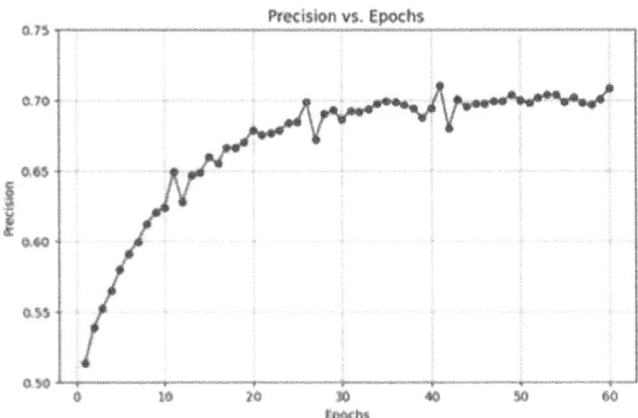

Fig. 8. Precision of the model versus epochs.

We utilized SHAP plots for model explainability, as detailed in reference [24]. In these plots, the color coding (red and blue) represents feature values' positive and negative impact on the prediction relative to the baseline value. The baseline value, the average of all model output values over the dataset, is a reference point. In the SHAP plots (Fig. 11, red indicates that a specific feature value increases the prediction value, while blue signifies a decrease. For example, in the SHAP plots, a feature value of 2.086 on the red side of the plot suggests that this feature positively impacts the FL model's prediction. The magnitude of SHAP values (the distance from the baseline) indicates the strength of a feature's influence. Higher magnitudes, positive or negative, signify a more substantial impact on the prediction. In the second SHAP plot, features with SHAP values of 2.15, 0.418, and 0.517 exhibit a more significant impact on the model prediction than features with SHAP values of 1.15 and -0.8. This analysis helps identify which features most influence the model's predictions, providing valuable insights into the model's decision-making process.

5   Conclusion

The implementation of FL for banking fraud detection has demonstrated significant potential in enhancing data privacy and model performance through decentralized model training. This approach effectively maintains data privacy while leveraging diverse insights from various data sources by enabling clients to train models on their local datasets and share only model updates with a central server. The project's architecture utilized Flask for efficient server-client communication and integrated multithreading to address potential scalability challenges. The client weights, represented as multidimensional arrays of learned neural network parameters, played a critical role in aggregating individual model insights to update the global model effectively. A key innovation in this project was the incorporation of SHAP for model interpretability. SHAP enhanced the accuracy of model predictions and provided valuable insights into the most influential features driving these predictions. This capability is particularly crucial in sensitive domains like banking, where the transparency and understandability of model decisions are as important as their accuracy. SHAP's interpretability fosters trust and ensures that the decisions made by the federated model are transparent and justifiable. This research underscores the efficacy and potential of FL in contexts where centralized data collection is impractical or undesirable due to privacy or security concerns. The decentralized approach facilitated robust model training while upholding high data privacy and security standards. This study highlights the importance of FL in developing privacy-preserving, scalable, and interpretable models for critical applications such as banking fraud detection.

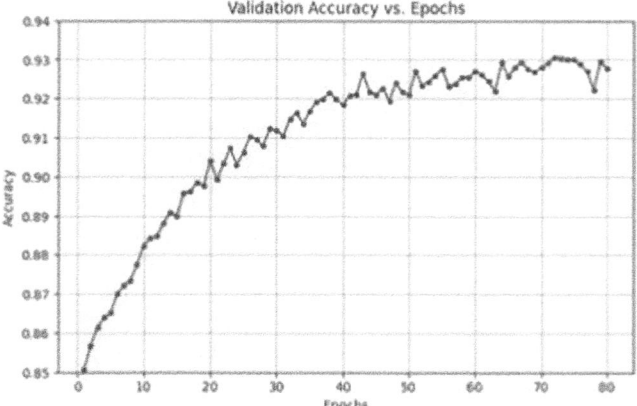

Fig. 9. Validation accuracy versus training epochs.

Future work could focus on optimizing communication efficiency and exploring advanced aggregation techniques to further enhance the performance and scalability of FL systems. Additionally, investigating the application of FL in other domains with stringent privacy requirements could broaden the impact and utility of this approach.

Fig. 10. Accuracy of all three models.

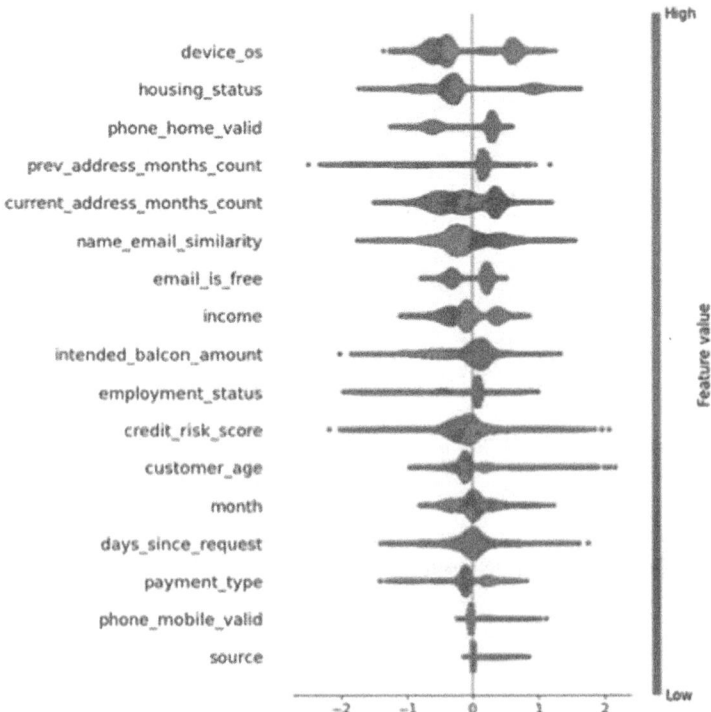

Fig. 11. Accuracy of all three models.

References

1. Smith, J., Liu, C.: Secure transactions, secure systems: regulatory compliance in internet banking. Technical report, EasyChair (2024)
2. Carminati, M., Caron, R., Maggi, F., Epifani, I., Zanero, S.: Banksealer: a decision support system for online banking fraud analysis and investigation. Comput. Secur. **53**, 175–186 (2015)
3. Dyck, A., Morse, A., Zingales, L.: How pervasive is corporate fraud? Rev. Acc. Stud. **29**(1), 736–769 (2024)
4. Abdallah, A., Maarof, M.A., Zainal, A.: Fraud detection system: a survey. J. Netw. Comput. Appl. **68**, 90–113 (2016)
5. Kumar, S.: A study of identity theft: intentions, connected frauds, methods and avoidance. ACADEMICIA: An Int. Multidisc. Res. J. **11**(10), 2044–2050 (2021)
6. Bhattacharyya, S., Jha, S., Tharakunnel, K., Westland, J.C.: Data mining for credit card fraud: a comparative study. Decision Support Syst. **50**(3), 602–613 (2011)
7. Rajesh, L.T., Das, T., Shukla, R.M., Sengupta, S.: Give and take: federated transfer learning for industrial iot network intrusion detection. In: 2023 IEEE 22nd International Conference on Trust, Security and Privacy in Computing and Communications (TrustCom), pp. 2365–2371. IEEE (2023)
8. Guan, H., Yap, P.-T., Bozoki, A., Liu, M.: Federated learning for medical image analysis: a survey. Pattern Recognit. 110424 (2024)
9. Bolton, R.J., Hand, D.J.: Statistical fraud detection: a review. Qual. Control Appl. Stat. **49**(3), 313–314 (2004)
10. Van Driel, H.: Financial fraud, scandals, and regulation: a conceptual framework and literature review. Business History (2019)
11. Trompeter, G.M., Carpenter, T.D., Desai, N., Jones, K.L., Riley, R.A.: A synthesis of fraud-related research. Auditing: A J. Pract. Theory **32**(Supplement 1), 287–321 (2013)
12. Raghavan, P., El Gayar, N.: Fraud detection using machine learning and deep learning. In: 2019 International Conference on Computational Intelligence and Knowledge Economy (ICCIKE), pp. 334–339. IEEE (2019)
13. Zareapoor, M., Shamsolmoali, P., et al.: Application of credit card fraud detection: based on bagging ensemble classifier. Procedia Comput. Sci. **48**(2015), 679–685 (2015)
14. Randhawa, K., Loo, C.K., Seera, M., Lim, C.P., Nandi, A.K.: Credit card fraud detection using adaboost and majority voting. IEEE Access **6**, 14277–14284 (2018)
15. Abhilash Sharma, M., Ganesh Raj, B.R., Ramamurthy, B., Hari Bhaskar, R.: Credit card fraud detection using deep learning based on auto-encoder. In: ITM Web of Conferences, vol. 50, p. 01001. EDP Sciences (2022)
16. Pumsirirat, A., Liu, Y.: Credit card fraud detection using deep learning based on auto-encoder and restricted Boltzmann machine. Int. J. Adv. Comput. Sci. Appl. **9**(1) (2018)
17. Kamei, S., Taghipour, S.: A comparison study of centralized and decentralized federated learning approaches utilizing the transformer architecture for estimating remaining useful life. Reliab. Eng. Syst. Saf. **233**, 109130 (2023)
18. McMahan, B., Moore, E., Ramage, D., Hampson, S., y Arcas, B.A.: Communication-efficient learning of deep networks from decentralized data. In: Artificial Intelligence and Statistics, pp. 1273–1282. PMLR (2017)
19. Benchaji, I., Douzi, S., El Ouahidi, B.: Credit card fraud detection model based on lstm recurrent neural networks. J. Adv. Inf. Technol. **12**(2) (2021)
20. Bharati, S., Mondal, M., Podder, P., Prasath, V.B.: Federated learning: applications, challenges and future directions. Int. J. Hybrid Intell. Syst. **18**(1–2), 19–35 (2022)

21. Yang, W., Zhang, Y., Ye, K., Li, L., Xu, C.-Z.: Ffd: a federated learning based method for credit card fraud detection. In: Big Data– BigData 2019: 8th International Congress, Held as Part of the Services Conference Federation, SCF 2019, San Diego, CA, USA, June 25–30, 2019, Proceedings 8, pp. 18–32. Springer (2019)
22. Doshi-Velez, F., Kim, B.: Towards a rigorous science of interpretable machine learning. arXiv preprint arXiv:1702.08608 (2017)
23. Bonawitz, K., Eichner, H., Grieskamp, W., Huba, D., Ingerman, A., Ivanov, V., Kiddon, C., Kone˘cny`, J., Mazzocchi, S., McMahan, B., et al.: Towards federated learning at scale: system design. In: Proceedings of Machine Learning and Systems, vol. 1, pp. 374–388 (2019)
24. Yang, Q., Liu, Y., Chen, T., Tong, Y.: Federated machine learning: concept and applications. ACM Trans. Intell. Syst. Technol. (TIST) **10**(2), 1–19 (2019)
25. Huang, H., Liu, B., Xue, X., Cao, J., Chen, X.: Imbalanced credit card fraud detection data: a solution based on hybrid neural network and clustering-based undersampling technique. Appl. Soft Comput. **154**, 111368 (2024)
26. Elreedy, D., Atiya, A.F., Kamalov, F.: A theoretical distribution analysis of synthetic minority oversampling technique (smote) for imbalanced learning. Machine Learn. **113**(7), 4903–4923 (2024)
27. Abdiweli, A.J.: Simulation study on the performance of robust outlier labelling methods. PhD thesis, Kampala International University, College of Economics and management (2023)
28. Wan, X., Wang, W., Liu, J., Tong, T.: Estimating the sample mean and standard deviation from the sample size, median, range and/or interquartile range. BMC Med. Res. Methodol. **14**, 1–13 (2014)
29. Jain, A.N., Dhanawat, V., Sukjunnimit, P.: Application programming interface endpoint analysis and modification, December 31 2019. US Patent 10,521,246

Enhancing Generative AI Chatbot Accuracy Using Knowledge Graph

Ajay Bandi[1]([⊠]), Jameer Babu[1], Ruida Zeng[2], and Sai Ram Muthyala[1]

[1] School of Computer Science and Information Systems, Northwest Missouri State University, 800 University Dr, Maryville, MO 64468, USA
ajay@nwmissouri.edu
[2] Department of Computer Science, Brown University, Providence, RI 02912, USA

Abstract. In recent years, generative AI chatbots have significantly improved in their ability to simulate human-like conversations. However, ensuring the accuracy and contextual relevance of their responses remains a challenge. This paper presents an innovative approach to enhancing the accuracy of generative AI chatbots by integrating knowledge graphs using Neo4j. We demonstrate how combining structured data from Knowledge Graphs with advanced large language models can result in more accurate and context-aware chatbot interactions. By implementing this approach, we aim to provide a robust framework for developing intelligent chatbots that can deliver precise and contextually appropriate responses. We created three categories of test cases: Data-Relevant Inquiries, Non-Contextual Queries, and Contextually Relevant but Data-Irrelevant Questions. The accuracy obtained for the data-relevant test cases was 91.44%.

Keywords: Retrieval and Augmented Generation (RAG) · Large Language Model (LLM) · Knowledge graphs · Chatbot · Generative AI · Word embeddings · Vector index · Cypher · Similarity search · Neo4j

1 Introduction

Generative AI refers to artificial intelligence systems that can create new content or data. Unlike traditional AI models, which primarily classify or predict outcomes based on existing data, generative AI models can generate text, images, music, and even complex designs from scratch [1]. Most generative AI models are built using deep learning techniques, particularly neural networks like Generative Adversarial Networks (GANs), Variational Autoencoders (VAEs), and Transformers.

A chatbot is a software application designed to simulate human conversation through text or voice interactions [6, 22]. Chatbots can be rule-based, following predefined scripts, or more advanced AI-powered, utilizing AI to understand and respond to user inputs dynamically. Rule-based chatbots operate based on a set of predefined rules. They can handle simple queries but struggle with more complex conversations. Whereas, AI-powered chatbots use natural language processing (NLP) and machine learning to understand and respond to user inputs more agility. They can learn from interactions

W. Feng et al. (Eds.): SEDE 2024, CCIS 2244, pp. 157–167, 2024.
https://doi.org/10.1007/978-3-031-75201-8_11

and improve over time [7]. Customer support, personal assistants, and e-commerce are a few applications.

Rule-based chatbots provide responses based on a fixed set of predefined options, typically using if-then logic or decision trees. They struggle with limited flexibility. Whereas, Generative AI chatbots use machine learning models, such as GPT (Generative Pre-trained Transformer), to generate responses on the fly. They understand context [26] and generate natural language responses providing high flexibility. Rule-based chatbots rely on keyword matching and pattern recognition to understand [26] user input. They lack awareness over complex phrasings and their interactions look artificial [2]. Generative AI chatbots use advanced NLP techniques to understand and interpret user input. They interact in a natural and coherent way. The knowledge and capabilities of rule-based chatbots are fixed and must be manually updated. They do not learn from interactions. They cannot improve their performance over time without human intervention. Any updates or improvements require reprogramming. Generative AI chatbots can learn from new data and interactions. They can be fine-tuned and updated with new information, improving their performance and accuracy. They can adapt to new types of queries and improve their responses based on user feedback and additional training data. One such adaptation is Retrieval Augmented Generation (RAG) [6]. RAG is an advanced NLP technique that combines the strengths of retrieval-based and generative models. It improves the accuracy and contextual relevance of generated responses by incorporating external knowledge through a retrieval component. RAG offers numerous advantages, including enhanced accuracy, better contextual understanding, scalability, flexibility, reduced hallucination, and efficient information retrieval [7]. These benefits make RAG a powerful tool for various applications, such as customer support, research assistance, content creation, and question-answering systems.

In this paper, we aimed to improve the accuracy by creating three different test categories namely three different test categories namely: *Data-Relevant*, which focuses on known data; *Non-Contextual*, which deals with out-of-context data; and *Contextually Relevant but Data-Irrelevant*, based on contextual data but previously not encountered by the chatbot. The remainder of the paper is organized as follows. Section 2 describes related work on chatbots, RAG, and knowledge graphs. Section 3 discusses the implementation of the chatbot, detailing the tools, technologies, and steps involved. Section 4 presents the results and evaluation. Section 5 provides research conclusions.

2 Related Work

Bandi and Kagitha in their article [2] presented the different phases of generative AI project life cycle with the implementation of chatbot using generative AI LLMs. While we used those different phases of generative AI project, we observed that there are limitations in the evaluating the responses of the chatbot. They have tested only on the contextually relevant data and their test cases are completely based on the trained data able to get one hundred percent accurate results. The same article did not address if the prompts are not relevant to the trained data and the results for such prompts from the chatbot can't be predicted.

LLMs are empowered with Retrieval Augmented Generation (RAG) [4] in enabling them to deliver correct and contextual answers. Particularly in the space of open-domain question answering [5], educational question-answering system [9], adaptable AI assistant for network management [15], medical consultation chatbot [3, 17]. RAG model has its own applications, methodologies and their effectiveness, techniques and challenges [6, 7]. LLMs utilising RAG have a proven ability in extracting relations from the text and corresponding models were proven effective [8].

These RAG enabled Chatbots when enhanced with Knowledge-Graphs [10, 18, 20] can improve customer service question answering [11]. LLMs are capable of performing generative graph analytics, focusing on query processing, learning [12]. Mainly, Also there are other approaches such as hybrid context retrieval-augmented generation, that combines knowledge graphs and vector databases [13], graph-based retrieval-augmented generation approach for query-focused summarization [16].

There is an inadvertent need to integrate large language models with vector databases [14]. Neo4j [24, 25] comes with the combination of Knowledge graphs and Vector indices [19]. These vector indices are built based on word embeddings [21].

Our research focuses on increasing the accuracy of Chatbot by implementing a Knowledge-Graph enabled RAG combined with vector indices by considering all the types of data such as relevant, irrelevant, contextually relevant but data irrelevant. We developed a chatbot for the MSACS program at Northwest Missouri State University, which constructs knowledge graphs and vector indices using data available on NWMSU websites related to courses, professors, schedules, and more. This chatbot utilizes RAG to provide responses to student prompts or queries.

3   Chatbot Implementation

This section presents the details of the chatbot implementation. We developed a chatbot for prospective students of the Master of Science in Applied Computer Science (MSACS) program. This AI-powered chatbot assists prospective and current students in obtaining information using the following tools and technologies.

3.1   Tools and Technologies

- **Python**: The primary programming language used to develop the chatbot
- **Neo4j**: A graph database that aids in constructing and managing the knowledge graph, with efficient storage and retrieval of entities and relationships within the MSACS program data.
- **LangChain**: LangChain is an open-source framework designed to aid developers in creating applications that utilize large language models (LLMs) for natural language processing (NLP). It offers a variety of tools, components, and interfaces that streamline the development process and facilitate the integration of language models with external data sources such as Neo4j.
- **OpenAI GPT-3.5-Turbo-0125 LLM**: OpenAI GPT-3.5-Turbo-0125 is an advanced version of the GPT-3 model, designed to be faster and more efficient. The "0125" indicates specific enhancements and adjustments in this version. It can handle a variety of language-related tasks, such as generating text, translating languages, summarizing content, and question-answering chats.
- **Tiktoken**: Library used for tokenizing the text.

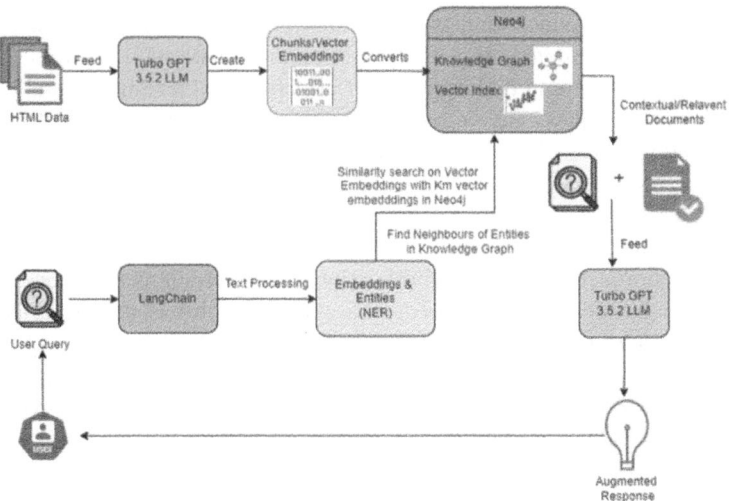

Fig. 1. Architecture of chatbot

3.2 Methodology

This section details the different steps in implementing the MSACS chatbot. Figure 1 represents the high-level architecture of the chatbot, illustrating how different components interact and integrate with each other, providing an easier understanding of the overall system layout and data flow. We implemented our chatbot by adopting practical guide to constructing and retrieving information from knowledge graphs in RAG applications with Neo4j and LangChain by Tomaz Bratanic [26]. Figure 2 shows the sequence diagram, which demonstrates the dynamic behavior of the system with different actors, visualizing interactions between components and representing the system behavior over time. All the files related to the implementation of the paper are provided in the GitHub repo.[1]

1. Extract data from the Html pages: Using data from MSACS websites, WebBase Loaders of *LangChain* fetch and load the content of multiple web pages. This content is stored in a buffer for further processing.
2. Split the data into chunks: Tokenizing data is essential for effectively leveraging large language models. It transforms raw text into a structured and standardized format that the model can process efficiently. By capturing semantic meaning, reducing complexity, and enabling efficient computation, tokenization plays a fundamental role in the performance and capabilities of LLMs. Using *TikToken*, the buffered data is split into chunks of 512 tokens with an overlap of 24 tokens. The overlap ensures that contextual relevance is maintained across the tokenized data. This step facilitates breaking down the content into more digestible parts while preserving context.

---

[1] https://github.com/bandiajay/Enhancing-Generative-AI-Chatbot-Accuracy-Using-Knowledge-Graph.

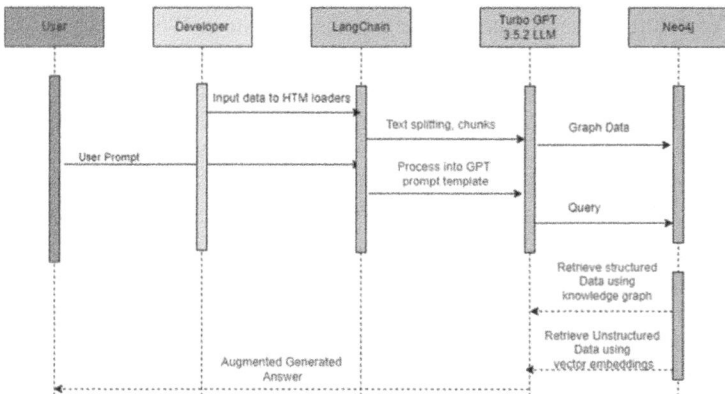

Fig. 2. Interactions of chatbot's components in sequence diagram

3. Transform the Data into Knowledge Graphs Using LLMs and Store in Neo4j Database: We use the *gpt-3.5-turbo-0125* LLM to implement the chatbot. By controlling the randomness of the model's responses, ensuring deterministic and consistent outputs. The tokenized data from the previous step is transformed into a graph-based format, known as a *Knowledge Graph*, as shown in Fig. 3. This aids in advanced document analysis, enhanced querying of textual data, and knowledge extraction using a graph transformer called *LLM- GraphTransformer*. The nodes in the graph contain primary entity information, and the original source of each document is retained within the graph, enhancing traceability and context preservation. This transformation is crucial for complex document analysis tasks, enabling more sophisticated knowledge extraction and representation. The entire pipeline—from loading and splitting documents to transforming them into graph documents—is designed to enhance the processing and analysis capabilities of textual data.

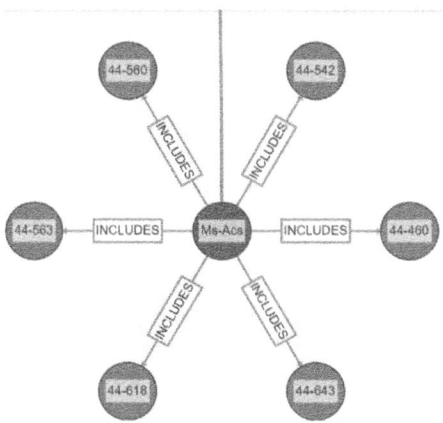

Fig. 3. Knowledge Graph of MSACS program courses

4 Create Vector Indices on Knowledge Graphs and Store Word Embed- dings: Vector indices enable rapid and scalable search and retrieval operations, and they help manage high-dimensional data, optimizing performance and enabling sophisticated data-driven solutions. A vector index is created from the existing graph developed in the previous step. OpenAI's embedding model is used to convert the data into vector representations. The search types are hybrid, effectively using both vector-based search methods like cosine similarity and traditional search methods. Full-text indices in Neo4j are also utilized for efficient text searches, enhancing query performance and enabling advanced search capabilities.

5. Give a Prompt: A prompt is provided, which may or may not be related to the extracted data. The LLM should respond with contextual knowledge derived from the previously developed knowledge graphs.

6. Retrieve Structured Context from Neo4j Using Knowledge Graphs: The structured retriever operates on the knowledge graph, extracting specific entities such as courses, professors, requirements, and projects using prompt-based entity extraction. For each extracted entity, it constructs a full-text search query and retrieves relevant nodes and their relationships from the Neo4j graph database, including both outgoing and incoming relationships. The results are formatted into a structured output.

7. Retrieve Unstructured Context from Neo4j Using Similarity Search on Vector Embeddings: The unstructured retriever performs a similarity search on the vector indices using the prompt. This search aims to provide flexible, content-based retrieval without focusing on predefined entity types or relationships.

8. Augment Both Contexts and Provide to LLM: The structured and unstructured retrievers extract and query entities related to the user's prompt, collecting their neighborhood in the graph database to create a single context. This augmented context is then passed to the LLM.

9. Get the Response from LLM: A template is created with the user's question and the RAG's context, forming a coherent prompt. The LLM then responds to this prompt.

4   Results and Evaluation

The chatbot's accuracy is evaluated based on the following three categories of test cases:

1. **Data-Relevant Inquiries**: These are questions directly related to the specific data provided. The chatbot needs to accurately retrieve and respond to queries based on the information it has been trained on or has access to within the dataset.
   Example: "Is a score of 105 in Duolingo sufficient for admission?" This question requires the chatbot to reference the admissions criteria data for Duolingo scores.

2. **Non-Contextual Queries**: These are questions that are not related to the context of the data provided. Such queries are outside the scope of the chatbot's intended knowledge base, and it should ideally recognize these and handle them appropriately, potentially by stating that the information is not available.
   Example: "Does the sun rise in the east?" This question is a general knowledge inquiry and not relevant to the specific dataset or context the chatbot is designed to address.

3. **Contextually Relevant but Data-Irrelevant Questions**: These questions are within the broader context, but are not specifically covered by the data the chatbot has. The chatbot should be able to recognize the context and acknowledge the relevance, yet correctly indicate that the specific data point is not available.

   Example: "How long does it take to commute from campus to downtown during rush hour?" This question is relevant to someone considering the practical aspects of attending the institution, but it falls outside the scope of the chatbot's knowledge on admissions criteria. The chatbot should acknowledge the relevance of commuting concerns, but state that it doesn't have specific data regarding commuting times.

By organizing the test cases in this way, we can thoroughly assess how well the chatbot handles different types of questions. This helps us gauge its strength in understanding and responding appropriately across various contexts. We've prepared a set of 1000 test cases using generative AI based on the following prompt. The test cases are designed to mimic the types of prompts the chatbot would encounter in real-life scenarios. To create a balanced dataset, we included an equal mix of 50% true prompts and 50% false prompts. The goal of using true/false format questions is to construct a confusion matrix. After inputting these prompts into the chatbot, we manually review the results to classify them as true positives (TP), false positives (FP), true negatives (TN), or false negatives (FN). This manual validation allows us to accurately calculate the confusion matrix values.

Precision:

$$P = \frac{TP}{TP + FP}$$

Accuracy:

$$Acc = \frac{TP + TN}{TP + TN + FP + FN}$$

Recall:

$$R = \frac{TP}{TP + FN}$$

Using the website URLs from the MSACS website, generate 1000 test cases, with nearly 330 each in all three categories such that the test case is similar to the prompt and the answer is always either True or False. 1. Questions relevant to the above data 2. Questions that are not in context to the data 3. Questions that are in context, but not related to the above data.

Each of these categories represents different types of questions the chatbot may encounter in real-world scenarios. To evaluate its performance, we used metrics such as precision, accuracy, and recall, which are crucial for assessing how effectively the chatbot handles various contexts. Table 1 presents the confusion matrix, which shows the number of true positives, false positives, true negatives, and false negatives for each category of test cases. Table 2 provides the final precision, accuracy, and recall values for all three categories of test cases.

In the Data-Relevant Inquiries group, the chatbot excelled with a precision of 95.33%, an accuracy of 91.45%, and a recall of 91.48%. These impressive metrics highlight the chatbot's effectiveness in dealing with straightforward questions directly related to the provided data. The high precision means that the chatbot's responses are mostly relevant and accurate, ensuring users get the correct information. The high recall indicates that the chatbot successfully retrieves a significant portion of relevant information, demonstrating its thoroughness. The accuracy score reflects the overall correctness of the chatbot's responses in this category, showing its reliability when answering data-specific questions.

By categorizing the test cases this way, we can comprehensively evaluate the chatbot's ability to understand and respond accurately across different types of inquiries. This approach helps us measure its robustness and contextual understanding in a variety of scenarios. We prepared a total of 1000 test cases using these criteria to ensure a thorough assessment. The Non-Contextual Queries group posed a significant challenge for the chatbot. While the precision was notably high at 98.92%, indicating that the chatbot correctly identified irrelevant queries with great accuracy, the recall dropped significantly to 54.12%. This means that the chatbot failed to identify nearly half of the irrelevant instances, missing a substantial number of them. This insight suggests that while the chatbot broadly classified positive and negative irrelevant queries correctly, it struggled to catch all irrelevant queries. The overall accuracy was 76.76%, showing that the chatbot could correctly identify a substantial proportion of instances, but still missed a significant number of relevant responses. This discrepancy indicates that although the chatbot performed well in recognizing true positives (correctly identifying irrelevant queries), it had difficulty in identifying all irrelevant responses, especially when the context of the queries did not match the available data. This performance gap highlights the need for improvements in the chatbot's ability to understand and classify non-contextual queries, ensuring it can better distinguish between relevant and irrelevant questions in various contexts.

Table 1. Confusion Matrix

	Predicted					
	Category I		Category II		Category III	
Actual positive	204 (TP)	19 (FN)	92 (TP)	78 (FN)	82 (TP)	141 (FN)
Actual negative	10 (FP)	106 (TN)	1 (FP)	169 (TN)	4 (FP)	104 (TN)

In the Contextually Relevant but Data-Irrelevant Questions group, the chatbot faced moderate difficulty. The main reason for it is *Hallucination*. **Hallucination** in the context of language models refers to the generation of text that is plausible-sounding but factually incorrect or nonsensical. GPT-3.5-Turbo-0125, like other large language models, can sometimes produce information that is fabricated or not grounded in its training data. It achieved a precision of 95.35%, indicating that when the chatbot made a prediction, it was highly likely to be correct. However, the recall dropped significantly to 36.77%, revealing that a large number of relevant responses were not retrieved by the chatbot. The overall accuracy was relatively low at 56.19%, suggesting that many of the chatbot's predictions

Table 2. Performance metrics for different categories of test cases

	Data-relevant	Non-contextual	Contextually relevant but data-irrelevant	Overall
Precision	95.327	98.93	95.348	97.512
Accuracy	91.445	76.76	56.193	75.698
Recall	91.479	54.12	36.771	61.583

were incorrect when considered in total. These performance metrics reflect the inherent challenge of dealing with questions that are contextually relevant but lack specific data within the chatbot's training set. This situation hampers the chatbot's ability to provide accurate and comprehensive responses. The lower recall and accuracy in this category underscore the difficulty the chatbot encounters when it needs to navigate incomplete or missing contextual data. This highlights the need for the chatbot to improve its ability to recognize and handle questions that are relevant to the context but fall outside the scope of its available data, ensuring it can better serve users with accurate information even when specific details are not directly available.

Overall, the chatbot's performance across all test cases was quite strong. For the data-relevant inquiries, an average precision of 95.32%, accuracy of 91.44%, and recall of 91.49%. These numbers show that the chatbot is performance is good at identifying relevant information when it's there, meaning its answers are generally reliable. However, there's room for improvement, especially in how it handles tricky questions. For instance, when it comes to Non-Contextual Queries and Contextually Relevant but Data-Irrelevant questions, the chatbot's recall is much lower. This means it often misses relevant information in these harder scenarios, even though it does well when it does make a prediction. The high precision shows that the chatbot's responses are accurate when it decides to answer, but the lower recall indicates it doesn't always catch everything it should. To make the chatbot even better, we need to focus on helping it deal with questions that are outside its usual scope or where the context is not clear. Moving forward, we should work on enhancing the chatbot's ability to understand and respond to a wider range of questions, particularly those that are more complex or less directly related to its data. This will help improve its recall and overall accuracy, making it more effective and reliable for users in all kinds of situations.

5   Conclusion

In conclusion, our methodology demonstrated significant progress in addressing the common limitations of LLMs, such as hallucinations, while retaining the benefits of a Graph-RAG. The chatbot performed well with data-relevant queries, showing a strong precision of precision of 95.32%, accuracy of 91.44%, and recall of 91.49%. However, it faced challenges with non-contextual queries and those that were contextually relevant but data-irrelevant, as evidenced by a lower recall of 61.58%. Improving the chatbot's ability to understand and manage context will be crucial for enhancing its performance in these more complex scenarios. By refining the algorithms to better handle these types of queries, we can boost both recall and overall accuracy, making the chatbot more effective and reliable. Our research establishes a promising framework for developing intelligent chatbots that leverage the strengths of Generative AI and Knowledge Graphs. This combination paves the way for creating more accurate, efficient, and reliable AI-driven communication tools. Such advancements have broad applications across various fields, including education and customer service, promising to revolutionize how we interact with AI in many aspects of our daily lives.

References

1. Bandi, A., Adapa, P.V.S.R., Kuchi, Y.E.V.P.K.: The power of generative AI: a review of requirements, models, input–output formats, evaluation metrics, and challenges. Future Internet **15**(8), 260 (2023)
2. Bandi, A., Kagitha, H.: A case study on the generative AI project life cycle using large language models. In: Proceedings of 39th International Conlererence, vol. 98, pp. 189–199 (2024)
3. Naseem, U., Bandi, A., Raza, S., Rashid, J., Chakravarthi, B.R.: Incorporating medical knowledge to transformer-based language models for medical dialogue generation. In: Proceedings of the 21st Workshop on Biomedical Language Processing, pp. 110–115 (2022)
4. Lewis, P., Perez, E., Piktus, A., Petroni, F., Karpukhin, V., Goyal, N., Ku¨ttler, H., Lewis, M., Yih, W.T., Rockt¨aschel, T.: Retrieval-augmented generation for knowledge-intensive NLP tasks. Adv. Neural Inf. Process. Syst. **33**, 9459–9474 (2020)
5. Siriwardhana, S., Weerasekera, R., Wen, E., Kaluarachchi, T., Rana, R., Nanayakkara, S.: Improving the domain adaptation of retrieval augmented generation (RAG) models for open domain question answering. Trans. Assoc. Comput. Linguistics **11**, 1–17. MIT Press (2023)
6. Zhao, P., Zhang, H., Yu, Q., Wang, Z., Geng, Y., Fu, F., Yang, L., Zhang, W., Cui, B.: Retrieval-augmented generation for AI-generated content: a survey. arXiv preprint arXiv:2402.19473 (2024)
7. Gao, Y., Xiong, Y., Gao, X., Jia, K., Pan, J., Bi, Y., Dai, Y., Sun, J., Wang, H.: Retrieval-augmented generation for large language models: a survey. arXiv preprint arXiv:2312.10997 (2023)
8. Efeoglu, S., Paschke, A.: Retrieval-augmented generation-based relation extraction. arXiv preprint arXiv:2404.13397 (2024)
9. Bui, T., Tran, O., Nguyen, P., Ho, B., Nguyen, L., Bui, T., Quan, T.: Cross-data knowledge graph construction for llm-enabled educational question-answering system: a case study at HCMUT. arXiv preprint arXiv:2404.09296 (2024)
10. Pan, J.Z., Razniewski, S., Kalo, J.C., Singhania, S., Chen, J., Dietze, S., Jabeen, H., Omeliya-nenko, J., Zhang, W., Lissandrini, M., et al.: Large language models and knowledge graphs: opportunities and challenges. arXiv preprint arXiv:2308.06374 (2023)
11. Xu, Z., Cruz, M.J., Guevara, M., Wang, T., Deshpande, M., Wang, X., Li, Z.: Retrieval-augmented generation with knowledge graphs for customer service question answering. arXiv preprint arXiv:2404.17723 (2024)
12. Shang, W., Huang, X.: A survey of large language models on generative graph analytics: query, learning, and applications. arXiv preprint arXiv:2404.14809 (2024)
13. Edwards, C.: Hybrid context retrieval augmented generation pipeline: LLM-augmented knowledge graphs and vector database for accreditation reporting assistance. arXiv preprint arXiv:2405.15436 (2024)

14. Jing, Z., Su, Y., Han, Y., Yuan, B., Liu, C., Xu, H., Chen, K.: When large language models meet vector databases: a survey. arXiv preprint arXiv:2402.01763 (2024)
15. Abane, A., Battou, A., Merzouki, M.: An adaptable AI assistant for network management. In: IEEE/IFIP Network Operations and Management Symposium. Seoul, KR (2024)
16. Edge, D., Trinh, H., Cheng, N., Bradley, J., Chao, A., Mody, A., Truitt, S., Larson, J.: From local to global: a graph RAG approach to query-focused summarization. arXiv preprint arXiv: 2404.16130 (2024)
17. Ni, P., Okhrati, R., Guan, S., Chang, V.: Knowledge graph and deep learning-based text-to-GraphQL model for intelligent medical consultation chatbot. Inf. Syst. Front. **26**(1), 137–156. Springer (2024)
18. Barrasa, J., Webber, J.: Building Knowledge Graphs. Inc, O'Reilly Media (2023)
19. Hodler, A.E., Needham, M.: Graph data science using Neo4j. In: Massive Graph Analytics, pp. 433–457. Chapman and Hall/CRC (2022)
20. Tamaˇsauskaiteˋ, G., Groth, P.: Defining a knowledge graph development process through a systematic review. ACM Trans. Softw. Eng. Methodol. **32**(1), 1–40. ACM (2023)
21. Galke, L., Saleh, A., Scherp, A.: Word embeddings for practical in- formation retrieval. In: Informatik 2017, pp. 2155–2167. Gesellschaft fu¨r Informatik (2017)
22. Kong, X., Wang, G., Nichol, A.: Conversational AI with Rasa: build, test, and deploy AI-powered, enterprise-grade virtual assistants and chatbots. Packt Publishing Ltd. (2021)
23. Palmonari, M., De Paoli, F.: Enabling data enrichment pipelines for AI-driven business products and services
24. Wita, R., Bubphachuen, K., Chawachat, J.: Content-based filtering recommendation in abstract search using neo4j. In: 2017 21st International Computer Science and Engineering Conference (ICSEC), pp. 1–5. IEEE (2017)
25. Mathew, A.B., Kumar, S.M.: An efficient index based query handling model for neo4j. IJCST **3**(2), 12–18. Citeseer (2014)
26. Bratanic, T.: Enhancing the accuracy of RAG applications with knowledge graphs. Medium (2024). https://medium.com/neo4j/enhancing-the-accuracy-of-rag-applications-with-knowledge-graphs-ad5e2ffab663

ReVisE: Emulated Visual Outfit Generation from User Reviews Using Generative-AI

Samar Rahimi Rosas[1]($\boxtimes$), Subash Neupane[2], Shaswata Mitra[2], and Sudip Mittal[2]

[1] The Mississippi School for Mathematics and Science, Columbus, MS, USA
`rahimirosass25@themsms.org`
[2] Department of Computer Science and Engineering, Mississippi State University, Starkville, MS, USA
`{sn922,sm3843}@msstate.edu, mittal@cse.mstate.edu`

Abstract. The fashion industry faces significant challenges due to overproduction and waste, often driven by uncertainty about consumer preferences. This paper presents ReVisE, a novel framework leveraging generative AI to address this issue by emulating outfit generation from user reviews. ReVisE combines a text-to-text Large Language Model (LLM) and a text-to-image Stable Diffusion (SD) model to create virtual outfits based on customer feedback. The LLM consolidates user reviews to extract desired improvements and feedback, and the SD model utilizes these insights to produce realistic visual representations of the improved product. Our framework allows designers to evaluate potential designs and identify areas for improvement without physically producing multiple prototypes, thereby reducing waste and accelerating the design process. Experimental results conducted on the Amazon fashion item reviews demonstrate the effectiveness of ReVisE, showing promising results with both multimodal and human evaluations.

Keywords: Outfit generation · Generative AI · LLM · Text-to-Text · Text-to-Image · Stable diffusion

1 Introduction

Fashion has continuously evolved over the centuries, reflecting changes in society, culture, and technology. Enriching customer experience has been the main driving force behind this development. However, the fashion industry faces extreme sustainability challenges due to issues of overproduction and waste. This is due to the constant changes in popular fashion trends, with producers not confident about the wants of consumers while designing their products. Hence, designers at clothing companies tend to quickly move from one fashion trend to another to acquire customer feedback while experimenting with their designs [1]. They are also unable to predict potential future trends, causing them to conduct trials with multiple trends and quickly jump from one design to another [2]. In order to obtain a directed approach, designers identify areas for improvement through customer feedback and try to address them in new designs. While addressing the feedback and creating new products, designers produce multiple variations of experimental copies to identify the most suitable ones. However, this manual trial-and-error design selection process often leads to waste in clothing, costs, and time [3]. Utilization of generative AI in the fashion industry can help address these issues and increase productivity and profitability through emulated outfit generation from customer reviews. Therefore, with emulated trials, designers can finalize the selected design and only produce a limited physical sample for further tests that require physical products such as fabric quality, etc.

Successfully addressing this problem requires a profound understanding of user interest, compatibility, and fashion sense. Hence, the problem consists of two main components: consolidating unstructured user reviews in natural language and generating relevant images addressing the consolidated review context and critical details. To address this, we developed a novel framework ReVisE consisting of two generative AI components: a natural language (Large Language Model (LLM)) and an image generation model (Stable Diffusion). Our framework differs significantly from other state-of-the-art approaches for outfit generation, such as those proposed by Forouzandehmehr et al. [4], Nakamura et al. [5], Bettaney et al. [6], and Xu et al. [7] (see Sect. 2.2 for details). Unlike these methods, our approach uniquely incorporates user reviews.

LLMs can consolidate reviews of a clothing item to produce a brief description of the specific qualities that customers desire in the product. This description can then be used by Stable Diffusion (SD) models to generate multiple derivative images of the sought-after product. This will allow fashion designers to obtain numerous realistic visual impressions without actually implementing the design and identify improvement scopes in their designs and obtain inspiration while creating new fashion pieces. The final approved design will be tailored to the audience, reducing the overproduction of trial designs. Furthermore, prompts and images generated from consumer preferences will help fashion designers optimize their designs to meet customer requirements. This data-driven approach will empower designers to streamline the design process and maximize fashion production. By leveraging generative AI capabilities, fashion industries can capitalize on emerging trends and make rapid decisions to ensure long-term success and sustainability.

We can formally define our problem statement and solution framework in the following. Let, $o_c \in \mathcal{O}|c_0^k$ be a fashion object in universal fashion item set $\mathcal{O}$. $r \in \mathcal{R}_{oc}$ represents a review of o_c and $\mathcal{I}$ denote all suggested improvements for o_c. Given $(\mathcal{R}_{oc})$, ReVisE is expected to generate a list of compatible fashion objects $\mathcal{O}_d \in \mathcal{O}|d_0^l$ that adhere to the suggested improvements $\mathcal{I}$, extracted from $\mathcal{R}_{oc}$. Hence, the ReVisE can be defined as:

$$\mathcal{O}_d = \theta(\mathcal{I}) \| \mathcal{I} = \lambda(\mathcal{R}_{oc}) \tag{1}$$

where λ is the language model and θ is the image generation model. The main contributions of this paper are as follows:

- We demonstrate the feasibility of generating virtual images of fashion apparels addressing the improvement areas identified from natural language reviews.
- We develop a robust outfit generation framework that combines a text-to-text Large Language Model (LLM) and a text-to-image model (diffusion) to create virtual outfits based on user reviews.
- We demonstrate the effectiveness of our approach through a qualitative assessment involving both LLMs and Subject Matter Experts (SMEs).

2 Background and Related Work

In this section, we provide the background on text-to-text and text-to-image models and explore the related literature pertaining to outfit generation.

2.1 LLM and Diffusion Models

Large Language Models (LLMs) are powerful Natural Language Processing (NLP) models designed to understand and generate human-like text. They are typically built on the Transformer architecture [8], utilizing self-attention mechanisms to process vast amounts of text data. This architecture, consisting of billions of parameters combined with extensive training datasets, enables LLMs to achieve remarkable capabilities. Capabilities include text generation, summarization, content moderation, language translation, and more [9] in both general and specific domains such as legal [10], medical [11], cybersecurity [12], and many more [13]. Examples of these models include Generative Pre-trained Transformer (GPT) based models such as OpenAI's GPT-3/GPT-4,[1] Meta's Llama 3,[2] and Google's Gemini.[3] LLMs demonstrate their prowess by comprehending natural language and performing complex tasks, such as generating text based on given inputs. LLM prompts are crucial to operating LLMs. Prompts are instructions given to LLMs to guide their behavior when performing tasks [14]. They serve as a form of instruction that enables the models to generate the desired output in response [9].

In order to attain the desired generated output from LLMs, prompting is notable among all the techniques. Prompting is a method used to create an effective sentence that can be used to interact and instruct LLMs to be able to understand the problem context. Prompts are given to LLMs as a form of instruction that allows the models to respond with the desired output [9]. Popular prompting techniques done by regular users include asking prompts in a question format, providing additional information to an already stated prompt, or using keywords to provide context. When going more in-depth, prompting techniques can be separated into two categories: prompt generation, which generates prompts that yield the desired answers, and post-processing, which tries to enhance the quality of the answers [14]. Zero-shot learning is a type of prompting technique that helps the model perform a task without any training data or direct examples of the required task. For LLMs, zero-shot prompting instructs a model to generate responses for tasks without any reference examples and also may not have previously trained for [15].

Diffusion models are mare a class of probabilistic generative models that generate data (images, text, or video) [16] by iteratively refining a noisy starting point until it matches the desired distribution. The generation process involves two main phases: the forward diffusion process and the reverse de-noising process. In the forward diffusion phase, noise is gradually added to the data over a series of time steps. Starting with a clean data sample (e.g., an image, encoded text, etc.), Gaussian noise is incrementally applied, resulting in a sequence of increasingly noisy versions of the original data. Mathematically, this is often represented as a Markov chain where each state in the chain

---

[1] OpenAI: https://openai.com/

[2] Llama 3: https://www.llama.com/

[3] Gemini: https://deepmind.google/technologies/gemini/

is a noisier version of the previous state. In the de-noising phase, the goal is to reverse the forward diffusion process, gradually removing the noise to recover the original data. A neural network, typically a type of U-Net [17] or other deep convolutional networks, is trained to predict the de-noised version of the data at each step. By iteratively applying the reverse process, starting from random noise, the diffusion model generates new data samples that resemble the input context. These models have shown significant success in generating high-quality images from text descriptions [18]. In this process, the text is encoded into a feature representation, which is then decoded into an image. Diffusion models are commonly used in text-to-image synthesis and creative content generation. One popular example of a text-to-image diffusion model is Stability AI's Stable Diffusion (SD).[4]

2.2 Related Works

The authors in [4] integrated LLMs with text-to-image models to recommend outfits based on user interests. They focus on Character-based Outfit Generation (COG) and interpret character information with customer specifications to generate personalized and cohesive outfits. The purpose of the research was to have e-commerce platforms generate outfit sets based on an item of interest, personal styles, color, and patterns. Three variants were proposed: baseline OG with LLM, vision-enhanced OG, and diverse style OG. Each variation generated looks for 29 fictional characters—separated by gender—and each outfit was evaluated by GPT2 and human evaluators. The main limitations found were that the model faced challenges in representing age and gender and sometimes lacked details in textures and accessories.

In another work, the researchers in [5] focused on style information that can be found in generated outfits. To do this, they incorporated an unsupervised style extraction module into a model, and using the style information of an outfit, the model generated outfits without any additional information. Four types of styles were created, Style A, B, C, and D, with each being easily distinguishable. Outfits were generated for each style, along with outfits that incorporated a mix of the two elements of the styles. The authors state that their future work is aiming to develop a recommender system that can extract someone's style preferences to recommend items and outfits.

In a similar vein, Bettaney et al. [6], presented an approach to generate fashion outfits for e-commerce. The authors used a multilayer neural network fed by visual and textual features to learn which items in a latent style are compatible with other items. Current research shows that researchers are utilizing diffusion models for outfit recommendation. For example, the authors in [7] introduced DiFashion that used diffusion models for the task of Generative Outfit Recommendation (GOR) intending to generate a set of fashion images and compose them into a compatible outfit tailored for specific users.

LLMs can be used to improve content generation quality and have gained frequent applications in e-commerce [19–22]. Their understanding of natural language improves item relevance. LLMs can label relationships between different products, as seen in [23], to find their compatibility. When using text-to-image generation, text and vision relevance become linked. This technique can be seen in the CLIP model [24], which uses

---

[4] Stability AI: github.com/Stability-AI/generative-models.

pre-trained language models to turn text into a format that can be used with images. Generative adversarial networks (GANs) are also used to connect text and image modeling [25]. The Stable Diffusion (SD) model in [26] can improve the text-to-image generation quality by using diffusion probability models (DMs). This allows for better vision-based recommender systems, such as those in [27] and [28]. LLMs and SD can be combined to streamline LLM-based preference understanding and vision-based augmentation and relevance, which was used in [6].

3   System Description

In this section, we describe the architecture of our framework, ReVisE, as shown in Fig. 1. Our architecture leverages the LLM and the SDM to generate outfits based on the suggested improvements i extracted from reviews r on fashion object O.

Novel research often starts with a small-scale dataset and limited infrastructure to assess the feasibility and practicality and then gradually expands to incorporate additional dimensions. Hence, the dataset (fashion object reviews) we used in this paper was sourced from a curated list of popular fashion objects (apparel) on Amazon Fashion. For each review of a given piece of apparel, we extracted the suggested improvements and associated persona (male, female, and kids) for further evaluation. ReVisE comprises two phases. The first phase utilizes the text-to-text LLM to identify suggested improvements. On the other hand, the second phase utilizes the improvements generated in the first phase to generate outfits leveraging diffusion models. In the following sections, we describe these phases in detail.

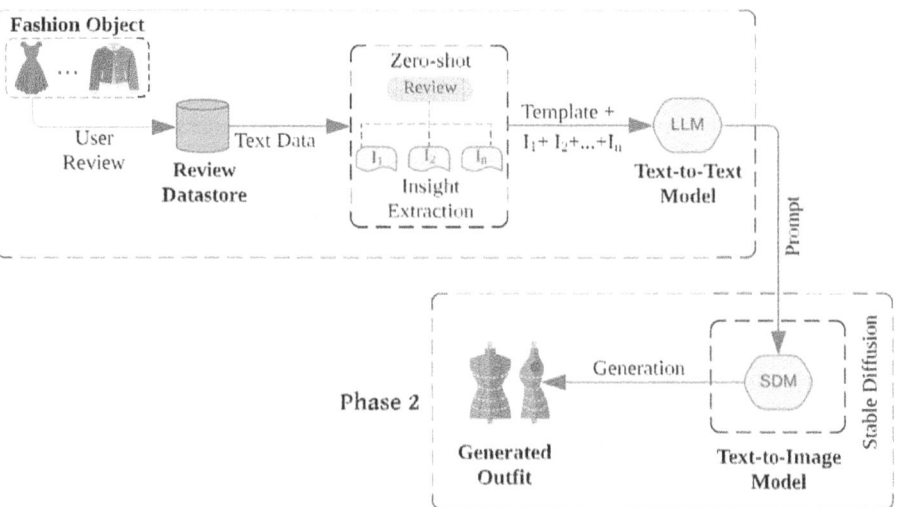

Fig. 1. An illustration of ReVisE architecture. Our framework comprises two phases. Phase 1 involves *improvement identification* from user reviews leveraging text-to-text models, while Phase 2 focuses on *outfit generation* addressing identified improvements utilizing text-to-image models.

3.1   Phase 1: Improvement Identification

The process begins with analyzing text-based reviews of fashion items. We utilize the zero-shot prompting strategies to extract the customer-suggested improvement on a particular fashion item. A review can have one or multiple suggested improvements. For example, given a review of *Men's Gym Running Shorts* such as *"Good fit but it needs the inside protective mesh. Especially if designed for running."* The suggested improvement in this case is to include a *protective mesh* in future design and production. Figure 2 illustrates the structure of our zero-shot prompt template. Such a prompt aims to extract customer's suggestions on a particular fashion object through LLM.

Fig. 2. An example prompt to extract customer-suggested improvement.

The output of the example prompt above is *"Needs the inside protective mesh"*. The extracted improvement suggestions are then stored in a list. We then combine suggested improvements and a custom template for the LLM (text-to-text) model to generate an SD prompt as illustrated in Fig. 3. The output of this phase is the prompt for the SD model.

```
prompt_template = """
Extract the customer feedback from the following review:
review: "{review}"
1. improvement suggestion for {gender}
"""
review = "Good fit but it needs the inside protective mesh.
Especially if designed for running."
```

Fig. 3. An example of template and improvement for LLM (text-to-text) model to generate a stable diffusion model prompt.

3.2 Phase 2: Outfit Generation

The second phase of our architecture is outfit generation. In this phase, the output from the first phase (SD prompt) serves as the input. Initially, prompts are generated by the text-to-text model in the first phase. These prompts are then passed to a text-to-image generator, which generates an image of the desired clothing based on the review. We employ the SD model for text-to-image generation to ensure high-quality and realistic images. This model interprets the prompts and generates detailed and accurate representations of fashion items. For instance, Fig. 4 illustrates a typical SD prompt for a review of men's running shorts from the first phase. This detailed and context-aware prompt ensures that the resulting image accurately reflects the described clothing item.

```
sd_template = """Improvements: {improvements}

Based on the suggested improvements provided for a gender,
generate a detailed prompt for a Stable Diffusion model. The
prompt should describe an image of a product that incorpo-
rates all the suggested improvements. Ensure the prompt is
clear and specific enough for the Stable Diffusion model to
create an accurate and detailed image."""
```

Fig. 4. An example SD prompt used for text-to-image model for outfit generation.

4 Experiments and Evaluation

In this section, we describe our experiments and results. ReVisE is a proof-of-concept framework capable of processing multiple data modalities. Specifically, it handles both text-to-text data and text-to-image synthesis, aiming to convert natural language text into realistic images.

4.1 Dataset

To evaluate the robustness of our framework, we conducted a manual curation of fashion object reviews sourced from Amazon Fashion. Table 1 represents a dataset of fashion reviews categorized by different fashion objects (Gym Shorts, Cargo Pants, Sunglasses, Dresses, Suits) and personas (Male, Female, Kids). It illustrates how a customer perceives and reviews fashion products, offering qualitative feedback on aspects such as fit, comfort, and design. These insights can potentially guide future product improvements and may shape development and marketing strategies.

4.2 Evaluation

To assess the effectiveness of our approach we took a dual-prong approach, including evaluation using LLMs and evaluation using fashion designers (Subject Matter Experts

Table 1. A sample dataset of fashion reviews representing diverse personas: male, female, and children.

Fashion Object	Persona	Review
Gym Shorts	Male	Good fit but it needs the inside protective mesh. Especially if designed for running.
Cargo Pant	Male	The black Cargo Joggers fit great and are comfortable. I've worn them hiking and traveling. I wish they had a chain to convert them into shorts for summer.
Sunglasses	Female	The sunnies are so cute! Love the rose gold. However, I wish the frame color would have been in black!
Dress	Female	Red Retro 1950s Vintage Style, Notched V Neck, Cute Cap Sleeves, Ruched Sheath Bandage Bodycon Design. Would be nice to have a golden pocket to carry out your mobile.
Suit	Kids	Super cute outfit. Wish to have suspenders. The bow tie wouldn't stay on.

(SME)). We kept evaluation criteria consistent for both evaluators wherein we asked raters to rate (on a scale of 1 and 5) the generated outfit based on the review of a fashion object by comparing them and checking if the suggested improvements are indeed present in the generated outfit.

Multimodal Evaluator: We utilize the Gemini-1.5-Flash model as a multi-modal evaluator to compare the fashion object with the generated outfit. Figure 5 presents the evaluation prompt that we use to compare two different images.

```
sd_prompt = """ Generate a realistic image of {gender} {fash-
ion object}, in studio light, white background, 35 mm, highly
detailed. The image should incorporate the suggested {im-
provements} as mentioned in the review: {review}."""
```

Fig. 5. A prompt for outfit evaluation utilizing Gemini-1.5-Flash model.

Human Evaluators: In addition to the LLM-based evaluation, we conducted a human assessment of the generated outfits. Due to the expensive nature of human evaluation, we selected a panel of three fashion SMEs. They were tasked to rate the generated outfits on a scale of 1 to 5 based on the inclusion of suggested improvements and overall aesthetic appeal.

Results: For our evaluation, we utilized both original and generated outfit samples for a specific fashion object, along with their respective reviews. Each evaluator was tasked with comparing two images and providing ratings. Figure 6 displays the original image of the fashion object alongside its review and the generated outfits. The red circle in the figure highlights the incorporation of suggested improvements in the generated outfit.

```
outfit_evaluation = """ You are given two images of an fash-
ion outfit {image}. The first is a real image with the re-
view: {review}. Compare the images to see if the generated
outfit incorporates the suggested improvement. Rate the gen-
erated outfit on a scale of 1 to 5."""
```

Fig. 6. An example of outfit generation using ReVisE framework. The red circle indicates the suggested improvement.

Table 2. Results

Avg multimodal evaluator score	STD Dev	Avg Human evaluator score	STD Dev
3.6	0.461	3.733	0.86

The evaluation results are summarized in Table 2. The average score from the AI model evaluator was 3.6 out of 5, with a standard deviation of 0.461, while human evaluators gave a slightly higher average score of 3.733, with a standard deviation of 0.86. Insights from human feedback, such as for a red dress, *"The generated image does a great job of incorporating customer feedback. It adds a stylish side pocket with a golden stripe. However, the execution of the pocket could be improved—it appears slightly too large and bulky for the sleek design of the dress"* can be valuable for designers aiming to further optimize their designs.

5 Conclusion

This paper proposes a novel framework, ReVisE, for emulated visual outfit generation using generative AI, addressing the overproduction and waste prevalent in the fashion industry. By leveraging the power of LLMs and text-to-image generation models, ReVisE effectively translates customer feedback into realistic visual representations of improved fashion products. Our experiments demonstrate the potential of this approach to streamline the design process, reduce waste, and empower designers to create more sustainable and customer-centric fashion products. While ReVisE offers a promising solution, there are opportunities for further development that can enhance its capabilities and fall under the scope of our future research. For example, in phase 1, the insight extraction and text-to-image prompt generation with object description and desired improvements heavily rely on provided product descriptions. Future research can focus on enhancing the model's ability to capture these finer nuances in an automated manner. Additionally, outfit generation is a multi-faceted research problem. Therefore, it is crucial to thoroughly evaluate all research frameworks using a baseline standardized benchmark to assess relative improvement. In the future, we plan to develop a robust dataset and benchmark to enable researchers reckon this problem uniformly. Besides, ReVisE is only capable of generating a 2D outfit. With the advancement of augmented reality solutions, designers now prefer 3D designs over 2D for better insights, opening up the potential for further research. Hence, future research can focus on improving the model's ability to capture all the aspects uniformly, expanding its capabilities to generate complete outfits with accessories, and exploring its integration with existing fashion platforms for real-world applications.

Acknowledgement. This work was supported by the Predictive Analytics and Technology Integration (PATENT) Laboratory at the Department of Computer Science and Engineering, Mississippi State University.

References

1. Kushel Digi Solutions LinkedIn. Why are trends important in stretch out fashion business. linkedin.com/pulse/why-trends-important-stretch-out-fashion-business-7jjxc (2024)
2. ADAM HAYES Investopedia. Fast fashion: How it impacts retail manufacturing. investopedia.com/terms/f/fast-fashion.asp (2024)
3. MARTINA IGINI EARTH.ORG. 10 concerning fast fashion waste statistics. earth.org/statistics-about-fast-fashion-waste (2023)
4. Forouzandehmehr, N., Cao, Y., Thakurdesai, N., Giahi, R., Ma, L., Farrokhsiar, N., Xu, J., Korpeoglu, E., Achan, K.: Character-based outfit generation with vision-augmented style extraction via llms. In: 2023 IEEE International Conference on Big Data (BigData), pp. 1–7. IEEE (2023)
5. Nakamura, T., Goto, R.: Outfit generation and style extraction via bidirectional LSTM and autoencoder. *arXiv preprint* arXiv:1807.03133 (2018)
6. Bettaney, E.M., Hardwick, S.R., Zisimopoulos, O., Chamberlain, B.P.: Fashion outfit generation for e-commerce. In: Machine Learning and Knowledge Discovery in Databases. Applied Data Science and Demo Track: European Conference, ECML PKDD 2020, Ghent, Belgium, September 14–18, 2020, Proceedings, Part V, pp. 339–354. Springer (2021)
7. Xu, Y., Wang, W., Feng, F., Ma, Y., Zhang, J., He, X.: Difashion: towards personalized outfit generation. arXiv preprint arXiv:2402.17279 (2024)
8. Vaswani, A., Shazeer, N., Parmar, N., Uszkoreit, J., Jones, L., Gomez, A.N., Kaiser, L., Polosukhin, I.: Attention is all you need. Adv. Neural Inf. Process. Syst. **30** (2017)
9. Carlini, N., Tramer, F., Wallace, E., Jagielski, M., Herbert-Voss, A., Lee, K., Roberts, A., Brown, T., Song, D., Erlingsson, U., et al.: Extracting training data from large language models. In: 30th USENIX Security Symposium (USENIX Security 21), pp. 2633–2650 (2021)
10. Adam Allen Bent: Large language models: Ai's legal revolution. Pace Law Rev. **44**(1), 91 (2023)
11. Neupane, S., Mitra, S., Mittal, S., Go lilarz, N.A., Rahimi, S., Amirlatifi, A.: Medinsight: a multi-source context augmentation framework for generating patient-centric medical responses using large language models. arXiv preprint arXiv:2403.08607 (2024)
12. Mitra, S., Neupane, S., Chakraborty, T., Mittal, S., Piplai, A., Gaur, M., Rahimi, S.: Localintel: generating organizational threat intelligence from global and local cyber knowledge. arXiv preprint arXiv:2401.10036 (2024)
13. Ge, Y., Hua, W., Mei, K., Tan, J., Xu, S., Li, Z.., Zhang, Y., et al.: Openagi: When llm meets domain experts. Adv. Neural Inf. Process. Syst. **36** (2024)
14. Alivanistos, D., Santamaría, S.B., Cochez, M., Kalo, J.-C., van Krieken, E., Thanapalasingam, T.: Prompting as probing: using language models for knowledge base construction. arXiv preprint arXiv:2208.11057 (2022)

15. Radford, A., Jeffrey, W., Child, R., Luan, D., Amodei, D., Sutskever, I., et al.: Language models are unsupervised multitask learners. OpenAI Blog **1**(8), 9 (2019)
16. Luo, C.: Understanding diffusion models: a unified perspective. arXiv preprint arXiv:2208. 11970 (2022)
17. Ronneberger, O., Fischer, P., Brox, T.: U-net: convolutional networks for biomedical image segmentation. In: Medical image computing and computer-assisted intervention–MICCAI 2015: 18th international conference, Munich, Germany, October 5–9, 2015, proceedings, part III 18, pp. 234–241. Springer (2015)
18. Kumari, N., Zhang, B., Wang, S.-Y., Shechtman, E., Zhang, R., Zhu, J.-Y.: Ablating concepts in text-to-image diffusion models. In: Proceedings of the IEEE/CVF International Conference on Computer Vision, pp. 22691–22702 (2023)
19. Cui, Z., Ma, J., Zhou, C., Zhou, J., Yang, H.: M6-rec: generative pretrained language models are open-ended recommender systems. arXiv preprint arXiv:2205.08084 (2022)
20. Geng, S., Liu, S., Fu, Z., Ge, Y., Zhang, Y.: Recommendation as language processing (rlp): A unified pretrain, personalized prompt & predict paradigm (p5). In: Proceedings of the 16th ACM Conference on Recommender Systems, pp. 299–315 (2022)
21. Bao, K., Zhang, J., Zhang, Y., Wang, W., Feng, F., He, X.: Tallrec: an effective and efficient tuning framework to align large language model with recommendation. In: Proceedings of the 17th ACM Conference on Recommender Systems, pp. 1007–1014 (2023)
22. Hou, Y., Zhang, J., Lin, Z., Lu, H., Xie, R., McAuley, J., Zhao, W.X.: Large language models are zero-shot rankers for recommender systems. In: European Conference on Information Retrieval, pp. 364–381. Springer (2024)
23. Chen, J., Ma, L., Li, X., Thakurdesai, N., Xu, J., Cho, J.H.D., Nag, K., Korpeoglu, E., Kumar, S., Achan, K.: Knowledge graph completion models are few-shot learners: an empirical study of relation labeling in e-commerce with llms. arXiv preprint arXiv:2305.09858 (2023)
24. Radford, A., Kim, J.W., Hallacy, C., Ramesh, A., Goh, G.., Agarwal, S., Sastry, G., Askell, A., Mishkin, P., Clark, J., et al.: Learning transferable visual models from natural language ReVisE13 supervision. In: International Conference on Machine Learning, pp. 8748–8763. PMLR (2021)
25. Reed, S., Akata, Z., Yan, X., Logeswaran, L., Schiele, B., Lee, H.: Generative adversarial text to image synthesis. In: International Conference on Machine Learning, pp. 1060–1069. PMLR (2016)
26. Rombach, R., Blattmann, A., Lorenz, D., Esser, P., Ommer, B.: High-resolution image synthesis with latent diffusion models. In: Proceedings of the IEEE/CVF Conference on Computer Vision and Pattern Recognition, pp. 10684–10695 (2022)
27. Sevegnani, K., Seshadri, A., Wang, T., Beniwal, A., McAuley, J., Lu, A., Medioni, G.: Contrastive learning for interactive recommendation in fashion. arXiv preprint arXiv:2207.12033 (2022)
28. Dong, Z., Chen, B., Liu, X., Polak, P., Zhang, P.: Musechat: a conversational music recommendation system for videos. arXiv preprint arXiv:2310.06282 (2023)

A Case Study on AI to Automate Simulation Modelling

Uchechukwu Obinwanne and Wenying Feng[(✉)]

Trent University Durham GTA (Greater Toronto Area)
55, Thornton Road South, Oshawa, ON L1J 5Y1, Canada
{uchechukwuobinwanne,wfeng}@trentu.ca

Abstract. We explore the use of Large Language Models (LLMs) for Discrete Event Simulation (DES). While DES typically involves both domain and technical expertise, our study demonstrates the potential of LLMs in generating queueing models in Python. The code outputs generated by the LLMs are compared to solutions implemented in GPSS (General Purpose Simulation System), a simulation language for DES. Prompt engineering is also reviewed, showcasing its impact on the quality of code generated by LLMs. Our results show that while LLMs assist in speeding up DES, they are far from replacing human experts. However, considering the steady advancements in Artificial Intelligence (AI), there is a promising future for more sophisticated and capable models.

Keywords: Artificial Intelligence · Large Language Models · Discrete Event Simulation · GPSS

1 Introduction

Large Language Models (LLMs) have garnered significant attention in recent times, bolstered by the emergence of generative Artificial Intelligence (AI) tools such as Chat-GPT and DALL-E [20], which are based on OpenAI's GPT (Generative Pre-trained Transformer); Google's Gemini, built on the LLM of the same name; Meta's Large Language Model Meta AI (Llama) and Code Llama models; and Microsoft Copilot. LLMs are trained on substantial corpora of text [5, 7, 10] and have shown remarkable proficiency in understanding human languages and generating human-like responses to prompts [16]. Besides text generation, they are also capable of producing images [12], audio [17], and code [21].

Discrete Event Simulation (DES) entails the stochastic modelling and simulation of a system's behavior with the aid of computational and mathematical techniques [1, 14, 18]. DES has been shown to have multifaceted applications across various domains. For instance, in healthcare, DES was employed to estimate the societal costs of strokes [11], for the operational management of Intensive Care Units (ICUs) [9], and facilitation of intra-hospital patient transfers [13]. In logistics, DES has been applied to redesign food supply chains [15]. In education, DES modelling was used to analyse and improve the performance of college counselling centres to support student mental health [3].

© The Author(s), under exclusive license to Springer Nature Switzerland AG 2025
W. Feng et al. (Eds.): SEDE 2024, CCIS 2244, pp. 179–186, 2024.
https://doi.org/10.1007/978-3-031-75201-8_13

Our study will explore the feasibility of DES with Large Language Models (LLMs). Presently, there is sparse literature investigating the role of AI in DES. [6] examined the collaboration between human and AI-based experts (LLMs) in creating simulation models of logistic systems, but OpenAI's Codex [4], a GPT-3 model that was fine-tuned for code generation and used in these experiments, has been deprecated. Moreover, far more sophisticated LLMs are currently available. For our study, we intend to harness the code-generating potential of GPT-4 and Llama 3 to generate queueing models based on descriptive prompts in the English Language. We have chosen Python as the programming language due to its simplicity, versatility, and readability. Furthermore, in a comparative study [2] using code generated by ChatGPT to solve a variety of tasks across different domains in ten different programming languages, ChatGPT generated more executable Python code than most of the common general-purpose programming languages including C and C++.

While simulation modelling provides the advantage of analysing complex processes to discover bottlenecks in a given system, developing these models can be a challenging process, requiring both technical and domain expertise. While this could foster collaboration among professionals possessing each of these skill sets, it can be an expensive endeavour and leads to delays in project execution [6]. The collaboration process typically involves the domain experts providing detailed model requirements and specifications to technical specialists. The technical specialists in turn translate these descriptions into computer programs [6]. This process can be facilitated using LLMs, which have displayed consistent improvements in code generation from natural language prompts and will be demonstrated in this paper.

2 Methodology

In this section, we introduce the Large Language Models (LLMs) to be used in our study, providing some background on their development, and reviewing their features and capabilities. Subsequently, we present General Purpose Simulation System (GPSS), a special-purpose simulation language for DES. The results obtained from GPSS will serve as a baseline for the outputs generated by the LLMs. Afterwards, we discuss the problem to be solved by the LLMs and the experimental design.

The first model selected is OpenAI's GPT-4o ("o" for "omni"). This model is an iteration of GPT-4 and is currently OpenAI's most advanced, having a context window of 128,000 tokens and a knowledge cut-off of October 2023. In the context of LLMs, a token is a unit of text processed by the model. Tokens can be as short as one character or as long as one word, depending on the tokenization method used. In other words, tokenization is the process of breaking down text into smaller pieces [28, 29]. A context window is the maximum number of tokens a model can take into account at any given time. A larger context window enhances the model's ability to generate responses based on the provided context or prompt. GPT-4o is faster and more efficient than its predecessor, GPT-4 Turbo, but has an earlier knowledge cut-off [22]. The exact number of training parameters (weights and biases that a model learns during training) has not been disclosed as of this time. For context, previous models such as GPT-3 and GPT-2 have 175 billion and 1.5 billion parameters, respectively [19], demonstrating performance improvements with increased scale [8].

The next LLM was created by Meta (formerly Facebook). Meta's latest LLM, Llama 3, is available in two variants: Meta-Llama-3-8B and Meta-Llama-3-70B, having 8 billion and 70 billion parameters, respectively. For this study, we will use the 70B ("B" for "billion") version, which has a context window of 8,000 tokens [25]. Akin to GPT-4o, it is capable of text and code generation from prompts [24]. A bigger parameter size generally allows the model to perform a wider range of language tasks because of its increased capacity. Ultimately, we will use GPSS as a benchmark for solving the given problem. GPSS was primarily designed for modelling discrete event systems and has various built- in features such as transaction generation and control, queue management, and delay handling among others. The outputs from GPSS will be compared to those generated by the LLMs to evaluate their performance.

3 Problem Statement and Experiment Design

We intend to analyse and optimize the operational efficiency of Minute Lube's (fictional) garage service to ensure they can meet their advertised promise of completing a filter, lube, and oil service within 10 min or providing the service for free. This involves solving the following three problems:

1. Calculating how long, on average, a customer has to wait from the moment they arrive until the service is completed.
2. Determining how effectively the mechanics (and their respective hoists) are being utilized during the garage's operational hours.
3. Evaluating the frequency at which the service time exceeds the 10 min guarantee, resulting in the need to provide the service for free.

The structure of the prompt fed to the LLMs has a significant impact on the quality of responses generated by them. Therefore, they require an effective use of prompt engineering. This involves crafting and optimizing the input to elicit better results from the model. Proper implementation of prompt engineering involves comprehension of how LLMs work, including their strengths and limitations. Moreover, it is an iterative process that involves experimentation with different prompts, sentence structures, and phrasings.

To demonstrate the impact of prompt engineering, our experimentation will follow three approaches:

1. The first approach will phrase the question as is, without making any adjustments to the phrasing.
2. The question is trimmed, removing details unnecessary for solving the problems.
3. The final approach will refine the instructions, concisely stating restrictions and breaking down the problem.

The prompts to be used in each case are stated below:

Case one: "You have been hired as a consultant by Minute Lube who advertises that they can do a filter, lube and oil in 10 minutes total (no appointment necessary) or its free. Their service has proved so popular that they are unable to meet this restriction and as a result they are giving away too many free services.

Upon your examination of the garage, you notice that it consists of three hoists (where a car must first be put on a hoist to do the filter, lube and oil) and three mechanics. The garage is open 5 days a week, 8 am to 6 pm. You also observe that on average, a mechanic can do a filter, lube and oil in 10 min and cars arrive at an average of 15/hr. You first decide to model this system by assuming that both the interarrival and service times are uniformly distributed. The interarrival times are average 1 and service times are average

2. Simulate this model on Python for 2000 customers and give the average time a car spends at the garage, the utilization of the mechanics (i.e., hoists), and the percentage of time a customer has to wait over 10 minutes."

Case two: "A garage has three hoists (where a car must first be put on a hoist to do the filter, lube, and oil) and three mechanics. On average a mechanic can do a filter, lube, and oil in 10 min and cars arrive at an average rate of 15/hr. This system should be modeled by assuming that both the interarrival and service times are uniformly distributed. The interarrival times are average

1 and service times are average 2.

Simulate this model in Python for 2000 customers and give the average time a car spends at the garage, the utilization of the mechanics (i.e. hoists), and the percentage of time a customer has to wait over 10 minutes."

Case three: "Task: Simulate a model in Python for 2,000 customers and calculate the following:

1. Calculate the average time a car spends at the garage.
2. Determine the hoist utilization percentage.
3. Compute the percentage of time the waiting time exceeds 10 min.

Conditions:

1. The garage has three hoists and three mechanics.
2. On average, a mechanic can complete a filter, lube, and oil change in 10 min.
3. Cars arrive at an average rate of 15/hr.
4. The interarrival time is uniformly distributed.
5. The service time is uniformly distributed.
6. The interarrival time is 4 ± 1 min.
7. The service time is 10 ± 2 min.
8. Print the average time in minutes.
9. Print the hoist utilization as a percentage.
10. Set a seed.

Terminology: A hoist is where a car must first be put to do the filter, lube, and oil change."

The prompt used in the third step employed some of the prompt engineer- ing strategies published by OpenAI [26]. Furthermore, some variables such as interarrival and service times were simplified, presented in minutes instead of "average 1" and "average 2" respectively. The statistics required by the user and conditions for the task were also outlined clearly to leave less room for misinterpretation.

The Python code generated by the LLMs will be executed within an inte- grated development environment (IDE) and compared to the correct output of the problem, which was solved by a human expert using GPSS. Additionally, the generated code will neither be modified nor debugged, and the model will not receive feedback if runtime errors occur. Since LLMs often produce varying responses to the same prompt, each prompt will be presented to each of the mod- els ten times, with their outputs compared. It is worth mentioning that these variations or randomness in output are influenced by several factors notably the temperature settings of the LLMs. The generated codes will be evaluated solely based on their output.

The tests for GPT-4 will be conducted on OpenAI's ChatGPT [27] and Llama-3 70B via Hugging Face's HuggingChat [23]. The instruction-tuned version of Llama-3 70B, Meta-Llama-3-70B-Instruct, will be used for inference, as this version has been "optimized for dialogue use cases" [25].

4   Results

The results will be presented as the percentage of correct outputs by each LLM. Codes generated by the LLMs that contained errors will be counted as incorrect (Table 1 and Fig. 1).

Table 1. Overview of Correct Outputs Generated by the LLMs.

Case	Problem	GPT-4o (%)	Meta-Llama-3-70B-Instruct (%)
Case one	One	50	0
	Two	10	0
	Three	50	0
Case two	One	70	20
	Two	30	0
	Three	10	10
Case three	One	90	50
	Two	70	0
	Three	0	10

5   Discussions and Future Work

The models performed the best in solving the first problem across all the cases, with the percentages of correct outputs increasing as the overall context was trimmed and modi-fied for clarity. However, their performance declined as the cases progressed, especially in the third question. This poor performance could be attributed to the additional steps involved in solving the third question, such as keeping track of the number of times a customer waited for more than ten minutes and converting these instances to percent-ages. Breaking down the problem further, outlining the steps required to reach a correct solution, or even modifying the prompt could yield more accurate results.

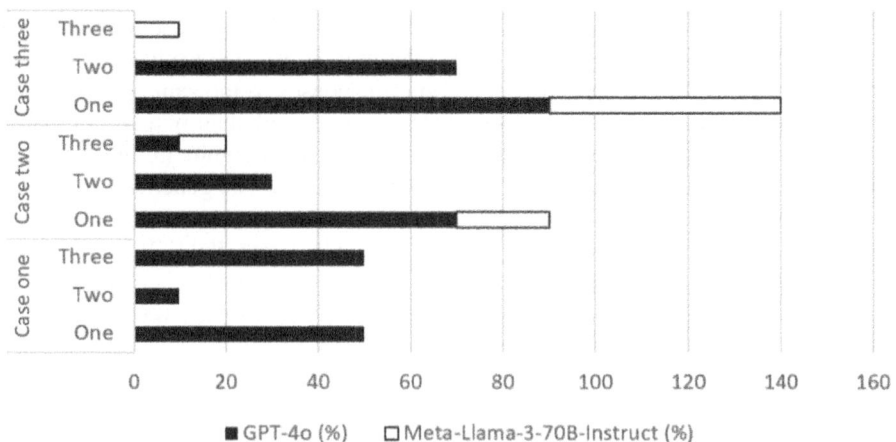

Fig. 1. Graphical Summary of Correct Outputs.

Upon reviewing the code samples, it was observed that GPT-4o generated three erroneous code samples out of sixty, whereas Llama-3 generated six. Furthermore, in several tests, Llama-3 created more variables (problems) than required. For example, it often treated hoist utilization and mechanic utilization as separate entities. Another frequent issue encountered in the first case was both models using the working hours of the garage to solve the problems, which led to misinterpretation and erroneous outputs. This issue did not recur in subsequent cases when the working hours were excluded from the problem formulation. Given more opportunities to arrive at a correct solution, supplemented with feedback on the incorrectness of generated outputs, the results would have significantly improved.

Like other domains, DES is not immune to the biases that LLMs are capable of reinforcing. They rely heavily on the large datasets on which they are trained, which can vary in quality and diversity, potentially skewing simulations toward certain viewpoints. Given the application of DES in different fields, this can lead to biased outcomes in generated simulations. Furthermore, there is the risk that the simulation code produced by LLMs could infringe on copyrighted data and information, leading to unintentional plagiarism. There is also an added layer of difficulty in identifying the sources of the generated content making it chal- lenging to properly attribute them. All these issues underscore the importance of maintaining a human-in-the-loop approach to oversee the simulation process and mitigate the ethical risks and biases.

In this paper, we have explored the use of LLMs for DES. We demonstrated the benefits of proper prompt engineering for improving simulation results. Our findings indicate that while LLMs can speed up workflows and aid in DES, they are presently unable to serve as substitutes for technical experts in performing simulations. Collaboration between domain and technical experts or possession of these two skill sets remains essential. Overall, these models exhibited an im- pressive capability of generating simple simulations from verbal cues, augmented with detailed explanations of the steps taken to obtain the presented output.

Generative AI is advancing rapidly, with new LLMs, updates, and optimization approaches released frequently. Consequently, larger and more competent models capable of advanced DES are bound to emerge. Smaller LLMs than those presented in this paper can produce better DES results from human prompts by fine-tuning them on Python code related to DES, thereby focusing their area of coding expertise and improving their proficiency in DES.

References

1. Babulak, E., Wang, M.: Discrete event simulation: state of the art. Discrete Event Simul. (2010). https://doi.org/10.5772/9894
2. Buscemi, A.: A comparative study of code generation using ChatGPT 3.5 across 10 Programming Languages 2023. Accessed 07 July 2024. [Online]. https://arxiv.org/pdf/2308.04477
3. Chatterjee, S., Hebaish, Y., Ntaimo, L., Deegear, J., Rucker, M., Aprahamian, H.: A quantitative simulation–based modeling approach for college counseling centers. SIMULATION **99**(8), 791–815 (2023). https://doi.org/10.1177/00375497231159675
4. Chen, M.I.-C., et al.: Evaluating Large Language Models Trained on Code. arXiv (Cornell University) (2021). https://doi.org/10.48550/arxiv.2107.03374
5. Devlin, J., Chang, M.-W., Lee, K., Toutanova, K.: BERT: Pre-training of Deep Bidirectional Transformers for Language Understanding. arXiv.org (2018). https://arxiv.org/abs/1810.04805
6. Jackson, I., Sáenz, M.J., Ivanov, D.: From natural language to simulations: applying AI to automate simulation modelling of logistics systems. Int. J. Prod. Res. 1–24 (2023). https://doi.org/10.1080/00207543.2023.2276811
7. Lewis, M., et al.: BART: Denoising Sequence-to-Sequence Pre-training for Natural Language Generation, Translation, and Comprehension. arXiv:1910.13461 [cs, stat] (2019). https://arxiv.org/abs/1910.13461
8. Naveed, H., et al.: A Comprehensive Overview of Large Language Models (2024). https://arxiv.org/pdf/2307.06435
9. Ortiz-Barrios, M., Arias-Fonseca, S., Ishizaka, A., Barbati, M., Avendan~o-Collante, B., Navarro-Jiménez, E.: Artificial intelligence and discrete-event simulation for capacity management of intensive care units during the Covid-19 pandemic: a case study. J. Bus. Res. **160**, 113806 (2023). https://doi.org/10.1016/j.jbusres.2023.113806
10. Peters M.E., et al.: Deep contextualized word representations, arXiv.org (2018). https://arxiv.org/abs/1802.05365
11. Patel, A., Berdunov, V., Quayyum, Z., King, D., Knapp, M., Wittenberg, R.: Estimated societal costs of stroke in the UK based on a discrete event simulation. Age Ageing **49**(2), 270–276 (2020). https://doi.org/10.1093/ageing/afz162
12. Sapkota, R., Ahmed, D., Karkee, M.: Creating image datasets in agricultural environments using DALL.E: generative AI-powered large language model. Soc. Sci. Res. Netw. (2024). https://doi.org/10.2139/ssrn.4770726
13. Meephu, E., Arwatchananukul, S., Aunsri, N.: Enhancement of Intra-hospital patient transfer in medical center hospital using discrete event system simulation. **18**(4), e0282592–e0282592 (2023). https://doi.org/10.1371/journal.pone.0282592
14. Vazquez-Serrano, J.I., Peimbert-García, R.E., Cárdenas-Barrón, L.E.: Discrete-Event Simulation Modeling in Healthcare: A Comprehensive Review," International Journal of Environmental Research and Public Health, vol. 18, no. 22, p. 12262, Nov. 2021. https://doi.org/10.3390/ijerph182212262

15. van der Vorst, J.G.A.J., Tromp, S.-O., van der Zee, D.-J.: Simulation modelling for food supply chain redesign; integrated decision making on product quality, sustainability and logistics. Int. J. Prod. Res. **47**(23), 6611–6631 (2009). https://doi.org/10.1080/00207540802356747

16. Wei, J., et al.: Emergent Abilities of Large Language Models, arXiv:2206.07682 [cs], (2022). https://arxiv.org/abs/2206.07682

17. Yuan, R., et al.: ChatMusician: understanding and generating music intrinsically with LLM, arXiv (Cornell University) (2024). https://doi.org/10.48550/arxiv.2402.16153

18. Ullrich, O., Lückerath, D.: An introduction to discrete-event modeling and simulation. SNE Simul. Notes Euro. **27**(1), 9–16 (2017). https://doi.org/10.11128/sne.27.on.10362

19. Zhang, M., Li, J.: A commentary of GPT-3 in MIT technology review 2021. Fund. Res. **1**(6), 831–833 (2021). https://doi.org/10.1016/j.fmre.2021.11.011

20. ChatGPT—Release Notes. https://help.openai.com/en/articles/6825453-chatgpt-release-notes

21. "Code Llama: Open Foundation Models for Code—Meta AI Research," ai.meta.com. https://ai.meta.com/research/publications/code-llama-open-foundation-models-for-code/

22. "Flagship models," Models—OpenAI API. https://platform.openai.com/docs/models/gpt-4-turbo-and-gpt-4

23. Hugging Face, "HuggingChat," huggingface.co. https://huggingface.co/chat/

24. Meta, "Meta Llama 3," Meta Llama. https://llama.meta.com/llama3/

25. Meta, "meta-llama/Meta-Llama-3-70B-Instruct Hugging Face," huggingface.co, Apr. 18, 2024. https://huggingface.co/meta-llama/Meta-Llama-3-70B-Instruct

26. OpenAI, "Prompt engineering," Prompt engineering—OpenAI API. https://platform.openai.com/docs/guides/prompt-engineering

27. OpenAI, "ChatGPT," ChatGPT, 2024. https://chatgpt.com/

28. "Tokenization," Stanford.edu, 2009. https://nlp.stanford.edu/IR-book/html/htmledition/tokenization-1.html

29. "Tokenization—Mistral AI Large Language Models," docs.mistral.ai. https://docs.mistral.ai/guides/tokenization/

Racial Disparity in Breast Cancer Prognosis

M. Mehdi Owrang O$^{(\boxtimes)}$ and Fariba Jafari Horestani

American University, Washington, DC 20016, USA
{Owrang,Fj9605a}@american.edu

Abstract. In this work, we looked at the significance of the race factor in breast cancer prognosis, using Association rules data mining technique. We utilized XLMiner data mining tool for our experiments. The data used is the National Cancer Institute's SEER Public-Use Data. Several experiments were conducted based on the prognostic factors including those of Age, Behavior code, Stage of cancer, Grade, and Marital status with respect to Race. Our discovered association rules indicate that Japanese patients have better survival rate than White patients and White patients have better survival rate than Black patients. The racial disparity in breast cancer prognosis is shown to be statistically significant.

Keywords: Data Mining · Association Rules · Breast Cancer Prognosis · Prognostic Tool · Hypothesis Testing

1 Introduction

Breast cancer is a malignant cancer-causing tumor that begins when cells in the breast tissue grow abnormally, without managing cell division and cell death rates. Breast cancer is the most common female cancer in the US, the second most common cause of cancer death in women, and the main cause of death in women ages 40–59 [6]. Approximately 232,340 new cases of invasive breast cancer are expected to be diagnosed in the United States in 2013, and almost 40,000 will die from the disease [7, 9]. The lifetime probability of developing breast cancer is one in six overall (one in eight for invasive disease) [8, 9, 25].

Breast cancer treatments can be classified as local or systematic. Surgery and radiation fall under local while chemotherapy and hormone therapy are examples of systematic therapies. Usually for the best results, the two types of treatments are used collectively [9]. Although breast cancer is the second leading cause of cancer death in women, the survival rate is high. With early diagnosis, 97% of women survive for 5 years or more [6–8].

Although cancer research is generally clinical and/or biological in nature, data mining research is becoming a common match. In medical domains where data and statistics driven research is successfully applied, new and fresh research directions are recognized to promote clinical and biological research.

Forecasting the result of a disease or discovering information previously unknown is one of the most inspiring and challenging tasks in which to develop data mining

© The Author(s), under exclusive license to Springer Nature Switzerland AG 2025
W. Feng et al. (Eds.): SEDE 2024, CCIS 2244, pp. 187–201, 2024.
https://doi.org/10.1007/978-3-031-75201-8_14

applications. Survival analysis is a field in medical prognosis that deals with application of various techniques to historical data to predict the survival of a particular patient suffering from a disease over a time [3, 10, 15]. With the advancement of technology, automated tools, storage and retrieval of large volumes of medical data are being collected and are being made available to the medical research community who has been interested in developing prediction models for survivability [3, 10, 15].

Existing literature considered many clinical factors, including tumor size, tumor grade, lymph nodes positives, different therapies among others, that may influence or correlate with prognosis for breast cancer patients [5, 10, 12, 21, 22, 24]. In our prior work [26], we have done experiments on breast cancer data set to discover association rules. In our analysis of the discovered rules, while most of the results were agreeable by domain experts, we did find some inconclusive patterns (i.e., in survivability by age >45, stage of cancer (localized)) that suggested that race factor may have some significance in the survivability prediction of the breast cancer patients. This has motivated us to further examine the significance of the race factor in the breast cancer prognosis. In this study, we present an analysis of the prediction of survivability rate of breast cancer patients using association rules mining technique and data mining tool of XLMiner [4]. Experimental results are analyzed. The results support the fact that race has a role in the prediction of the survivability rate of the breast cancer patients.

This paper is organized as follows. Section 2 looks at the current research activities in this area. Section 3 explains the data preparation. Section 4 overviews the prognostic factors in breast cancer. Section 5 discusses the Association Rules mining on breast cancer dataset. Section 6 provides a discussion on the breast cancer prognostic tool. Finally, Sect. 7 presents a conclusion.

2 Related Research

Several studies have been carried out on the survivability prediction of breast cancer using Naïve Bayes and Classification Trees, Artificial Neural Networks and statistical techniques of regression [3, 10–18]. In their study, Delen et al. [10] preprocessed the SEER data (1973–2000 with 433,272 records contained in a flat file breast.txt) for breast cancer. They removed redundancies and missing information resulting in a data set with 202,932 records, which then pre-classified into two groups of "survived" (93,273) and "not survived" (109,659) depending on the Survival Time Recode (STR) field. The "survived" class is records that contain value greater than or equal 60 months in the STR field and the "not survived" class represents the remaining records. In this study, authors have used data mining algorithms Artificial Neural Networks, decision trees, and logistic regression to develop the breast cancer prediction models. The results indicated that the decision tree (C5) is the best predictor with 93.6% accuracy on the sample, artificial neural networks came second with 91,2% accuracy and the logistic regression models came to be the worst of the three with 89.2% accuracy.

In the study of Bellaachia et al. [11] (period of 1973–2002 with 482,052 records) the approach takes into consideration, besides the Survival Time Recode (STR), the Vital Status Recode (VSR) and Cause of Death (COD) fields as well. They achieved a classification rate of about 87%. Authors have investigated three data mining techniques:

the Naïve Bayes, the back-propagated neural network, and the C4.5 decision tree algorithms. In their experiment, the Neural Networks and Decision tree had comparable performance with 86.5% and 86.7% accuracy.

In [18], authors applied seven data mining algorithms, artificial neural networks, Naïve Bayes, Decision Trees (ID3), Decision Trees (J48), DT with Naïve Bayes, Bayes Net, and Logistic Regression on SEER breast cancer data set. In their experiments, logistic regression model had the highest accuracy (85.8%) and Decision Trees (ID3) had the worst accuracy (82.3%).

The use of Association rules for breast cancer prediction has been sparse. The main advantage of this method is that it generates clear and simple rules of the form "IF X THEN Y", which is very transparent and easy to understand by medical people. This motivated us to explore the use of Association Rules for breast cancer survivability prediction [16]. In this study, we used the commercial data mining tool XLMiner [4] for our experiments.

3 Data Preparation

We have used the data contained in the Surveillance, Epidemiology, and End Results (SEER) Program Cancer Incidence Public-Use Database for the years 1973–2004 [5]. We queried the SEER database using the SEER Stat software which is a front-end tool that connects to the SEER database. Our selection criteria include all records where site recode equals "Breast" the sex is "Female" for the above period. A total of 770,000 records were generated by the SEER database based on our selection criteria. The SEER Breast cancer data consisted of 115 variables [5]. These variables provide sociodemographic and cancer specific information regarding incidence of cancer. Based on SEER personnel advice, 16 variables/attributes have been selected as shown in Table.

1. In the literature, these attributes are considered (using attributes/features selection techniques including PCA (Principal Component Analysis) [41]) to have prognostic and predictive significance on the survival analysis of breast cancer patients [22, 38].

After eliminating redundancy and missing information, and selecting records for the year greater than 1988, we narrowed our selection to 71,077 records. Due to the limitation of XLMiner, the selection was further reduced to 60,000 records. We should note that XLMiner data mining tool [4] can only handle a maximum of 60,000 patients' records at a time in searching for discovered patterns.

The reader is referred to the SEER documents for detailed descriptions and values of all the variables defined in Table 1 [19].

4 Prognostic Factors in Breast Cancer

Medical prognosis is a field in medicine that encompasses the science of estimating the complication and recurrence of disease and to predict survival of patient [3, 10, 11, 14, 15, 18]. Survival analysis is a field in medical prognosis that deals with the application of various methods to estimate the survival of a particular patient suffering from a disease.

Although scientists do not know the exact cause of most breast cancer, they do know some of the risk factors that increase the likelihood of a woman developing breast

Table 1. Variables used for Knowledge Discovery

Categorical Variable Name	Distinct Values
Behavior Code	4
Race	19
Marital Status at Diagnosis	6
Extension of Tumor	23
Radiation	9
Lymph Node Involvement	10
Grade	5
Diagnostic Confirmation	8
Stage of Cancer	5
Cause of Death	2
Primary Site	10
Continuous Variables	**Range**
RX Summ-Surgery Primary Site	0–99
Number of Primaries	1–8
Number of Positive Nodes	0–50
Age at Diagnosis	17–102
Survival Time Recode Total Months	0–83

cancer. These factors include such attributes as age, genetic risk, and family history among others.

A prognostic factor may be defined as a measurable variable that correlates with the natural history of the disease. The prognostic factors used in the prediction of survival of breast cancer can be separated into two categories: chronological (based on the amount of time present, i.e., Stage of Cancer), or biological (based on the potential behavior of the tumor, i.e., Histological Grade) [6, 20–22].

Lymph node status, tumor size, histological grade are among the prognostic factors in use today [6, 20–22]. Lymph node status is a time-dependent factor and is directly related to survival. One of the most significant prognostic factors in breast cancer is the presence or absence of axillary lymph node involvement, which is usually assessed at the time of surgery using sentinel lymph node biopsy or axillary dissection [22]. Macrometastases (>0.2 cm in size) have clearly been shown to have prognostic significance.

Survival is inversely related to the size of the tumor. The probability of long-term survival is better with smaller tumors than with larger tumors [6, 20, 21]. Tumor size has long been recognized as an independent prognostic factor and as a predictor of axillary node status, with larger tumors being associated with a worse prognosis and an increased likelihood of nodal metastasis. In [11], authors have used Weka mining tool and ranked the survivability attributes. The result indicates that Extension of Tumor has a higher rank than the tumor size. Histological grade is being identified as being highly correlated with long term survival. Patients with a grade 1 tumor have a much better chance of surviving than patients with grade 3 tumor [9]. In [10], authors also conducted sensitivity analysis on artificial neural networks model to gain insight into the relative contribution of the independent variables to predict survivability. The sensitivity results indicated that the prognosis factor "Grade" is by far the most important predictor, which is consistent with the previous research, followed by "Stage of Cancer", "Radiation", and "Number of Primaries". Why these prognostic factors are more important predictors than the other is a question that can only be answered by medical professionals and further clinical studies.

Other factors include the patient's age, general health, and estrogen-receptor and progesterone-receptor levels in the tumor tissue.

5 Association Rules Mining on Breast Cancer Dataset

Medical databases are often analyzed with classification trees, clustering, artificial neural networks, and regression techniques [3, 13–15, 17, 18]. Association rules mining technique is used here for predicting the survivability rate of breast cancer patients. In contrast to other data mining techniques, it is adequate to discover combinatorial patterns that exist in subsets of the data set attributes.

5.1 Association Rules

Association rules show attributes value conditions that occur frequently together in each dataset [1, 2, 4]. Association rule mining finds interesting associations and/or correlation relationships among large set of data items. That is, given a collection of items and a set of records, each of which contain some number of items from the given collection, an association function can find rules such as 70% of all the records that contain items A, B, and C also contain items D and E.

There are several numbers that are associated with an association rule. The first number (a) is called the support for the rule. The support is simply the number of transactions that include all items in the antecedent and consequent parts of the rule. The other number (b) is known as the confidence of the rule. Confidence is the ratio of the number of transactions that include all items in the consequent as well as the antecedent (namely, the support) to the number of transactions that include all items in the antecedent. Lift is one more parameter of interest in the association analysis. Lift is nothing but the ratio of Confidence to Expected Confidence [1, 2, 4]. It is defined as Lift = Confidence of the rule/(ratio of the records containing the consequent to the total number of the records in the data set).

Several iterations of model generation were done to achieve an optimized model that had good support for the rules and corresponding confidence of the rules. Unlike the if-then rules of logic, association rules are probabilistic in nature.

5.2 Experimental Results

As we noted, it was our intension, through experiments, to study the significance of the established prognostic factors and their combinations on the prediction of the survivability rates of the breast cancer patients. We have done many experiments using XLMiner data mining tool and Association Rules data mining technique. Most of the results from our experiments support the available clinically established prognostic factors.

We were intrigued with the result that survival was high when Race = Japanese. Table 2 shows the survivability distribution by Race, where a value "Alive" for the Cause of death means patient survived and a value "Breast" means patient died. We explored the data for Japanese only but could not determine from the available fields/data any pattern that could explain it. After talking with domain experts, the result could possibly be highlighted to other factors including those of genetic, food habit, environment and Climate which are not part of the SEER data. Existing studies show that a lifelong diet rich in soy foods reduces the risk of breast cancer in women [42, 43]. Soy contains the full complement of amino acids, can be made to fit with a low-fat diet, and Japanese women who eat a lot of soy have less breast cancer than women in the U.S.

Table 2. Survivability by Race.

Race	Cause of death	Total	Conf. %
Japanese	Alive	1085	89%
Japanese	Breast	134	11%
White	Alive	40296	75.1%
White	Breast	13385	24.9%
Black	Alive	3671	58.1%
Black	Breast	2652	41.9%

As noted by Newman [23], breast cancer pathogenesis and epidemiology is complex and influenced by a great number of environmental and lifestyle factors that impact on lifetime hormone exposures. Also, the genetic, socioeconomic, and cultural features associated with ethnic background could further complicate the picture. For African American women, these different elements tend to generate the unusual kind of patterns of a relatively lower cancer incidence, higher mortality rate, and younger age distribution (age of 45 years have a greater incidence of breast cancer than Caucasian-American women at this young age range) [23, 24]. Our association rule discovery based on race and age indicates that Japanese women, at age of 45 or older, have the highest and black women have the lowest survivability rate. The survivability rate of black women at age of 45 or less is much lower than the white women, as shown in Table 3. For the age group of "45 or Less", the Asian women (Japanese, Chinese, etc.) did not have enough records to satisfy the threshold set for the support/confidence for the rule.

Considering the survivability by Behavior Code and Race, we'll see that white women have slightly better chance of survival than the black women in In Situ cancer (97.97%–95.41%), but a much higher chance of survival in Malignant cancer (70.70%–51.92%). We should point out that Japanese patients, surviving with a confidence of 86.29% are doing better than white and black patients in Malignant cancer.

Considering the survivability by Stage of Cancer and Race, we'll see that white women are doing better than the black women in In Situ cancer (97.97%–95.41%),

Table 3. Survivability by Race and Age.

Race	Age	Cause of Death	Confidence %
Japanese	45 Plus	Alive	89.27
Chinese	45 Plus	Alive	85.63
Pilipino	45 Plus	Alive	81.23
White	45 Plus	Alive	74.82
Black	45 Plus	Alive	59.23
White	45 or Less	Alive	76.48
Black	45 or Less	Alive	54.01

Table 4 Shows the survivability by Race and Behavior Code.

Race	Behavior Code	Cause Death	Conf. %	Lift Ratio
White	In Situ	Alive	97.97	10.09
Black	In Situ	Alive	95.41	9.83
White	Malignant	Alive	70.70	7.28
Black	Malignant	Alive	51.92	5.34
Japanese	Malignant	Alive	86.29	8.89

Localized cancer (88.86%–79.95%), Distant cancer (90.36%–95.41%. We should point out that again, Japanese patients, surviving with a confidence of 95.17%, are doing better than white and black patients in localized cancer. Table 5 shows the survivability by Race and Stage of Cancer.

Histological grade is another important factor for breast cancer prognosis. Based on a biopsy, the grade could take a value of Poorly Differentiated, Grade III which gives a poor prognosis. Patients with a Well differentiated Grade I have a much better chance of survival. Table 6 shows that White women are doing better that the Black women regarding histological prognostic factor.

In our experiments (Table 7), we have found out that Marital Status has some significance (although not conclusive) in the patients' breast cancer prognosis. Our analysis of the data showed that survival rates among breast cancer were generally higher among married women. This value varied between racial and age groups but was on average 10.03 percent among racial groups and 3.62 percent average across age groups.

5.3 Statistical Analysis

Our data mining experiments suggest that the race of the patient has some significance in the survivability rate of the patient. The "confidence" levels of the association rules can be verified by statistical assessment of the hypotheses (or rules). The more widely

Table 5. Survivability by Race and Stage of Cancer.

Race	Stage Cancer	Cause of Death	Conf.%	Lift Ratio
White	In Situ	Alive	97.97	26.55
Black	In Situ	Alive	95.41	28.03
Japanese	Localized	Alive	95.17	9.80
White	Localized	Alive	88.86	9.15
Black	Localized	Alive	79.95	8.23
White	Regional	Alive	63.58	6.55
Black	Regional	Breast	54.19	15.92
White	Distant	Breast	90.36	26.55
Black	Distant	Breast	95.41	28.03
White	Unstaged	Breast	81.40	23.91

Table 6. Survivability by Race and Grade.

Race	Grade	Cause of Death	Conf. %	Lift Ratio
White	Poorlydiff., Grade III	Alive	62.15	6.40
Black	Poorlydiff., Grade III	Breast	53.31	15.66
White	Moderately Diff., Grade II	Alive	83.65	8.62
Black	Moderately Diff., Grade II	Alive	72.27	7.44
White	Unknown	Alive	65.70	6.77
Black	Unknown	Alive	50.56	5.21
White	Well Diff., Grade I	Alive	93.07	9.58

accepted statistical methods are Odds Ratio (OR) [28] and P-value from hypothesis testing [29].

The OR evaluates whether the odds of a certain event or outcome is the same for two groups. Specifically, the OR measures the ratio of the odds that an event or result will occur (i.e., cause of death = Alive) to the odds of the event not happening (cause of death = Breast). Clinically, that often means that the researcher measures the ratio of the odds of a disease occurring or a death from a specific injury or illness happening to the odds of the disease or death not occurring.

Considering the Survivability by race data in Table 2, calculation of the Odds Ratio is shown in Eq. 1, where "PG1" represents the odds of the event of interest for Group 1 (Japanese patients), and "PG2" represents the odds of the event of interest for Group 2 (White patients).

$$\text{Odds ratio} = \frac{PG_1 / (1 - PG_1)}{PG_2 / (1 - PG_2)} \tag{1}$$

Table 7. Survivability by Race and Marital Status.

Race	Marital Status	Cause of Death	Conf. %	Lift Ratio
Japanese	Married	Alive	91.69	9.44
White	Married	Alive	80.47	8.29
Black	Married	Alive	64.78	6.67
White	Divorced	Alive	74.71	7.69
Black	Divorced	Alive	60.30	6.21
White	Single	Alive	72.65	7.48
Black	Single	Alive	54.20	5.58
White	Widowed	Alive	63.31	6.52
Black	Widowed	Alive	50.91	5.24

Odds ratio = (odds for Japanese survival)/(odds for White survival).

Odds ratio = ((1085/1219)/(1–1085/1219))/((40296/53681)/(1–40296/53681)).

Odds ratio = ((.89/.11))/((.75/.25)) Odds ratio = 8.10/3.0 = 2.697.

Thus, for a Japanese breast cancer patient, the odd of survival is 2.697 larger than the odds for a White patient. Likewise, for a White patient, the odd of survival is 2.172 larger than the odds for a Black patient. Based on Table 2 (the contingency table), we have done Chisquare tests (using StatCrunch software) to determine whether the results for the ORs are statistically significant. The significance tests resulted in a Chi-square = 124.81985 and P-value < 0.0001 for the Japanese/White groups and a Chi-square = 835.54407 and P-value < 0.0001 for the White/Black groups. The high values of the Chi-squares and very low values for P-values indicate that the differences are statistically significant.

Hypothesis testing is a well-established tool for scientific discovery. It enables us to distinguish results that represent systematic effects in the data from those that are due to a random chance. Hypothesis testing involves a comparison of two or more sub-populations.

Using StatCrunch software [27], we have done proportions hypothesis testing with two samples (Japanese and White) summary data of Table 2. The hypothesis was to see if the disparity in the survival rate of the Japanese and White breast cancer patients was statistically significant. The calculated P-value was <0.0001, which resulted in the rejection of the null hypothesis that there is no difference in the survival rate between the two populations. Similarly, for the proportions hypothesis test for the White and Black patients' survival rates difference, the P-value was again <0.0001, causing the null hypothesis (no differences in the survival rate between the two groups) to be rejected.

The statistical methods validate the data mining result that the race factor is in fact statistically significant in the survivability rate of breast cancer patients.

6   Breast Cancer Prognostic Tool

There have been efforts in building breast cancer risk assessment and prognostic tools. For example, National Cancer Institute (NCI) Breast Cancer Risk Assessment Tool [32, 33] uses a Woman's risk factors (i.e., age, menstruating at early age, older age at first birth or never having given birth, etc.) to estimate her risk for breast cancer during the next 5 years and up to age 90. It considers seven key risk factors for breast cancer:

- Age
- Age at first period
- Age at the time of the birth of her first child (or has not given birth)
- Family history of breast cancer (mother, sister or daughter)
- Number of past breast biopsies
- Number of breast biopsies showing atypical hyperplasia
- Race/ethnicity

The original model was based on data from white women. Recently, the model was updated to estimate risk for:

- African American women using data from the Contraceptive and Reproductive Experiences (CARE) Study
- Asian American and Pacific Islander women using data from the Asian American Breast Cancer Study (AABCS)

Multiparametric tools have been developed for breast cancer prognosis. These include TNM staging [37], Nottingham prognostic index (NPI) [30, 31] Adjuvant! Online [34], PREDICT [35, 36]. For our experiments, we have used NPI prognostic tool to see if race has any impact on the overall patient's prognosis.

6.1   Nottingham Prognostic Index (NPI)

The Nottingham Prognostic Index (NPI) [30, 31] is a tool used, widely in Europe, to determine prognosis following surgery for breast cancer. Its value is calculated using three pathological criteria: the size of the tumor; the number of involved lymph nodes; and the grade of the tumor.

The index is calculated using the formula:

$$NPI = \left[0.2 \times S \right] + N + G$$

where:

- S is the size of the tumor in centimeters
- N is the number of lymph nodes involved:$0 = 1$, $1\text{--}3 = 2$, $> 3 = 3$
- G is the grade of tumor: Grade I $= 1$, Grade II $= 2$, Grade III $= 3$

The interpretation is as follows:
Score 5-Year Survival Prognosis.

> = 2.0to < = 2.4	93%	Excellent Prognosis
> 2.4 to < = 3.4	85%	Good Prognosis
> 3.4 to < = 5.4	70%	Moderate Prognosis
> 5.4	50%	Poor Prognosis

6.2 Experimental Results and Analysis

We have used SEER's breast cancer dataset for the years 1977–2013 (401,056 records). Table 8 shows the calculated prognosis using NPI tool for different races.

Table 8. Calculated prognosis using NPI prognostic tool.

Race/Ethnicity	Prognosis				
	Excellent	Good	Mode	Poor	Total
Japanese	861	1161	1379	423	3824
Percent%	22.52	30.36	36.06	11.06	
White	58044	80600	117634	44310	300588
Percent%	19.31	26.81	39.13	14.74	
Black	4263	6882	16595	8387	36127
Percent%	11.80	19.05	45.94	23.22	
Chinese	882	1323	2063	724	4992
Percent%	17.67	26.50	41.33	14.50	
Others	2135	3558	6057	2427	14177
Percent%	15.06	25.10	42.72	17.12	

The results suggest that there are differences in the survivability rates among races. For example, a white patient has 19.31% chance of survival compared to a black patient with an 11.8% in the" Excellent prognosis" category.

To see if this disparity in the prognosis among races is statistically significant, we have done hypothesis testing using StatCrunch statistical package [27]. For the "Excellent Prognosis" category, the hypothesis testing for the groups Japanese/White, White/Black, Japanese/Black, Japanese/Chinese, the calculated P-Value was <0.0001 in every case. As for the White/Chinese group, the P-value was 0.0035. The very small P-value indicates that the differences between groups are statistically significant (another words, we reject the hypothesis that there is no differences between groups). Likewise, for the "Poor Prognosis" category, the hypothesis testing for the groups Japanese/White, White/Black, Japanese/Black, Japanese/Chinese, the calculated P-Value was <0.0001 in every case. Therefore, we conclude that the differences among races in the prognosis are statistically significant.

7 Problems with Association Rule Mining

The problem of mining association rules in a high dimensional data set with numeric and categorical attributes is challenging, due to the large number of patterns rather than to dataset size. Most approaches are exhaustive in the sense that they find all rules above the user-specified thresholds. Such an approach produces a huge number of rules which may contain redundant or irrelevant information or describe trivial knowledge. In addition, Association rules that involve many items are hard to interpret.

Association rule can be constrained to have a maximum number of attributes in the IF part, if the data mining tool allows you [1, 2, 4]. We can specify a minimum % confidence value to reduce the number of rules produced. Likewise, we can increase the value for the support to reduce the number of rules. We should be careful, however, not to set too low values for confidence and too high values for support as we may inadvertently eliminate the chance of discovering unusual patterns. For example, in our survivability by race experiment, if we set the minimum support value to 2000, we would not find that Japanese patients have higher survivability rate than other races. Finally, use the rules with higher lift value, to reduce the number of rules.

If the number of discovered rules is large, then it is desirable to obtain a few representative rules so that many rules can be derived from them. It is recommended then that a cover of association rules with the same consequent be generated. Given two rules with the same consequent:

R1: X1 = > Y and R2: X2 = > Y, such that X1 X2, it is said that R1 covers R2. Then, R2 can be included and R1 omitted. When there are several rules covered by R2, this will produce a concise summary. This approach is applied to each set of rules with the same consequent but different antecedent item sets. Covers included rules whose antecedent was a superset of the antecedent of simple rules.

Finally, in the absence of a global/standard breast cancer dataset, the reliance on the SEER dataset limits the generalizability of the findings to other populations or regions. Therefore, we need to do similar experiments with other breast cancer datasets to see if they support the findings using SEER dataset.

8 Conclusion

In this paper, we have done experiments on breast cancer data to study the significance of the prognostic factor of race in the overall survivability of breast cancer patients. The data mining tool of XLMiner and the Association rule mining technique have been utilized in this effort.

The observations can be summarized as characteristics of survived vs. not survived with respect to prognostic factors of Race, Age, Stage of cancer, Grade, and Marital Status. In general, several factors such as Race, Age at Diagnosis, Survival Time Recode can have influences for breast cancer survivability. In terms of survivability rate amongst different races, Asian, especially Japanese have a better rate of survivability. Factors such as food habits, work/occupational environment, and genetics could influence the survivability rate. However, such information was not available on SEER breast cancer data that we used for our experiments.

Currently, we are evaluating additional prognostic factors and/or combination of factors that might be used to predict patient survivability rate. We also need to find breast cancer data sets which include other factors including those of genetic and family history, hormone therapy, information about late or no pregnancy, eating habits to better predict the survivability rate of breast cancer patient.

New strategies and approaches are needed to promote breast cancer prevention, improve survived rates, reduce breast cancer mortality, and ultimately improve the health outcomes of racial/ethnic minorities. In addition, it is vital that medical professionals from minority population groups be represented in decision-making in research so that racial disparity in breast cancer can be well-studied, fully addressed, and ultimately eliminated in breast cancer.

References

1. Han, J., Kamber, M., Pei, J.: Data Mining: Concepts and Techniques, 3rd edn. The Morgan Kaufmann Series in Data Management Systems (2011)
2. Ian, H.W., Frank, E.: Data Mining: Practical Machine Learning Tools and Techniques, 3rd edn. The Morgan Kaufmann Series in Data Management Systems, San Francisco (2011)
3. Jonsdottir, T., Hvannberg, E.T., Sigurdsson, H., Sigurdsson, S.: The feasibility of constructing a predictive outcome model for breast cancer using the tools of data mining. Expert Syst. Appl. **34**(1), 108–118 (2008)
4. "XLMiner Online, User Manual" [Online], Available: http://www.solver.com/xlminer-data-mining. Accessed 01 September 2013
5. "Surveillance, Epidemiology, and End Results (SEER) Program Public-Use Data (1973–2004)", National Cancer Institute, DCCPS, Surveillance Research Program, Cancer Statistics Branch, [Online], Available: www.seer.cancer.gov. Accessed 15 January 2013
6. Costanza, M.E., Chen, W.Y.: "Epidemiology and risk factors for breast cancer", [Online], Available: http://www.uptodate.com/contents/epidemiology-and-risk-factors-for-breastcancer. Accessed 10 Feb 2013
7. Siegel, R., Naishadham, D., Jamal, A.: Cancer statistics. CA Cancer J. Clin. **62**(10), 2012 (2012)
8. "Seer Cancer Statistics Review, 1975–2010", [Online], Available: http://seer.cancer.gov/csr/1975_2010/. Accessed 01 September 2013
9. "Breast Cancer Q & A/Facts and Statistics,", [Online] Available: http://www.komen.org/bei/bhealth/QA/q-and-a.asp. Accessed 01 March 2013
10. Delen, D., Walker, G., Kadam, A.: Predicting breast cancer survivability: a comparison of three data mining methods. Artif. Intell. Med. **34**(2), 113–127 (2005)
11. Bellaachia, A., Guven, E.: Predicting breast cancer survivability using data mining techniques. In: Ninth Workshop on Mining Scientific and Engineering Dataset in Conjunction with the Sixth SIAM International Conference on Data Mining (SDM 2006)
12. Kharya, S.: Using data mining techniques for diagnosis and prognosis of cancer disease. Int. J. Comput. Sci. Eng. Inf. Technol. (IJCSEIT) **2**(2), 55–56 (2012)
13. Delen, D.: Analysis of cancer data: a data mining approach. J. Knowl. Eng. Expert Syst. **26**(1), 100–112 (2009)
14. Thongkam, J., Xu, G., Zhang, Y., Huang, F.: Breast cancer survivability via AdaBoost algorithms. In: HDKM '08 Proceedings of the Second Australasian Workshop on Health Data and Knowledge Management, vol. 80, pp. 55–64 (2008)
15. Gupta, S., Kumar, D., Sharma, A.: Data mining classification techniques applied for breast cancer diagnosis and prognosis. Indian J. Comput. Sci. Eng. **2**(2) (2011). Issn: 0976-5166

16. Mamura, T., et al.: A technique for identifying three diagnostic findings using association analysis. Med. Biol. Eng. Comput. **45**, 51–59 (2007)
17. Gadewadikar, J., Kuljaca1, O., Agyepong, K., Sarigul, E., Zheng, Y., Zhang, P.: Exploring Bayesian networks for medical decision support in breast cancer detection. African J. Math. Comput. Sci. Res. 3(10), 225–231 (2010)
18. Endo, A., Shibata, T., Tanaka, H.: Comparisons of seven algorithms to predict breast cancer survival. Biomed. Soft Comput. Hum. Sci. **13**(2), 11–16 (2008)
19. "SEER Extend of Disease, 1988: Codes and Coding Instructions, Third Edition", [Online] (2014). Available: http://seer.cancer.gov/manuals/EOD10Dig.pub.pdf. Accessed 20 July 2013
20. Soerjomataram, I., Louwman, M.W.J., Ribot, J.G., Roukema, J.A., Coebergh, J.W.W.: An overview of prognostic factors for long-term survivors of breast cancer. Breast Cancer Res. Treat. **107**(3), 309–330 (2008)
21. Maskarinec, G., Pagano, J., Lurie, G., Bantum, E., Gotay, C.C., Issell, B.F.: Factors affecting survival among women in hawaii with breast cancer. J Womens Health (Larchmt) **20**(2), 231–237 (2011)
22. Bradley, K.T.: "Prognostic and Predictive Factors in Breast Cancer", [Online] (2007). Available: http://www.cap.org. Accessed 10 March 2013
23. Newman, L.A.: "Breast Cancer in African American Women", Oncologist, [Online] (2004). Available: http://theoncologist.alphamedpress.org/content/10/1/1.full. Accessed 01 Sep 2013
24. Baquet, C.R., Mishra, S.I., Commiskey, P., Ellison, G.L., DeShields, M.: Breast cancer epidemiology in blacks and whites: disparities in incidence, mortality, survival rates and histology. J. Natl. Med. Assoc. **100**(5), 480–488 (2008)
25. "American Cancer Society Breast Cancer Facts & Figures 2011–2012", [Online], Available: http://www.cancer.org/. Accessed 01 Oct 2013
26. Owrang O., M.M., Hosseinkhah, F.: Association rules mining for breast cancer survivability prediction. In: Proceedings of the 28th International Conference on Computers and Their Applications (CATA-2013), pp. 159–165. Honolulu, Hawaii (2013)
27. StatCrunch, [Online], Available: http://www.statcrunch.com. Accessed 10 Oct 2013
28. McHugh, M.L.: The odds ratio: calculation, usage, and interpretation. Biochemia Medica, The Journal of Croatian Society of Medical Biochemistry and Laboratory Medicine, [Online], Available: http://www.biochemia-medica.com/content/odds-ratio-calcul ationusage-and-interpretation. Accessed 01 Oct 2013; Moore, D.S., McCabe, G.P., Craig, B.A.: Introduction to the Practice of Statistics, 7th edn. W.H Freeman and Company (2012); Cancer Research **72**(24, supplement 3) (2012)
29. Galea, M.H., Blamey, R.W., Elstone, C.E., Ellis, I.O.: The Nottingham index in primary breast cancer. Breast Cancer Res. Treat. **22**(3), 207–219 (1992)
30. National Cancer Institute, Breast Cancer Risk assessment Tool. http://www.cancer.gov/bcr isktool/
31. Breast Cancer Risk AssessmentTool (Gail Model). http://ww5.komen.org/BreastCancer/Gai lAssessmentModel.html
32. www.adjuvantonline.com/breast.jsp
33. http://www.predict.nhs.uk.technical.shtml
34. Wishart, G.C., Azzato, E.M., Greenberg, D.C., Rashbass, J., Kearins, O., Lawrence, G., Caldas, C., Pharoah, P.D.P.: PREDICT: a new UK prognostic model that predicts survival following surgery for invasive breast cancer. http://www.breast-can cerresearch.com/content/12/1/R1
35. American Cancer Society, "How is Breast Cancer Staged". http://www.cancer.org/cancer/bre astcancer/detailedguide/breast-cancer-stagin
36. Schwarz, G., Horestani, F.J.: Prediction of breast cancer recurrence with machine learning. In: Encyclopedia of Information Science and Technology, 6th edn., pp. 1–33. IGI Global (2025)

37. Horestani, F.J., Schwarz, G.: Survival Analysis of Young Triple-Negative Breast Cancer Patients (2024). arXiv:2401.08712
38. Horestani, F.J.: Predicting diabetes with machine learning analysis of income and health factors detection. CS & IT Conf. Proc. **14**(7) (2024)
39. Song, F., Guo, Z., Mei, D.: Feature selection using principal component analysis. In: 2010 International Conference on System Science, Engineering Design and Manufacturing Informatization. 978-0-7695-4223-2/10 $26.00 © 2010 IEEE Xplore. https://doi.org/10.1109/ICSEM.2010.14
40. MOLLY ADAMS; MDAnderson Center, March 29, 2022, Is soy safe for patients with breast cancer? https://www.mdanderson.org/cancerwise/is-soy-safe-for-patients-withbreast-cancer.h00-159538167.html
41. Xiao Ou Shu, MD, Ph.D.,1 Ying Zheng, MD, M.Sc,2 Hui Cai, MD, Ph.D,1 Kai Gu, MD,1 Zhi Chen, MD, Ph.D,1 Wei Zheng, MD, Ph.D,1 and Wei Lu, MD, Ph.D.2
42. Soy Food Intake and Breast Cancer Survival. JAMA **302**(22), 2437–2443 (2009). https://doi.org/10.1001/jama.2009.1783, PMID: 19996398

Author Index

W. Feng et al. (Eds.): SEDE 2024, CCIS 2244, p. 203, 2024.
https://doi.org/10.1007/978-3-031-75201-8

GPSR Compliance

The European Union's (EU) General Product Safety Regulation (GPSR) is a set of rules that requires consumer products to be safe and our obligations to ensure this.

If you have any concerns about our products, you can contact us on ProductSafety@springernature.com

In case Publisher is established outside the EU, the EU authorized representative is:

Springer Nature Customer Service Center GmbH
Europaplatz 3
69115 Heidelberg, Germany

The manufacturer's authorised representative in the EU is Springer
Nature Customer Service Centre GmbH, Europaplatz 3, 69115 Heidelberg,
Germany. If you have any concerns regarding our products, please
contact ProductSafety@springernature.com

Printed and bound by CPI Group (UK) Ltd, Croydon, CR0 4YY
05/05/2026
02102981-0007